D0214253

In Discordance with the Scriptures

Recent Titles In

RELIGION IN AMERICA SERIES
Harry S. Stout, General Editor

The Frank S. and Elizabeth D. Brewer Prize Essay
of the American Society of Church History

IN DISCORDANCE WITH THE SCRIPTURES

American Protestant Battles over Translating the Bible

Peter J. Thuesen

NEW YORK   OXFORD   OXFORD UNIVERSITY PRESS   1999

HOUSTON PUBLIC LIBRARY

R01135 46866

Oxford University Press

Oxford   New York
Athens   Auckland   Bangkok   Bogotá   Buenos Aires   Calcutta
Cape Town   Chennai   Dar es Salaam   Delhi   Florence   Hong Kong   Istanbul
Karachi   Kuala Lumpur   Madrid   Melbourne   Mexico City   Mumbai
Nairobi   Paris   São Paulo   Singapore   Taipei   Tokyo   Toronto   Warsaw

and associated companies in
Berlin   Ibadan

Copyright © 1999 by Peter Johannes Thuesen

Published by Oxford University Press, Inc.
198 Madison Avenue, New York, New York 10016

Oxford is a registered trademark of Oxford University Press, Inc.

All rights reserved. No part of this publication may be reproduced,
stored in a retrieval system, or transmitted, in any form or by any means,
electronic, mechanical, photocopying, recording, or otherwise,
without the prior permission of Oxford University Press.

Library of Congress Cataloging-in-Publication Data
Thuesen, Peter Johannes, 1971–
    In discordance with the scriptures : American Protestant
battles over translating the Bible / Peter J. Thuesen.
       p.   cm.
   Includes bibliographical references and index.
   ISBN 0-19-512736-6
   1. Bible—Translating—History.   2. Bible.
English—Versions—History.   3. Protestant churches—United
States—Doctrines.   4. Bible—United States—History.   I. Title.
   BS455 .T55   1999
   220.5′2′00973—dc21   99-24447

9 8 7 6 5 4 3 2 1

Printed in the United States of America
on acid-free paper

For my parents,

MARY WISE THUESEN

and

THEODORE JOHANNES THUESEN

Acknowledgments

My foremost academic debts are to John F. Wilson and to my other mentors at Princeton University, Albert J. Raboteau, Leigh Eric Schmidt, and Robert Wuthnow. James H. Moorhead of Princeton Theological Seminary also deserves special thanks. This project would not have been possible without the generosity of Bruce M. Metzger, the Collord Professor Emeritus at Princeton Seminary, who granted me unrestricted access to the uncatalogued RSV Committee Papers and who first shared a prospectus of my manuscript with Oxford University Press. I owe longer-standing debts to those teachers at the University of North Carolina at Chapel Hill who introduced me to religious studies: Bart D. Ehrman, Peter Iver Kaufman, Gerhard Lenski, Laurie F. Maffly-Kipp, and Grant Wacker. Crucial financial support came at various stages along the way from the Andrew W. Mellon Foundation, the Mrs. Giles Whiting Foundation, the Louisville Institute, the Center for the Study of American Religion at Princeton University, and finally, the venerable Graduate School of "Nassau Hall." After this book was accepted for publication in Oxford's Religion in America Series, I was hired by the series general editor, Harry S. Stout, as assistant editor of another publishing project, *The Works of Jonathan Edwards*. I am grateful to him and to executive editor Kenneth P. Minkema for helping in various ways during the preparation of this volume. For guiding the book through Oxford's editorial process, I thank Cynthia A. Read, Jessica A. Ryan, and Martha Ramsey. A number of people made suggestions or offered other assistance: Stephen D. Crocco, Christine Deming, Lorraine Fuhrmann, Marie Griffith, Ruth Weigle Guyton, William O. Harris, E. Brooks Holifield, Jack Kenyon, Janie Kenyon, Anita Kline, James W. Lewis, David J. Lull, Constance Weigle Mann, Claire McCurdy, Jeanene

Moore, Mark A. Noll, Donna Potts, Margaret Weigle Quillian, Dan Sack, Kate Skrebutenas, Stephen J. Stein, Harriet Stuart, Brad Verter, Marta Weigle, Diane Winston, and especially my sister and co-Americanist, Sarah Caroline Thuesen. My debt to my parents, Mary Wise Thuesen and Theodore Johannes Thuesen, is expressed in the dedication to this volume. Finally, I am ever grateful for the love and support of my wife, Jane Allen Kenyon, and my son, Isaac Kenyon Thuesen, who was born just nine days after I defended the dissertation that would become this book.

Portions of chapter 2 appeared as "Some Scripture Is Inspired by God: Late-Nineteenth-Century Protestants and the Demise of a Common Bible," *Church History* 65 (December 1996): 609–23, copyright 1996 by the American Society of Church History. I gratefully acknowledge the society's support of the publication of this book through the Frank S. and Elizabeth D. Brewer Prize.

Contents

A gallery of photos appears after page 66.

Abbreviations

ACCC	American Council of Christian Churches
ASV	American Standard Version (1901)
CRC	Christian Reformed Church in North America
ETS	Evangelical Theological Society
FCC	Federal Council of Churches
ICCC	International Council of Christian Churches
ICRE	International Council of Religious Education
KJV	King James Version (1611)
NAE	National Association of Evangelicals
NASB	New American Standard Bible (1963–71)
NCC	National Council of the Churches of Christ in the United States of America
NIV	New International Version (1973–78)
NRSV	New Revised Standard Version (1989)
NYBS	New York Bible Society
RSV	Revised Standard Version (1946–52)
RSVCE	Revised Standard Version, Catholic Edition (1965–66)
RV	Revised Version (1881–85)

In notes, the Papers of the Revised Standard Version Bible Committee, Princeton Theological Seminary Archives, are abbreviated throughout as RSV Committee Papers.

In Discordance with the Scriptures

Sharper Than Any Two-Edged Sword

The Bible in Modern American Protestantism

✠

For the word of God is living and active, sharper than any two-edged sword . . .

—Hebrews 4:12 (RSV)

It cannot be said often and emphatically enough that liberals and fundamentalists are siblings under the skin in identifying or rather confusing . . . literalism about Jesus at the level of understanding the text, with . . . literalism at the level of knowing historical reality.

—Hans W. Frei (1922–88)
Types of Christian Theology (compiled posthumously, 1992)

A NEWSPAPER ADVERTISEMENT placed in late 1952 by the First Baptist Church of Babylon, New York, sounded a sentinel's alarm: "Beware: Do Not Buy the RSV Bible for Christmas Because It Destroys the Virgin Birth." The Revised Standard Version of the Bible, sponsored by the National Council of Churches, had just appeared amid great fanfare—President Harry Truman received his copy at a White House ceremony—yet conservative Protestants in Babylon were not feeling festive. The "virgin" in the King James Bible's rendering of Isaiah 7:14 ("Behold, a virgin shall conceive, and bear a son") had been changed in the RSV to "young woman," and to conservatives, this was an affront not only to Jesus' miraculous birth but to one of the key prophetic links between the Old and New Testaments. How dare the liberals lay waste to a cardinal proof-text of the Nativity— and during the Christmas season no less!

The outcry in Babylon, one of many similar episodes in the greatest Bible translation controversy in American religious history, was about more than the RSV's rendering of Isaiah 7:14. Below the surface-level dispute over an isolated Hebrew term lurked troubling questions about America's Book: Who has the authority to translate Scripture? How authoritative is the Bible in translation? Can translation be divorced from interpretation? These problems seemed to demand philological, even philosophical, expertise, but at their heart stood a purely practical question: Which version do you believe? The allegedly liberal RSV competed with the inherited King James Version, and later, the evangelical New International Version for Protestant loyalties, even as a welter of lesser known versions glutted the market. Many Protestants, of course, used the versions unconsciously, even interchangeably. But to scholars and church executives, the choice of a version often signaled one's allegiances in the struggle between conservatives and liberals for the soul of American Protestantism.[1]

In this study, I shall consider the theological implications of Bible translation controversies in modern American Protestantism. "Modern," for my purpose, denotes in its most narrow sense the period since 1870, when work began in England and the United States on the first major revision of the King James Bible, the Revised Version (1881–85). Although the Revised Version generated intense excitement and not a little opposition, starker conflicts erupted over its primary American successor, the RSV, during the years 1946–65. In a broader sense, "modern" denotes the period since the Reformation and Enlightenment, the two events that most profoundly reshaped the scripturalism of English-speaking Christians. I shall argue that Bible translation controversies between conservatives and liberals arose in the nineteenth century from modern assumptions that both groups held in common and resulted by the mid-twentieth century in the tacit repudiation of some of the same assumptions by combatants on both sides. Throughout the period in question, Bible controversies were less about actual translation than about the peculiarly modern modes of authority and interpretation that had developed since the sixteenth century. Indeed, though all historical categories involve oversimplification, the terms "modern" and its conceptual companion "premodern" remain indispensable for understanding the place of the Bible in Protestant culture. These terms therefore deserve elaboration before I sketch an outline of this study.

Premodern and modern Christians were, in many instances, equally scriptural. Though worlds apart in piety, the medieval Catholic parishioner and the modern Protestant fundamentalist both viewed reality through the biblical template of the Fall, redemption, and the second coming. Though worlds apart in methodology, the twelfth-century scholastic theologian and the twentieth-century feminist theologian both explicated biblical stories in light of contemporary philosophy. In each of these cases, the Bible exerted a unique claim to authority: it was *the* book to be reckoned with, *the* measuring rod of religious authenticity. The actual degree of the Bible's authority—that is, the extent of its normative power—changed far less over time than the regnant modes of biblical authority and interpretation.[2]

The Bible's authority in a premodern world tended to assume iconographic and ecclesiastical forms. Biblical stories were represented first of all in images: wall paintings, statuary, illuminated books of hours, and perhaps most characteristically, in the stained-glass windows of the Gothic cathedrals. The very idea of the image, informed by the Platonic notion of light as the most noble of natural phenomena, was central to medieval thought. Theologians regarded both the Scriptures themselves and the stained-glass windows depicting biblical stories as images (alternately termed screens or veils), which the Divine Light illuminated from behind. The entire perceptible or visual realm was an "image of the invisible," a representation of the higher realm of ideas, meanings, and ultimately the Godhead itself. Images functioned both mystically and didactically, serving simultaneously as windows to the Divine and as Bible-story books for the illiterate.[3]

Second, biblical stories in the premodern period were conveyed by ecclesiastical rites, principally the reenactment of the Eucharist. The elevation of the Host was the highpoint of the Mass, dramatically transporting parishioners to the scene of the Crucifixion while reinforcing the priest's authority to reenact the Paschal sacrifice. Biblical stories not represented in the Mass found popular expression in religious plays, which reflected what one scholar has called the medieval church's "catechetical preoccupations."[4] Indeed, premodern Christians rarely experienced the Scriptures apart from their corporate ecclesiastical setting. Even those educated persons able to read the Bible privately did so through the mediation of the church, which attempted during the Middle Ages, though not without difficulty, to standardize the Latin biblical text already established by long-standing liturgical precedence. The Latin Bible was the symbolic unifier of diverse national communions, representing the authority of the visible ecclesia, the earthly City of God.[5]

The Christian Middle Ages have rightly been termed a "culture of the Book," yet how was Scripture, whether encountered verbally, pictorially, or dramatically, actually "read"? The premodern mode of biblical interpretation was so different from most present-day exegesis that it requires careful elaboration, and no scholar is more helpful for this purpose than Hans W. Frei (1922–88).[6] In his classic study *The Eclipse of Biblical Narrative* (1974), Frei epitomized medieval interpretations of the Bible as "precritical," meaning they did not look *beyond* the biblical narrative for underlying historical facts. In other words, the Bible and history were regarded as a unified whole, and the very concept of "history" lacked the fully differentiated sense taken for granted by late-twentieth-century minds.

Influenced by the literary analysis of Erich Auerbach, Frei argued that only with the dawn of critical historical consciousness during the eighteenth and nineteenth centuries did Christians begin to regard the biblical world and the "real" world as separable. The precritical conception of history, according to Auerbach, was "magnificent in its homogeneity"; present reality melded with scriptural reality to form an all-encompassing, providential universe.[7] This does not mean, to take an American example, that the seventeenth-century Puritans believed themselves literal inhabitants of the biblical Israel; rather, they regarded the New Israel's history and the biblical Israel's history as continuous, or parts of the same truth.[8] In a precritical world, the truth (that is, the conformity to reality) of the biblical stories was an assumed quality. That God created Adam and Eve; that God imputed Adam's sin to all humanity; that God saved Noah and his family from the Flood; that God made an everlasting covenant with Abraham and his descendants; that God gave the Law to Moses on Sinai; that God led the children of Israel out of Egypt into the Promised Land; that God established a great kingdom under David and Solomon; that God exiled the Hebrew people in Babylon and announced their apostasy through the prophets; that God sent Jesus, the foretold Messiah, whose death purchased righteousness for the elect—all these events were assumed to be part of the same history in which God renewed the church under Luther and Calvin and then entrusted the light of the Reformation to the Puritans, founders of the New Israel. This entire epic, to borrow a term from R. G. Collingwood, constituted an "absolute presupposition," a story whose truth was simply taken for granted.[9]

Exegetically, this unitary view of Bible and history meant an emphasis on typological, or figural, interpretation, according to which events related to each other by a grand system of interlocking "types" and "antitypes." As Frei observed, the exact relation between type and antitype was not usually articulated, although it often took the form of prophecy-fulfillment. In most cases the "sheer juxtaposition" of type and antitype was enough to convince precritical readers of the providential connection between the two.[10] The precedent for typology was found in the New Testament itself, as in Matthew 12:40, where Jesus compares Jonah's three days and nights in the belly of a whale to the Son of Man's three days and nights in the grave.[11] In this and many other instances, Christ appeared as the Great Antitype, unifier of the biblical canon. The unity of Old Testament and New Testament events, as Auerbach explained, depended not on direct "horizontal" linkages, whether temporal or causal, but on a "vertical" connection to Divine Providence. Similarly, Providence united biblical and extrabiblical history in an elaborate, inscrutable figural structure.[12]

Typological or figural interpretation, as Frei pointed out, not only survived the Reformation but was in fact strengthened by the reformers, especially Calvin. In this sense the Reformation was a premodern event, a refinement of medieval exegesis.[13] Yet in another crucial respect—religious authority—the Reformation represented a partial transition to the modern age. In a rebellion against the iconographic and ecclesiastical authority of medieval Christendom, the Reformation substituted authority of an iconoclastic and biblicistic nature. Iconoclasm, especially in Reformed Protestantism, attacked the visible church in nearly all its manifestations, from stained-glass windows and episcopal vestments to the five lesser sacraments and, above all, the papacy itself. In place of these old authorities, iconoclasts elevated the authority of the Bible and the authority of "the people" (however vaguely defined) as the Bible's only legitimate interpreters. Biblicism was iconoclasm's constant companion, and the synthesis of the two inspired the work of the English Bible's first great translator, William Tyndale.

Ironically, the Bible's authority in Tyndale's England was sometimes represented iconographically in images of the monarch promulgating vernacular Scripture to the masses. Whereas premodern Catholic images depicted the biblical story, early modern Protestant images depicted the Bible itself. Biblicism, in other words, sometimes subverted iconoclasm in practice, even though Protestants remained iconoclastic in theory. This tension was lost on most Protestants, who regarded their movement as fully emancipated from the tyrannical authority of medieval Catholicism.

The reformation of authority in Protestantism was the prelude to an equally momentous reformation of interpretation. Modern biblical interpretation emerged at various times, depending on geographical and intellectual circumstances. In the European context, according to Frei, the seeds of change are manifest in seventeenth-century figures as dissimilar as Benedict de Spinoza, the Dutch Jewish philosopher, and Johannes Cocceius, the German-born Dutch Calvinist theologian.[14] Frei remarked upon a further transformation in the work of eighteenth-century English Deists such as Anthony Collins, who rejected prophecy-fulfillment arguments as proofs of the canon's unity.[15] In the American context, which Frei did not examine, the shift occurred a bit more slowly amid the persistence of essentially precritical interpretation in eighteenth-century figures such as Jonathan Edwards. Edwards in some sense represents the last flowering of premodern interpretation in America's high intellectual culture, for within a few decades of his death, New World Deists—among them Benjamin Franklin, Thomas Jefferson, and other founders of the republic—were openly challenging the veracity of biblical miracle stories.[16]

Frei identified a common feature of all critical, or modern, interpretations of Scripture: the tendency to mine the Bible for evidence of historical facts. Critical readers, including most people today, treat Scripture as referential (that is, referring to something independent of itself) whereas precritical readers accepted biblical stories at face value (as, so to speak, self-referential). In a critical worldview, scriptural stories are either true or false depending on their perceived degree of correspondence to historical reality. Moreover, critical readers reduce the biblical narratives' literal sense (what Frei called their "history-likeness") to an aspect of their historical reference: Jesus' feeding of the five thousand, for example, is read literally if and only if the reader accepts the story as accurately corresponding to historical reality. The detachment of biblical history and "real" history forces interpreters to take sides on whether the two histories correspond with each other completely (fundamentalism) or loosely (liberalism). In popular understanding, fundamentalist belief in complete correspondence is equated with literal interpretation, while liberal belief in loose correspondence is equated with symbolic interpretation; yet these stereotypes obscure the fact that neither fundamentalists nor liberals are as concerned with bare literary sense (whether literal or symbolic) as they are with the all-consuming question of historical reference. As Frei explained this peculiarly modern problem,

> [t]he real events of history constitute an autonomous temporal framework of their own under God's providential design. Instead of rendering them accessible, the [biblical] narratives, heretofore indispensable as means of access to the events, now simply verify them, thus affirming their autonomy and the fact that they are in principle accessible through any kind of description that can manage to be accurate either predictively or after the event.[17]

A host of factors contributed to the rise of critical hermeneutics in America. Certainly the eighteenth-century Enlightenment played a crucial role when it discredited, on rationalistic grounds, biblical supernaturalism.[18] A related factor was the inductive method of Francis Bacon, which belatedly came to the New World during the eighteenth century via Scottish Common Sense philosophy and then became the epistemological foundation for much nineteenth-century theology. When applied by Protestants to biblical exegesis, "Baconianism" meant searching the Scriptures for fulfilled prophecies and other objective "evidence" of Christianity's truth.[19] As one nineteenth-century Presbyterian theologian, James Waddel Alexander, put it: "A book comes to us purporting to be a revelation from God. Examine the proofs which it brings to substantiate this claim. If they are incontrovertible, believe the book. . . . If they are insufficient, burn the volume."[20] Other recent accounts point to the influence of Darwinism and Comtean positivism, two strains of evolutionary thinking that many Protestants resisted but nevertheless unwittingly internalized.[21] Protestants disagreed, of course, about the consequences of evolutionary theory for biblical history; many dismissed the claims of science as irrelevant for faith, even as their theologies absorbed the developmental vocabulary of Darwinists and Comteans. A similar reception awaited German biblical "higher" criticism, which found its way to America during the nineteenth century as American scholars apprenticed at Germany's leading universities. Like other modern intellectual currents, higher criticism subtly transformed even its professed opponents by further infusing Protestantism with the empiricist lexicon of "evidence" and "proof." Whereas evolutionary theory attacked biblical history on natural-scientific grounds, higher criticism attacked it on literary-historical grounds, pointing to textual inconsistencies that raised such questions as whether Moses really wrote the Pentateuch, whether Jesus was really born in Bethlehem, or—and this question strained both methodology and soteriology—whether Jesus really rose from the dead. Yet in the final analysis higher criticism was simply the byproduct of that more fundamental revolution in human thought, the dawn of historical consciousness. The emergence of the modern concept of history, with its realization that societies and their texts are conditioned by time and circumstance, meant that Bible-readers never again would be oblivious to the truth-question.[22]

The truth-obsessed reading of Scripture took shape in the eighteenth and nineteenth centuries, which were the focus of Hans Frei's groundbreaking *Eclipse of Biblical Narrative,* although Frei speculated that had he carried his hermeneutical research into the twentieth century the story would have remained essentially the same. To Frei, the persistent modern or critical reading of the Bible had increasingly amounted to two things: "grammatical and lexical exactness in estimating what the original sense of a text was to its original audience, and the coincidence of the description with how the facts really occurred."[23] And this was the initial impetus of the Bible revision movement: a desire for textual and historical veracity. Truth-value—the common currency of modern Protestantism—was the price placed on every biblical story, every Bible version. Disagreements over truth-value, as Frei predicted, remained the stock in trade of twentieth-century theological disputation, as in the battle over Isaiah 7:14. Frei cited this verse as an example of the critical dispute over prophecy-fulfillment that emerged in eighteenth-century England. Had he continued his story into twentieth-century America, he would have found that the terms of the debate had changed only insofar as the Isaiah text figured in contemporary fundamentalist constructions of biblical "inerrancy."[24] What had not changed were the modern critical presuppositions that transformed every question of translation into a question of historical truth. The actual lexical problem of Isaiah 7:14—whether the Hebrew *almah* meant "young woman" or "virgin"—was a mere surrogate for debates over the possibility of prophecy-fulfillment, miraculous birth, and other phenomena whose reality in a precritical world had been taken for granted.

To return to my original argument, then, Bible translation controversies between conservative and liberal Protestants stemmed first of all from modern assumptions that, ironically, both groups held in common. As Frei put it in another context, conservatives and liberals are "siblings under the skin" in confusing literalism at the level of understanding the biblical text with literalism at the level of knowing historical reality.[25] In this logical confusion, conservatives and liberals betray themselves as equal heirs of a critical epistemology that subjected every text to the test of historical reference.[26]

It was precisely their epistemological agreement that plunged conservatives and liberals into conflict and prompted them to reconsider Protestantism's centuries-old iconoclastic rejection of ecclesiastical authority. The bitter translation controversies of the nineteenth and twentieth centuries highlighted the need for some extrabiblical authority to certify the orthodoxy (whether liberal or conservative) of Bible translations. For liberals, the primary authority was the National Council of Churches; for conservatives, the National Association of Evangelicals. Neither organization wielded regulatory power over its constituent churches, but both enjoyed symbolic power as the standard-bearers of liberal and conservative Protestantism, respectively. The stamp of approval of either the NCC or the NAE assured Protestant laypeople that a Bible translation would not transgress their preconceptions of biblical history. In the wake of modern Bible battles, then, a significant segment of American Protestantism tacitly repudiated the Reformation axiom of "Book over Church" and rehabilitated a premodern model of religious authority.

In exploring the origins of this historical irony, I turn in chapter 1 to the modern English Bible's formative period: sixteenth-century England. More than its German cousin, the English Reformation replaced traditional forms of religious authority with iconoclastic biblicism, a peculiarly modern valorization of the translated and printed word. The chief Bible translator and theorist of iconoclastic biblicism was William Tyndale, whose martyrdom rendered sacrosanct the saga of vernacular Scripture in England. Tyndale's shadow loomed large as English Puritans brought the Bible to American shores, but not until the late nineteenth century did an idea of the "Tyndale tradition" emerge in the form of a popular new literary genre, the English Bible history. Dozens of these histories appeared after 1870 as American and British Protestants were embarking upon the first major revision of the English Bible since 1611. The nascent Bible revision movement looked to the Bible histories for legitimation, and found therein an eminently usable past: the story of word's triumph over image, modernity's triumph over medievalism, and Protestantism's triumph over Catholicism.

The sixteenth century gave Protestantism the translated word and a piety of "Scripture alone," but the nineteenth century transformed the English Bible tradition into a relentless biblical empiricism. The intellectual currents issuing from the Enlightenment of the previous century had by 1870 refashioned biblical studies into a virtual science employing the evidence of "codices" and "variants" to retrace the Bible's textual evolution and to reconstruct the real history behind the Bible's stories. Out of this critical-historical milieu sprang the Revised Version (1881–85), perhaps the most celebrated book in the annals of nineteenth-century publishing. In chapter 2, I analyze Protestant reactions to the new Bible, hailed by the press as King Truth, anointed successor to King James. Besides the nearly millennialistic fervor about a supremely accurate Bible, the Revised Version was the harbinger of modern Bible translation controversies. Conservatives who had initially supported Bible revision were by the early years of the twentieth century questioning the "liberal" revisers' textual conclusions; yet these arcane disputes over textual accuracy masked a more fundamental concern for historical truth.

Conservative discontent did not temper the enthusiasm of liberal scholars who, spurred by new text-critical discoveries, began in 1937 a revision of the Revised Version, to be known as the Revised Standard Version. Appointed by the International Council of Religious Education, the RSV committee was headed by Luther Weigle, dean of Yale Divinity School and chairman of the World's Sunday School Association. Weigle and his colleagues differed in subtle but important ways from their late-nineteenth-century counterparts; in chapter 3, I explore some of these differences. Though nearly as empiricist and scientific in temper as the Revised Version translators, the RSV committee hoped to balance text-critical exactness with the literary elegance of the old Authorized Version. Moreover, the RSV committee members sought to dispel the unyielding biblicism that had so long characterized Protestantism. This meant repudiating some of the old Protestant historiography of the English Bible that equated Protestantism with the word and Catholicism with the image. When the newly founded National Council of Churches assumed sponsorship of the RSV project in 1951, the translators redoubled their ecumenical efforts: Might the RSV become a common text for American Protestants and perhaps even one day for American Catholics? Never before, it seemed, had history given English-speaking Christians such an opportunity for an ecumenism of the Book.

Such universalistic zeal infuriated conservatives, and with the publication of the complete RSV in 1952 their frustrations came to a head. A variety of figures, from the Presbyterian controversialist Carl McIntire to Baptist radio evangelist Edgar Bundy, published articles and tracts assailing the National Council of Churches for presuming to grant any Bible its "imprimatur." A few preachers, despite widespread cries of sacrilege, even burned copies of the RSV in a futile attempt to vanquish the strange specter of unholy Scripture. In chapter 4, I analyze the RSV controversy as a simultaneous struggle over authority and interpretation. To conservatives, the National Council usurped the authority of the Bible as the "people's book"; like Communist regimes, the NCC seemed to reserve the right of censorship over the printed word. Allegations that the RSV was a "Communist Bible" soon proliferated, even appearing as late as 1960 in a U.S. Air Force training manual. At the same time, conservatives anathematized the RSV on interpretive grounds, seizing on passages where the new translation strained the King James Version's account of biblical history.

A single verse, Isaiah 7:14, soon came to symbolize the interpretive debate, which is the subject of chapter 5. Conservatives insisted that such passages should be translated to conform to their New Testament citations (in this case, Matthew 1:23) and that to translate otherwise was to deny the unity and inerrancy of the testaments. A 1953 article by Dallas Seminary professor Merrill F. Unger chided the RSV translators for supposing that Bible translation is a "linguistic science" that "knows no theology." Unger, whose article reflected the opinion of many conservatives, insisted that correct translation of verses such as Isaiah 7:14 required the theological guidance of the Holy Spirit. Meanwhile, leaders of the National Association of Evangelicals were calling for a new conservative version of Scripture. Born of dissatisfaction with the RSV, this proposed translation was distinctive for the doctrinal oath required of its translators: an agreement that the

Scriptures are "inerrant in the autographs." The nascent New International Version thus acquired the evangelical *nihil obstat,* just as a modified edition of the RSV, in an unprecedented moment of ecumenism, was receiving the imprimatur of the Catholic Church.

The NIV would eventually restore the "virgin" to Isaiah, but in the controversy over the RSV, the translation of Protestantism's Book had finally ruptured along ideological lines. To this day the choice between RSV and NIV often serves as a marker of liberal or conservative loyalties, even as dozens of other versions compete for the allegiances of particular constituencies. In the epilogue, I consider this and other legacies of modern Bible battles. Although the balkanization of Bible publishing is the RSV controversy's most visible legacy, the struggles of the 1950s also laid bare the problems of authority and interpretation that six centuries of English Bible translation had failed to resolve. The ongoing engagement with these problems will continue to define and enliven the scripturalism of American Protestants.

Before proceeding with the narrative of modern translation controversies, I must place this study in the context of other scholarship on the Bible. As a historian rather than a translator, I am not primarily concerned with the accuracy of particular Bible versions or with the technical debates of textual critics. Only rarely will I consult a Greek or Hebrew lexicon, for such tools of true linguistic specialists are easily misused by amateurs or by interloping historians. Neither will I undertake extensive comparisons of different English versions, for this laborious but important exercise is best left to biblical scholars and literary critics.[27] American Protestant battles over Bible translation, after all, have usually been fought only incidentally over technical issues of translation or textual criticism. The true points of contention have most often been theological and institutional.

This work is a cultural and intellectual history of the RSV translation lineage and its discontents. In tracing this particular trajectory of Bible revision since 1870, I do not mean to obscure the tremendous diversity of lesser known translations appearing throughout American religious history. Historians have shown that the publishing marketplace was a Babel of ideologically diverse Bibles long before the RSV controversy. Baptists, Campbellites, Christian Scientists, Lutherans, Mormons, and Unitarians were just a few of the groups that boasted their own translations, annotations, or even whole new canons of Scripture. A variety of erudite and sometimes eccentric individuals also translated new editions of Holy Writ.

In no period of American history did a single Bible version, such as the King James, enjoy a complete market monopoly, and this will surely remain the case as long as Americans continue to read Scripture.[28]

My concern in the pages that follow is not primarily to enumerate the various versions of the Bible but rather to examine the assumptions about biblical authority and interpretation that have made Bible translation controversies such a ubiquitous feature of American religion. On the question of interpretation in particular, the reader may have detected a hint of approval in my explication of Hans Frei's "precritical" model, and indeed I am partial to this approach for reasons not wholly historiographical. The modern critical reading of Scripture—whether a conservative embrace of "verbal inerrancy" or a liberal quest for the "historical Jesus"—has long since outlived its usefulness. At the same time, I fully admit a serious flaw in what we might call Frei's neomedievalism: our critical presuppositions constantly work against the renewal of precritical exegesis. The historian Carl Becker recognized as much in 1931 when he spoke of the inescapability of "historical-mindedness" in the modern context. When Becker tried to imagine a conversation between a modern person and Thomas Aquinas, he concluded that the two would hopelessly talk past each other: while Thomas would ponder the intricate interconnections comprising a teleological universe, the modern person would focus on history's "irreducible brute fact[s]."[29] There is, then, something profoundly quixotic about Frei's lament over the eclipse of biblical narrative. To borrow a biblical metaphor, Scripture in the modern world seems irreparably rent asunder by the two-edged sword of conservative-liberal conflict. Yet in moments of quixotic fancy, I still envision with Frei a world where the Bible is "sharper than any two-edged sword," a world where the translated word enlivens the Christian imagination rather than plunging fellow pilgrims into discordance with the Scriptures.

Chapter 1

The Blood of the Martyr

History, Hagiography, and the Consecration of the English Bible

✠

What say I then? that the image is anything? or that it which is offered to images is anything? Nay, but I say, that those things which the gentiles offer, they offer to devils, and not to God.

—1 Corinthians 10:19–20
(William Tyndale's New Testament, 1534)

No other Christian people can show a vernacular Bible with such a history as ours; so consecrated by high purpose and noble sacrifice, so baptized in the tears and blood of faithful souls, so linked with the inmost life and history of the people.

—Hannah Chaplin Conant,
The Popular History of the Translation of the Holy Scriptures into the English Tongue (1856, 1881)

RARELY IN ITS six-hundred-year history has the English Bible functioned merely as a book. During the sixteenth century it became an icon, the object represented in paintings and woodcuts to replace the defaced images of saints. During the nineteenth century it became an idea, the historiographical construct of Protestants bent on glorifying the Anglo-American imprint upon God's Word. During this century the English Bible has lost none of its paradoxical force; at once concrete and abstract, it provides justification for religious movements working both evil and good.

In this chapter, I explore the "English Bible" as a Protestant historical idea. This largely nineteenth-century concept emerged from the Bible's sixteenth-century role as a literal and figurative icon; I therefore reexamine the work of the theologians and translators who first codified Protestant biblicism and gave English speakers vernacular Scripture. Because Protestant biblicism was often indistinguishable from anti-Catholicism, interreligious tensions are the subtext—the rumbling bass—of this narrative. Above the bass line is the unending contrapuntal play of word and image.

THE VARIETIES OF SIXTEENTH-CENTURY CONTINENTAL BIBLICISM

A striking illustration of the ambiguous Protestant relationship to the written word is on display in Wittenberg, Germany, where Luther posted his Ninety-five Theses. The original wooden door in the Castle Church's north portal, destroyed during the Seven Years' War, was replaced a century later, in 1858, at the behest of Prussian king Friedrich Wilhelm IV, by two massive bronze doors inscribed with all ninety-five theses. Even more extraordinary than the doors is the tympanum mosaic depicting the crucified Christ flanked by Luther, who holds a large open Bible, and Melanchthon, who holds the Augsburg Confession.[1] Here is word glorified in an image; iconography in a town whose Reformation rallying cry was *sola scriptura*.

Any study of the Protestant veneration of the word must consider the German Reformation, for Luther is the figure most associated with the maxim "Scripture alone." For many Protestants after Luther, "Scripture alone" came to denote an inflexible biblicism that often amounted to little more than thinly veiled iconoclasm. But was Luther himself, as the most famous Bible translator in history, a thoroughgoing biblicist? It is true that he devoted years of his life to giving Germans the Bible in their own tongue, and his labor was not in vain: his 1522 New Testament went through fifty printings in just four years as his followers expounded a theology whose "only rule and norm" was Holy Writ.[2]

Yet to understand the origins of Bible translation among Anglo-American Protestants, one must first understand the thoroughgoing biblicism that formed the deep backdrop to their work, and here the historical connection to Luther grows tenuous. Lutheran theology has always occupied a marginal position in the history of American religious thought, partly because of the immigrant status of its leading lights. With the exception of the "Americanizing" followers of Samuel Simon Schmucker (1799–1873), most Lutherans refused to abandon Old World liturgical forms in favor of New World evangelical simplicity.[3] Lutheran resistance to biblical primitivism frustrated some famous figures in American theology. John Cotton, patriarch of New England Puritanism, complained that "many and great Nations" had followed Luther in the "notorious errors of his way." The Lutheran countries, in Cotton's estimation, were among those who had failed to restore "Primitive Christianity . . . according to the word of Christ." A later advocate of primitive Christianity, Alexander Campbell, insisted that the world owed more to John Wycliffe than to Martin Luther because the former came closer to restoring Christianity to its simple New Testament ideal.[4] Indeed, for Luther, the New and Old Testaments were valuable only insofar as they conveyed Christ ("soweit sie Christum treiben").[5] By this criterion, Luther relegated to inferior status the Epistle of James; he also insisted that John is "the one, fine, true, and chief gospel, and is far, far to be preferred over the other three." Furthermore, he believed that the message of the crucified Christ was meant to be preached, not written. The gospel was codified in written words merely to prevent heresy. In this sense, according to Heiko Oberman, Luther regarded the printed Bible as a "necessary evil."[6]

The Lutheran maxim *sola scriptura* did not, therefore, denote a thoroughgoing biblicism. Nor was Luther's scriptural principle the doctrinal innovation that some Lutherans have claimed. Recent scholarship has demonstrated the continuities between Luther's treatment of the Bible and that of his medieval predecessors. Thomas Aquinas identified Scripture as the "ground of faith," and the later Augustinians, particularly Gregory of Rimini (d. 1358), held that Scripture was the sole basis of Christian theology.[7] To a lesser but still significant extent, Luther also stood in continuity with his late medieval predecessors on the question of images. Condemning the iconoclasm of Andreas Bodenstein von Karlstadt, Luther asserted that images in themselves "are neither here nor there, neither evil nor good" and that they might have pedagogical value for some people.[8] In fact, the Lutheran Reformation was notable for its use of didactic imagery. Woodcuts by Lucas Cranach the Elder filled Luther's edition of the Bible and appeared on thousands of pamphlets distributed by the German reformers.[9]

If Luther was not the precursor of Anglo-American iconoclastic biblicism, then who was? Clues begin to emerge in the two representatives of the early Reformed tradition, Huldrych Zwingli and Martin Bucer, who bore important affinities with the chief humanist of the age, Desiderius Erasmus. More than did Luther, Zwingli and Bucer imbibed the moralism and rationalism characteristic of the Erasmian approach to the Bible. Though Luther had relied on Erasmus's Greek New Testament for his own translation, he adopted little of the humanist's tendency to treat the Bible as a book of moral precepts but instead viewed Scripture through the doctrinal lens of justification. Zwingli and Bucer, on the other hand, read the Bible with an eye toward the moral regeneration of society. Like the humanists, they placed great value on Scripture's antiquity: its origin in an allegedly purer time.[10] In their campaign to strip away the accretions of tradition and return to Christianity's essence, Zwingli and Bucer regarded Scripture as the blueprint for a holy commonwealth. This Reformed preference for biblical simplicity led to widespread iconoclasm during the 1520s in Zwingli's Zurich and Bucer's Strasbourg. Music, as well as images, came under attack: Zwingli banned the use of chant and shut down all of Zurich's organs in 1524.[11] Similar efforts to purify church and society took place in Geneva, home of the great second-generation reformers John Calvin and Heinrich Bullinger. Indeed, historian Carlos Eire has identified opposition to idolatry as the "Calvinist shibboleth," the great unifying concern of the Geneva reformer and his successors.[12]

Zwingli, Bucer, Calvin, and Bullinger also differed from Luther on the crucial matter of the biblical canon. Applying the principle of *sola scriptura* more consistently, the Reformed tradition treated the Bible in its entirety as normative. Unlike Luther, who privileged (among other books) the Psalms, John, and Romans, Reformed exegetes reinterpreted the humanist rallying cry *ad fontes* ("to the sources") as a mandate to immerse themselves in the sum total of Scripture. The Reformed theologians believed that it was not for humans to judge Scripture; rather, humans themselves must be judged by it.[13] Reformed confessions of faith consequently stressed more than Lutheran statements the authority of the whole canon of Scripture.[14]

Thus was Anglo-American biblicism foreshadowed in Zurich, Strasbourg, and Geneva. Yet the impact of these Reformed strongholds on American culture was filtered through a final critical locale: England, where biblicism and iconoclasm were amalgamated into a peculiarly durable alloy. The cultural durability of this alloy was exceeded only by the symbolic efficacy of iconoclastic biblicism's patron saint, William Tyndale. To understand the peculiarities of the "Tyndale tradition" in Bible translation, one must first examine the man in his national context.

ICONOCLASTIC BIBLICISM AND THE
BIBLE IN SIXTEENTH-CENTURY ENGLAND

The Reformation in England will always remain something of an enigma, thanks in part to the enigmatic monarch at its center, Henry VIII. On the one hand, the events of 1527–34 were simply a matter of political intrigue. When Pope Clement VII denied Henry's request for an annulment of his marriage to Catherine of Aragon, Henry won the backing of the English court; Clement excommunicated Henry, but Henry retaliated by severing the English church's ties with Rome, thereby asserting the primacy of state over church. At the same time, the Henrician Reformation had theological as well as political consequences. A man of somewhat Erasmian religious sympathies, Henry recognized his dispute with Rome as an opportunity to purge the English church of excessive devotionalism while in the process consolidating his power over the ecclesiastical realm. Toward this end Henry supported vernacular Scripture if translated under royal supervision—William Tyndale lacked such authorization—and in 1538, through his vicegerent Thomas Cromwell, he ordered the placement of an English Bible in every parish church. Henry and Cromwell went on to dissolve the monasteries, seizing in the process their extensive assets, and to abolish all "abused" images in the churches. These sweeping reforms left a religious void that would soon be filled by a more thoroughgoing biblicism.[15]

The English people were neither biblicists nor iconoclasts by nature. Eamon Duffy has demonstrated the luxuriance of late-medieval religion in England, where burghers invested much time and money so that their lo-

cal parish churches would have rood screens and other iconography wor-
thy of cultic devotions. The saints loomed large in the imagination of the
late-medieval English. At every turn, worshippers encountered iconic re-
minders of the heavenly hierarchy. Yet the dominance of image over word
began to erode with the invention of the printing press and the phenomenal rise of literacy in English society. As in Germany, the availability in
Britain of cheap printed materials—catechisms, devotional manuals, tracts,
and pocket editions of Scripture—had an incalculable influence on popular culture. In time the text would replace the picture as the religious vernacular, and the idea of "vernacular Scripture" would become a virtual by-
word of English Protestantism.[16]

John Wycliffe, apologetically dubbed the "morning star of the Reformation," led the early movement for an English translation of the Latin
Vulgate, although many modern historians suspect that his followers, especially Nicholas of Hereford, produced most of what came to be known
as the Wycliffe Bible (1380–82). Hand-copied in Middle English prior to
the invention of printing, the Wycliffe Bible was revised around 1400, probably by John Purvey, Wycliffe's secretary, who added a prologue explaining the translation procedures.[17] Although banned in 1408 by Thomas
Arundel, the Archbishop of Canterbury, the Wycliffe Bible and other writings of the Lollard movement continued to circulate in England, popular-
izing a theology based on the supremacy of "God's Law" (the Wycliffite
term for Scripture) over ecclesiastical authority. The anticlericalism of the
Lollards, as Wycliffe's followers were known, helped pave the way for the
Reformation, as did Wycliffe's argument that the Bible, like the apostles on
the day of Pentecost, should speak in the native tongue of every nation.[18]

But it was William Tyndale who gave the English-speaking world the
first Bible translated from the original Greek and Hebrew. Probably born
in Gloucestershire in 1494, about forty years after the dawn of printing,
Tyndale first appears in the historical record in 1512–15, when he took
his bachelor's and master's degrees at Magdalen Hall, Oxford. In the years
immediately following Luther's Ninety-five Theses (1517), Tyndale is
thought to have studied at Cambridge, then the center of Erasmian and, to
a lesser extent, Lutheran learning. Ordained a priest, Tyndale spent two
years as a tutor and preacher in Gloucestershire, where he also translated
into English Erasmus's *Enchiridion Militis Christiani* (1504). Erasmus's
Greek-Latin New Testament, the *Novum Instrumentum* (1516; second edition, 1519), was then current as the basis of Luther's New Testament, and

in this milieu Tyndale went to London to seek the permission of Bishop Tunstall to undertake an English Bible translation. When Tunstall refused, Tyndale sailed to the Continent, settling first in Germany, where he produced his 1526 Worms New Testament, and finally in Antwerp, Flanders, where he completed revisions for his better known 1534 New Testament.[19]

Tyndale's theological genealogy remains a topic of serious debate. Traditionally, the primary influence was thought to have been Lutheran because of Tyndale's stint in Germany and his extensive borrowings from Luther's writings. More recently some scholars have traced significant continuities with Lollard thought, while others have pointed out Zwinglian parallels, thus painting Tyndale as a progenitor of seventeenth-century Puritan theology. Like Zwingli, Tyndale rejected eucharistic "real presence" and other holy mysteries in favor of what might be termed today, according to A. G. Dickens, a less "superstitious" religion.[20]

Crucial to Tyndale's thought, whether Lollard or Zwinglian in origin, was an emphasis on "God's Law" (Scripture, taken in its entirety) rather than "man's law" (the authority of the church).[21] In Tyndale's view, a biblical polity excluded the notion of papal primacy; a biblical piety excluded ritualism and the devotional use of images. Thus in his 1534 New Testament he deprived the papacy of its favorite proof-text (Matt. 16:18, "you are Peter, and on this rock I will build my church"), by translating the Greek *ekklēsia* as "congregation."[22] And leveling his opposition to the shape and hue of late-medieval piety, he translated the Greek *eidōlolatrēs* (1 Cor. 5:11) not as "idolater" but as "worshipper of images."[23] He went on to render the related Greek term *eidōlothuton* (food offered to idols) as "it which is offered to images" ("What say I then? that the image is anything? or that it which is offered to images is anything?"). He thereby transformed 1 Corinthians 10:19 from a passage about cultic food sacrifice to a denunciation of images and image worship.[24] This reflected Tyndale's opinion that "God is a spirit, and will be worshipped in his word only, which is spiritual."[25]

The anti-Catholic bias in Tyndale's New Testament incurred the wrath of a powerful adversary, Sir Thomas More, Lord Chancellor of England from 1529 to 1532. Though sympathetic to Christian humanism, More was an unshakable defender of ecclesiastical authority. He sized up Tyndale as a "drowsy drudge drinking deep in the devil's dregs" who would destroy the edifice of fifteen hundred years of church tradition.[26] No matter that More's friend Erasmus also had translated *ekklēsia* as "congregatio" in his

Latin New Testament; More smelled in Tyndale's "untrue translating" the unmistakable odor of "malicious intent." In addition to thumbing his nose at the papacy, according to More, Tyndale cast aspersions upon the "good folk which worship images of Christ and his saints." Tyndale, More added, failed to appreciate that "image is a term indifferent to good and bad" and that only idols, or abused images, were proscribed by the biblical writers.[27]

Ironically, Tyndale and More both fell into displeasure with King Henry VIII, whose own views of church authority and popular piety shifted like a weathervane in the political wind. As he began to dissolve the monasteries, Henry adopted an iconoclastic stance, but this came too late to save the life of the iconoclastic translator Tyndale, who was executed at Vilvoorde Castle, near Brussels, by agents of Emperor Charles V while the English crown looked the other way. Meanwhile More, the Catholic stalwart, already had proven too big a thorn in Henry's side. Because of his steadfast opposition to the royal divorce, More was beheaded in 1536, a year before Tyndale was strangled and burned at the stake. In the end the execution of Tyndale, the opponent of images, was immortalized for all time by an image. A lurid woodcut depicting his ceremonial strangulation, along with his alleged last words ("Lord, open the King of England's eyes"), was among the illustrations printed in the many editions of John Foxe's *Acts and Monuments.* No doubt it was one of the images that captivated Sir Francis Drake, victorious foe of Catholic Spain's navy, who lovingly colored the illustrations in his own copy of Foxe. More important, the icons of Tyndale and other Protestant martyrs inspired generations of Puritans, who brought iconoclastic biblicism to American shores.[28]

Although Tyndale and the iconography devoted to him indelibly imprinted English (and later, American) attitudes toward word and image, iconoclastic biblicism became an official article of faith only when the monarchy, influenced by the theology of the Continental reformers, embraced a thoroughgoing piety of the word.[29] The transformation began in 1547 when Henry VIII died and his nine-year-old son succeeded him as Edward VI. Having received a thoroughly Protestant education—one of his tutors was a correspondent of Calvin—young Edward was hailed upon his accession as a latter-day Josiah, the Judean king and reformer who took office at the age of eight. Comparison of English monarchs with biblical figures was familiar practice; indeed, such parallels were implied in a precritical, typological reading of Scripture. For his opposition to idolatry, Henry VIII had been eulogized as the new Hezekiah, destroyer of the "brasen serpent" (2 Kings 18:4). Now the "Tudor Josiah" Edward VI, following the biblical pattern, sought to complete the purification of religion begun by his father; he wrote out a list of Old Testament passages against images and presented the manuscript to his regent and uncle, Lord Protector Edward Seymour, duke of Somerset. King Edward proceeded through Somerset to issue a series of injunctions ordering parish priests to destroy all images, even stained glass, that had functioned as objects of pilgrimages or offerings. Edward's injunctions went beyond those of his father, which granted the power of iconoclasm only to diocesan officials, not parish clergy, and proscribed a narrower range of objects. Soon Edward himself became an icon for Protestant iconoclasts. A famous image by an unknown painter shows Edward on his throne with the fallen pope at his feet, surmounted by a Bible open to 1 Peter 1:25, "The worde of the Lorde endureth for ever"; to Edward's left is a depiction of the destruction of a religious statue.[30]

Edwardian iconoclasm went hand in hand with the ascendancy of Reformed theology in the English church during the episcopacy of Thomas Cranmer, archbishop of Canterbury. Cranmer counted among his friends some eminent Reformed divines, including Calvin, whom he urged to "write to the king frequently," and Bucer, whom he invited to live in England. Bucer, appointed Regius Professor of divinity at Cambridge, offered editorial suggestions for Cranmer's first *Book of Common Prayer* (1549), nudging the archbishop toward a more Reformed stance.[31] Among the Calvinist innovations in the revised prayer book (1552) was the stipulation that the Ten Commandments be read prior to Holy Communion. Particularly significant was the Decalogue's actual arrangement in the prayer book, which, favoring the Reformed pattern over the Catholic and Lutheran, treated the clause against "graven images" as a separate second commandment rather than subsuming it under the first.[32] With its prohibition against images, the Hebrew Law thus became a focal point of English worship during Edward's reign. (Later, during the Elizabethan period, Archbishop Matthew Parker ordered the placement of the commandments on the east wall of every church and chapel.) Cranmer's liturgical revolution also drew a great deal of ammunition from the New Testament. Influenced by Bucer among others, Cranmer was persuaded that eucharistic vestments were unscriptural, that the altar was simply the "Lord's table," and that transubstantiation was rank superstition. Cranmer's words of eucharistic administration in the 1552 prayer book ("Take and eat this, in remembrance that Christ died for thee, and feed on him in thy heart, by faith with thanksgiving") confounded high churchmen and Lutherans alike, who along with many later historians regarded the terminology as an example of Zwinglian memorialism.[33] Yet in eucharistic and other matters, Cranmer believed himself an advocate of biblical simplicity and considered the Bible the linchpin of the church's reformation. During the reign of Henry VIII, Cranmer had highlighted Scripture's importance in the English church in a famous preface to the 1540 edition of the Great Bible, the official version of the time, by referring to the words of Holy Writ as "a better jewel in our house than either gold or silver." The Great Bible's title page also highlighted Scripture's importance—this time iconographically—with a depiction (possibly by Hans Holbein) of King Henry handing Bibles to Archbishop Cranmer and Vicegerent Cromwell. All told, Cranmer's effort to strip away liturgical and doctrinal accretions and return to the biblical practices of the primitive church left a lasting mark on English piety. Although the archbishop himself was burned at the stake during the Catholic interlude under Mary Tudor, his prayer book was restored with few changes during the long reign of Elizabeth. His dying words—a repudiation of the pope as "Christ's enemy and antichrist"—excited anti-Catholic sentiment just as Tyndale's martyrdom had done twenty years earlier.[34]

Historians generally agree that the Marian return to Roman Catholicism (1553–58) served only to breed a resistant strain of hyper-Protestantism. Many English divines sought refuge in Reformed strongholds such as Geneva, Strasbourg, and Zurich, where they produced an important corpus of anti-Catholic literature. Chief among the exiles' works were the Geneva Bible and Foxe's *Acts and Monuments*. The former, heavily dependent upon Tyndale's translation, betrayed its antipapal bias at the outset when the translators noted the recent "horrible backesliding and falling away from Christ to Antichrist, from light to darcknes, from the liuing God to dumme and dead idoles." Similar digs at the papacy peppered the edition's extensive marginal notes, as at Revelation 17:4, where the annotation identified the Whore of Babylon as "the Antichrist, that is, the Pope." From 1560 to 1611, over 120 editions of the Geneva Bible appeared, more than three times the number of all other English editions combined. Later editions of the Geneva New Testament, edited by the Puritan member of Parliament Laurence Tomson, included notes by Theodore Beza and Franciscus Junius reinforcing the book's Calvinist and anti-Catholic character. In all its manifestations, the Geneva Bible proved a formidable influence on Anglo-Protestant culture. It was the first English Bible to introduce verse numbering, an innovation that would facilitate all future proof-texting. Moreover, it was the first truly popular Bible among the English people, thanks to its affordable quarto format, and was used widely in England well into the seventeenth century.[35]

The other important literary product of the Protestant exiles at Geneva was John Foxe's *Acts and Monuments,* better known as the *Book of Martyrs,* which remains to this day the only significant contemporaneous source—how accurate is not clear—on Tyndale's career. Recent Tyndale biographer David Daniell insists that Foxe is usually trustworthy, echoing the much earlier judgment of J. F. Mozley, who claimed that Foxe's errors were mere "spots on the sun."[36] Yet even Mozley admitted that Foxe was "temperamentally incapable of writing what is now called a scientific history."[37] Indeed, Foxe's representation of Tyndale and his Catholic opponents, not the accuracy of that representation, is of greatest relevance to this study. Foxe's anti-Catholic animus, though understandable in the wake of the Marian persecution, continued to influence constructions of the Tyndale tradition long after the fires of martyrdom had cooled.

In recounting the life of Tyndale, Foxe continually contrasted the translator's impeccable character with the "abominable doings and idolatries maintained by the pharisaical clergy." He scoffed at the "mist" of the English priests' "sophistry"; he decried their "false hypocrisy," their "froward devices," their "vain superstition," and their "insatiable covetousness." Standing in stark relief was Tyndale, "a man of most virtuous disposition, and of life unspotted." Tyndale was no less than "the apostle of England in this our later age," whose righteousness was sealed by the blood of martyrdom.[38] Foxe's hagiography of Tyndale even brought to mind the Synoptic Gospels' account of the centurion who witnessed the Crucifixion (Matt. 27:54; Mark 15:39; Luke 23:47). Concerning the scene of Tyndale's imprisonment and death at Vilvoorde, Foxe wrote: "The procurator-general, the emperor's attorney, being there, left this testimony of him, that he was 'Homo doctus, pius, et bonus,' that is, 'a learned, a good, and a godly man.'"[39] Subsequent historians repeatedly cited this and other details from the *Book of Martyrs,* conferring on Foxe's Tyndale an almost mythical status. Likewise, Foxe's anti-Catholicism persisted throughout many generations, enlivened by a particular notion of Rome's great sin—that it had kept "the Scriptures of God . . . hidden from people's eyes."[40]

By 1583, when a fourth edition of *Acts and Monuments* appeared, Roman Catholic exiles at Rheims, France, were at work on an English Bible of their own, and this development would soon harden the resolve of Protestant historiographers. The Rheims New Testament had appeared in 1582 at the instigation of William Allen, who was later created cardinal, and translator Gregory Martin, who died shortly after the book's completion.[41] In 1593, the English College at Rheims returned to its original home at Douay, Flanders, where work on the Old Testament continued until 1609. With its preface and extensive annotations, the Douay-Rheims Bible challenged the emerging Protestant version of history, namely, that Rome had always suppressed vernacular Scripture. English Bibles were never "wholly forbidden," according to the preface to the Rheims New Testament; yet even the great Jerome recognized the potential perils of translating Scripture from one tongue to another. The Catholic Church neither forbade authorized translation nor encouraged the "licentious tossing" of the vernacular Bible before untrained laypersons or, worse, "sect-masters." That the Protestant sect-masters had produced unauthorized and doctrinally corrupt Scripture necessitated a Catholic corrective: an English Bible adhering as closely as possible to the only authentic version, the Latin Vulgate. Invoking the Council of Trent, the Rheims translators enumerated ten reasons why the Vulgate was used as the translation's basis, most notably that the Latin text "is truer than the vulgar Greek itself" by virtue of its patristic and Counter-Reformation sanction.[42] The Douay-Rheims translation therefore abounded in ecclesiastical Latinisms (e.g., "Pasche"), with notes refuting their Protestant renderings ("Passover").

The Douay-Rheims Bible opened the floodgates to Protestant polemic, especially by leaders of the Puritan party. Treatises published during the 1580s by William Fulke, William Whitaker, George Wither, and Thomas Cartwright all sought to refute the Rheims renderings and annotations, as did Fulke's parallel edition of the Rheims and Bishops' Bibles (1589). Fulke, a fellow of St. John's College, Cambridge, had distinguished himself during the 1560s Vestiarian Controversy (in which Puritan divines refused to wear the surplice and other clerical vestments) as an ardent opponent of "Romish rags." Two and a half centuries later, American Protestants resurrected his *Confutation of the Rhemish Testament* as part of a flurry of no-popery publications, the most infamous being Maria Monk's *Awful Disclosures of the Hotel Dieu Nunnery of Montreal* (1836).[43]

THE EMERGENCE OF A "NATIONAL" BIBLE
IN ENGLAND AND AMERICA

The controversy of the 1580s increased public awareness of the Bible as a translated book and therefore one subject to dogmatic bias, yet English Protestants had so far failed in the face of Rheims to unite behind a single version of their own. In the early seventeenth century, the Geneva Bible still competed with the officially sanctioned Bishops' Bible (1568, revised 1572) for the loyalty of the average reader, even as scholars of Hebrew and Greek pointed out the deficiencies of both versions. Change came when James I accepted a Puritan proposal for a new translation, evidently because he feared that the "seditious" Geneva annotations questioned the divine right of kings. The new Bible, which came to be known as the Authorized (or King James) Version, eliminated the alleged threat to national security by removing all doctrinal glosses. And because the Authorized Version project brought together Puritan and conformist scholars, it symbolized, in historian Christopher Hill's estimation, a significant moment of national unity prior to the turmoil of the 1640s.[44] The English Civil War temporarily reignited the battle of the versions: soldiers of Cromwell's New Model Army carried a pocket booklet of Geneva Bible excerpts, while Royalists relied on Bible verses and propers culled from the *Book of Common Prayer*.[45] Yet with the Restoration, the tide turned decisively against Geneva, and the Authorized Version finally became *the* Bible for the English people. The overthrow of England's last Catholic king in the Glorious Revolution of 1688 confirmed Britain's status as a Protestant nation and laid the groundwork for a new triumphalist historiography of the English Bible.

Meanwhile, across the Atlantic, the King James Bible also was winning the hearts of the New World Puritans. Puritanism had been born of dissatisfaction with the Elizabethan Settlement, which tempered the iconoclasm of Edward's reign. The Puritans of New England, despite internecine theological disputes, all agreed that the Church of England had stopped far short of New Testament ideals of piety. The Bible, on a Puritan reading, mandated a "plain style" of worship that contrasted sharply with the periodically ascendant high church style. In Puritan meeting-houses the communion "table" was subordinate to the pulpit, and the only true altar was the prepared human heart.[46] Puritan theology centered not on corporate doctrines of the Eucharist but on the "covenant of grace"—God's conversion and redemption of the individual believer through Christ's atoning sacrifice. Yet soteriological individualism quickly proved perilous as Puritans struggled to maintain social order in the wilderness of the New World. Soon a parallel notion of the "federal covenant," a system of divine reward and punishment for national conduct, emerged as an integral part of the New England Way. And with the federal covenant, as Harry Stout has suggested, came the gradual decline of the old Geneva Bible, whose footnotes reflected the popular theology of the sixteenth century, with its emphasis on individual justification, rather than the more establishmentarian thought of the seventeenth century, with its emphasis on national election. Lacking doctrinal marginalia, the King James Bible was suggestive of simplicity and restraint; it won the loyalty of the New World authorities in no small part because of its unimpeachable credentials as a document of national unity.[47] Indeed, as Liah Greenfeld has pointed out, the Authorized Version was a particularly notable example of nationalism in the English Bible tradition: the English word "nation" (whose modern geopolitical sense has no exact equivalent in Hebrew or Greek) appeared in the King James Bible 454 times, whereas the Latin *natio* appeared only one hundred times in the Vulgate.[48]

With the Puritan adoption of the King James Bible, the words of 1611 became America's sacred lexicon, the language in which divinity addressed humanity. Puritan clergy effectively became America's first language teachers, and their method of instruction was homiletical. Preaching, New England's primary public means of communication, imprinted biblical language in the minds of the lettered and unlettered alike. Since literacy rates in New England were among the world's highest, most people reinforced aural exposure to Scripture with visual.[49] Indeed, Puritan fluency in Scripture's "great code"—Northrop Frye's term for the biblical well of normative stories and idiom—can scarcely be overestimated.[50]

Nearly all American Protestants internalized in some way the Puritan glorification of word over image, although what once was a native command of biblical language often degenerated into a mere bibliolatry. And this bibliolatry, while taking a variety of forms, usually included an implicit (or explicit) anti-Catholicism. In some cases anti-Catholicism rested on the belief that the American republic was founded on the King James Bible, which "papists" continually sought to exclude from the public schools. In other cases, anti-Catholicism lurked in the very text of Scripture, as in

Cyrus Scofield's famous annotated King James edition, which followed the Geneva Bible in identifying the Whore of Babylon with the papacy.[51] In most cases anti-Catholicism took the form of an unarticulated assumption, deep-seated in the Protestant psyche, that Catholic religion was the stuff of human fancy while Protestantism was built on the unchangeable testimony of Scripture.

CONSECRATED HISTORY: MODERN REPRESENTATIONS OF THE TYNDALE TRADITION

The equation of Protestantism with the Word, though often an unarticulated assumption of the Protestant mind, found vivid expression in the English Bible history, an oft-imitated genre in Anglo-Protestant nonfiction after the late-nineteenth-century explosion in Bible publishing. Almost invariably catering to a general readership, these histories typically ranged over five centuries of Bible translation, tracing the provenance and distinguishing characteristics of the various versions. The very idea of a Bible "version," with the corollary notion that one version could be truer than another, was popularized by these histories. At the same time, these volumes constructed an idea of a unified "Tyndale tradition" whose progress toward perfection resembled the ascent of the human species. With titles such as *How We Got Our Bible* and *The Bible and the Anglo-Saxon People,* these histories presupposed the existence of a monolithic Anglo-Protestant establishment that by the 1950s would no longer exist, as powerful liberal and conservative institutions competed for denominational and individual loyalties. Yet conservative and liberal Protestants were branches of the same tree—inheritors of the same unyielding biblicism that staggered the sixteenth century and practitioners of the same critical epistemology that elevated "fact" above all else in religion.

A few English Bible histories appeared in print as early as the eighteenth century, adopting such contemporary Enlightenment bywords as "reason" and "common sense" to describe the Protestant partiality for vernacular Scripture.[52] But the Bible history genre began to flower only in the latter half of the nineteenth century, particularly after 1870, when at least two new histories (and often many more) appeared in every succeeding decade. This proliferation of histories had a variety of causes, but probably the most decisive single factor was the rapid development of textual criticism, especially of the New Testament, during the period. As will become clear in the next chapter, the findings of textual critics spurred the Bible revision movement, which in turn stimulated intense public curiosity about the burgeoning Babel of Bibles. The English Bible histories therefore filled a significant market demand, and multiple print runs of the more popular books were not uncommon.[53]

Although some of the Bible histories were written by translators themselves, more were penned by well-informed clergy or laypersons from across the spectrum of oldline Protestant denominations. These amateur historians rarely questioned each other's basic conclusions, and their works often revealed a striking interdependence, the shorter volumes sometimes being little more than condensations of the more detailed ones. These histories also manifested certain common historiographical themes, and in the remainder of this chapter I shall examine four, drawing examples from across the literature except those histories by members of the Revised Standard Version committee, whose work I consider later. In some respects, the RSV translators modified the regnant historiography, and these subtle changes contributed indirectly to the RSV controversy of the 1950s. On the whole, however, the Bible histories published from the late nineteenth century onward articulated similar ideas of the English Bible that in turn helped give shape to Anglo-American Protestant biblicism.

The first theme of the English Bible histories, and probably the most important, was anti-Catholicism. Sometimes overt, sometimes subtle, anti-Catholic bias seemed to flow as naturally from the historians' pens as the ink itself. In many cases, this anti-Catholicism assumed the guise of a generalized antimedievalism, for the Middle Ages were equated with the Constantinian synthesis—the promiscuous union of church and state—and the virtually enforced religious ignorance of the laity. Typical of this view was Hannah Chaplin Conant's *Popular History of the Translation of the Holy Scriptures into the English Tongue,* originally published in 1856 and updated in 1881 by her husband, Thomas Jefferson Conant, a member of the Revised Version committee. A northern Baptist, Hannah Conant edited for many years the *Mother's Monthly Journal* and was a prolific translator of works from the German. In her view, medieval people had been mere tools of a priesthood that purposefully kept Scripture—"the only Magna Charta of the weak"—hidden in the cloister. Without the biblical "charter of their rights as men," medieval laypeople groped in the blindness of deepest midnight, deprived of the "very consciousness of their manhood."[54] Conant's interpretation begged the question of why priests wanted to hide the Scriptures, and John W. Lea, author of a copiously illustrated English Bible history for Sunday school classes, offered the typical answer—that Scripture denounced the priesthood and its claims—though he cited no Bible verses in support of this allegation.[55] Meanwhile John Eadie, a Presbyterian member of the Revised Version committee, buttressed his anti-Catholicism in a two-volume history of the English Bible by appealing not to Scripture but to the Puritan William Whitaker, one of the anti-Rheimists of the 1580s. On the first page of his history, Eadie juxtaposed epigraphs from Whitaker and Francis Bacon. Whitaker's was a predictable tongue-lashing of the Catholic opposition to Scripture's popularization; Bacon's was more philosophical:

> Howsoever these things are in men's depraved judgments and affections, yet Truth which only doth judge itself, teacheth that the inquiry of truth, which is the love-making and the wooing of it, and the belief of truth, which is the enjoying of it, is the sovereign good of human nature.[56]

Eadie's implication in juxtaposing the two epigraphs might have been boiled down to a syllogism: the words of Scripture are the only truth; Catholics suppress the words of Scripture; therefore, Catholics are enemies of the truth. Indeed, at the heart of many English Bible histories was the old sixteenth-century iconoclasm that equated Protestantism with "word" and Catholicism with "image." Or, as H. W. Hamilton-Hoare, in *The Evolution of the English Bible,* put it, "Medievalism asked not for a book but for religion externalized in an institution." The church in those distant days presented its teaching not in "a spiritual but in a sensuous, in a symbolic, and in a materialized form." This had a numbing effect on the popular mind: "So low indeed had sunk the general mental level that men were well-nigh incapable of any abstract conceptions at all."[57]

A REPRESENTATIVE SAMPLE OF PROTESTANT HISTORIES OF THE ENGLISH BIBLE, 1845–1956

1845　Christopher Anderson, *The Annals of the English Bible*

1856　Hannah C. Conant, *The English Bible: History of the Translation . . .*

1868　†B. F. Westcott, *A General View of the History of the English Bible*

1876　†John Eadie, *The English Bible: An External and Critical History . . .*

1878　John Stoughton, *Our English Bible: Its Translations and Translators*

1881　H. C. and †T. J. Conant, *A Popular History of the Translation of the Holy Scriptures into the English Tongue*

1883   J. I. Mombert, *A Hand-Book of the English Versions of the Bible*

1886   J. Paterson Smyth, *How We Got Our Bible*

1888   J. R. Dore, *Old Bibles: An Account of the Early Versions . . .*

1889   Andrew Edgar, *The Bibles of England: A Plain Account for Plain People of the Principal Versions of the Bible in English*

1894   T. Harwood Pattison, *The History of the English Bible*

1895   George Milligan, *The English Bible: A Sketch of Its History*

1896   Blackford Condit, *The History of the English Bible: Extending from the Earliest Saxon Translations to the Present Anglo-American Revision*

1901   H. W. Hamilton-Hoare, *The Evolution of the English Bible: An Historical Sketch . . .*

1905   †B. F. Westcott, *A General View . . .* (Rev. by William Aldis Wright)

1906   Ira M. Price, *The Ancestry of Our English Bible: An Account . . .*

1909   Samuel McComb, *The Making of the English Bible*

1911   †W. F. Moulton, *The History of the English Bible* (5th ed.)

1911   J. D. Payne, *The English Bible: An Historical Survey . . .*

1911   John Brown, *The History of the English Bible*

1911   Alfred W. Pollard, *Records of the English Bible: The Documents Relating to the Translation . . . of the Bible in English, 1525–1611*

1914   William Canton, *The Bible and the Anglo-Saxon People*

1922   John W. Lea, *The Book of Books and Its Wonderful Story: A Popular Handbook for Colleges, Bible Classes, Sunday Schools . . .*

1925   *Edgar J. Goodspeed, *The Making of the English New Testament*

1928   James Baikie, *The English Bible and Its Story: Its Growth, Its Translators, and Their Adventures*

1929   P. Marion Simms, *The Bible from the Beginning*

1936   P. Marion Simms, *The Bible in America: Versions that Have Played Their Part in the Making of the Republic*

1940   *Edgar J. Goodspeed, *How Came the Bible?*

1949   *Luther A. Weigle, *The English New Testament from Tyndale to the Revised Standard Version*

1952   *Herbert G. May, *Our English Bible in the Making*

1956   Ira M. Price, *The Ancestry of Our English Bible: An Account . . .* (Rev. by *William A. Irwin and *Allen P. Wikgren)

†Member of the Revised Version Committee
*Member of the Revised Standard Version Committee

Observations of this sort infuriated Father Hugh Pope (1869–1946), one of the relatively few American Catholic historians of the English Bible, who insisted that there was no proof that Rome forbade or even discouraged vernacular Bibles. In any case, Pope wrote, literate persons in the Middle Ages usually read Latin, and the Latin Bible had been available for centuries.[58] Yet Pope's objections could not stem the tide of a historiography that regarded the English Bible, and even the written word itself, as intrinsically Protestant and intrinsically modern. The converse of this historiography—a story of medieval Catholic decay and decline—was the narrative constructed by Renaissance humanists, from whom historians in the nineteenth and early twentieth centuries borrowed their own interpretation of the "Dark Ages." Discourses of modernity invariably depended for a foil on an idea of the Middle Ages as a time of stagnant traditionalism that, beginning with the Reformation, yielded to Hegelian ideals of historical change and individual self-realization. The darker subtext of this discourse, influenced by Victorian-era social Darwinism, was that certain peoples of the world were the beneficiaries of modernity while others were hopelessly benighted and thus subject to religious or political conquest.[59]

The idea of national or racial superiority leads to the second theme of the English Bible histories, ethnocentrism, which usually amounted to little more than an ethnically specific anti-Catholicism. Hamilton-Hoare's *Evolution of the English Bible* again provides an excellent example. Writing of the transitional period to the modern world, Hamilton-Hoare contrasted the "Latin" and "Teutonic" branches of Christianity, the former representing tradition, the latter representing Scripture. Elsewhere he referred to the "Teutonic love of truth," and explained that "it is not by the grace of either Roman, or Dane, or Norman, that we are what we are today, but mainly through that ireradicable instinct of race which courses so strongly in our Saxon blood."[60] Another writer, James Baikie, noted the inferior position of the Bible among the "Southern Europeans." In contrast, he added, "the English race is emphatically 'The People of the Book.'"[61] Similarly, John Stoughton, in *Our English Bible,* observed that Jews and Muslims either discouraged or forbade Scripture's translation: "It is otherwise in this country, thank God!"[62]

Perhaps the most revealing example of ethnocentrism is Christopher Anderson's massive two-volume *Annals of the English Bible* (1845), cited for decades by other Bible historians as a standard reference. Anderson was minister of a Baptist congregation at Edinburgh, and although he frequently betrayed his Scottish nationalist sentiments in his *Annals,* he nevertheless adopted a multinational perspective, recounting in 1,348 pages the English Bible's evolution and influence in England, Scotland, and North America. Looking upon the worldwide expanse of the British Empire and its current and former colonies, Anderson triumphantly proclaimed the English Bible "the only version in existence on which the sun never sets." He quickly conceded that the sun never set on the Spanish language either, and yet, what terrible neglect had the Bible suffered in Catholic Spain as compared to Protestant Britain! "Let the contrast, the indescribable contrast, at once humble and inspirit a people whom God has so distinguished," he wrote.[63] For Anderson, the people whom God had distinguished were not only the Scottish but all English-speaking Protestants. Wherever the English Bible had taken root, it had borne great fruits, as in the work of such American theologians as Roger Williams, Cotton Mather, and Jonathan Edwards, who participated in an unbroken transatlantic Bible tradition.[64] Anderson's apparent ease in knitting together a unified English-speaking religious culture would take on additional significance in the 1880s and 1890s as leading Americans articulated concepts of Anglo-Saxon civilization. From Josiah Strong's *Our Country* (1885) to Theodore Roosevelt's *Winning of the West* (1889–96), popular publications heralded the inevitable triumph of the evolutionarily superior, English-speaking Protestant "race." Though theories of this race's Anglo-Saxon origins varied, it was usually clear what this race was not: "colored" or Catholic. Many of the histories of the English Bible appeared precisely at this high point of Anglo-Saxon racial theorizing, and some degree of mutual influence may be assumed.[65]

At the same time, the English Bible translation tradition acted as a culturally homogenizing force, occasionally obscuring differences between Anglo and other Protestants. Non-Anglo Protestants, including some of the leaders of the African Methodist Episcopal (AME) Church, were among the supporters of the Bible revision movement of the 1880s. And among ethnic white Protestants, American Lutherans, who wrote their own histories glorifying Luther's German Bible, nevertheless readily embraced the Tyndale English Bible tradition, usually taking pains to stress Tyndale's "Lutheran" credentials.[66] The Tyndale translation tradition therefore became in certain respects the American religious tradition par excellence, uniting all American Protestants, if only superficially, in an imagined linguistic community.[67] In addition to North America, this community vaguely encompassed Britain and its state church, despite the relative minority status of Anglicans in the United States since disestablishment. American and British historians of the English Bible, by virtue of a common language and intimately linked national pasts, simultaneously reached audiences on both sides of the Atlantic; Bible histories published in London were reprinted in New York, and vice versa. In short, the Anglo notion of "our English Bible" was eminently pliable, depending as it did upon a perceived common enemy, the Catholic peril.

The third theme of the English Bible histories was hagiography, specifically, the veneration of English Scripture's patron saint, William Tyndale. Without Tyndale, the anti-Catholicism and ethnocentrism of the English Bible tradition might have remained dry, even perfunctory. But the blood of Tyndale's martyrdom colored the Anglo-Protestant imagination, transforming Tyndale's story into the most usable of pasts. Tyndale's martyrdom distinguished him from John Wycliffe, universally acknowledged as the first translator of the English Bible. Such was the opinion of the Bible historian and renowned textual critic Brooke Foss Westcott, Regius Professor of divinity at Cambridge, member of the Revised Version committee, and later bishop of Durham. Like other Bible historians, Westcott identified Wycliffe's contribution in the fourteenth century as the yielding of the "time of tutelage" to the "time of maturity"; yet also like his colleagues, Westcott believed that it was with Tyndale that the history of the English Bible really began. To Westcott, Tyndale almost seemed incapable of sin, so suffused was he with the divine Protestant purpose. "Not one selfish thought mixed with his magnificent devotion," Westcott wrote. "No treacherous intrigues ever shook his loyalty to his king: no intensity of distress ever obscured his faith in Christ." Nor was Westcott himself ambivalent about his own national and denominational loyalties, noting that Tyndale exhibited "a simple humility which Luther rarely if ever shews." It is true that Luther gave Germans the vernacular Bible, but one thing set Tyndale apart from the Wittenberg reformer: "the seal of martyrdom." Along with the executions of John Rogers (Tyndale's associate) and Archbishop Cranmer, the martyrdom of Tyndale lent the English Bible a peculiar authority. In Westcott's view, no other book was ever so consecrated.[68]

Yet the consecration of the English Bible through the person of Tyndale was not without problems. Anyone who had read his unedited polemics knew that Tyndale's mouth was as foul as those of his contemporaries, and the Parker Society, sponsor of a nineteenth-century edition of Tyndale's works, had occasionally excised lewd passages, noting in the margin that "a coarse expression is here omitted."[69] Other writers, like Hannah Conant, nodded indulgently at Tyndale's propensity for "homely, racy humor," which she judged to be "well adapted to influence the popular mind."[70] Most authors, however, seemed content simply to ignore the sharp edge of Tyndale's polemic, often invoking the judgment of the famous historian James Anthony Froude that Tyndale's "spirit, as it were divorced from the world, moved in a purer element than common air."[71]

So high were the estimations of Tyndale's humility that comparisons to Moses and Christ were not uncommon. John Eadie invoked a story from Exodus when he wrote of Tyndale's willingness "to remain an unrecognized benefactor, to be hidden 'in a cleft of the rock' as the divine glory passed by and settled at length over his beloved fatherland."[72] The fatherland mingled again with biblical imagery in John Brown's *History of the English Bible,* a King James tercentenary volume published at Cambridge. Recalling the execution scene at Vilvoorde, Brown wrote that Tyndale's "*via dolorosa* had come to its end, and his prayer, like that of his Master, was for those who had wronged him. His last thought was for the fatherland he had left so long and loved so well. 'Lord,' cried he, 'open the King of England's eyes.'"[73] In like manner, J. Paterson Smyth claimed that there was "no grander life in the whole annals of the Reformation than that of William Tyndale—none which comes nearer in its beautiful self-forgetfulness to His who 'laid down His life for His sheep.'"[74] For Eadie, Brown, and Smyth, Tyndale's martyrdom effectively ruled out of order any misgivings about the translator's character. If his death were not proof enough of his righteousness, his resurrection in the form of his Bible, whose words lived still, appeared to the historians as Tyndale's—and Protestantism's—ultimate vindication.

Nowhere did this Tyndale Bible mystique receive more high-flown expression than in Froude's multivolume history of England (1856–70), cited repeatedly by Bible historians despite (or possibly because of) Froude's reputation for Protestant zealotry. Of the English Bible tradition, Froude wrote:

> The peculiar genius—if such a word may be permitted—which breathes through it—the mingled tenderness and majesty—the Saxon simplicity— the preternatural grandeur—unequalled, unapproached, in the attempted improvements of modern scholars—all are here, and bear the impress of the mind of one man—William Tyndal.[75]

Yet Froude's disdain for the "attempted improvements of modern scholars" betrayed him as a relative outsider to the guild of English Bible historians, most of whom believed in the Bible's perfectibility through successively improved versions.

The fourth theme of the English Bible histories, therefore, was evolutionism, or the idea that Protestant biblical scholarship was an ever-ascending march toward a more perfect Bible. Bishop Westcott had encapsulated this notion in 1868 when he spoke of the English Bible's "assimilative power of life," that is, its ever-evolving, ever-improving quality.[76] The Bible's assimilative power derived largely from ongoing research in textual criticism, and many Bible historians could boast at least limited schooling in the science of "codices" and "variants." To demonstrate their insiders' knowledge, historians sometimes appended to their works brief "popular" introductions to text-critical principles. A case in point was P. Marion Simms, author of two widely distributed English Bible histories, who included in his first book "A Lesson in Textual Criticism" based on the example of Matthew 6:13, the latter half of which read in the Authorized Version, "For thine is the kingdom, and the power, and the glory, for ever. Amen." Simms explained that the two important codices, Vaticanus and Sinaiticus, did not have this concluding doxology, and for this reason the translators of the American Standard Version (1901) had relegated the phrase to a footnote.[77] To Simms, such changes in the biblical text, though potentially upsetting to the uninformed, were not only permissible but necessary. Simms had little patience for those who treated the Authorized Version as sacrosanct. Recalling an ill-fated attempt by the American Bible Society during the 1850s to correct minor typographical errors in the King James text, Simms suggested that the vociferous opposition to the corrections was "only an example of how ignorance often betrays Christian people into making donkeys of themselves."[78]

The English Bible's evolution, as Simms and other historians conceived of it, was a paradoxical process. On the one hand was the inexorable march toward perfection, the gradual removal of errors and obscurities. Yet this progression required retrospection, or ever more precise conjecture about the long-lost original biblical manuscripts. The twin enterprises of textual criticism and English Bible revision were therefore simultaneously evolutionary (imagining textual development toward a higher form) and primitivist (imagining textual restoration of an earlier form). At its height of evolution, the translated English Bible paradoxically would mirror the primitive Greek and Hebrew texts. Simms represented this unique evolution with a diagram on the frontispiece of his first book, but he credited J. Paterson Smyth for the diagram's conception. Smyth's frontispiece depicted a line beginning with the nebulous text-critical primordium ("Original Manuscripts Lost") and culminating with the then-latest Bible, the Revised Version of 1881–85. As beneficiary of the late-nineteenth-century revolution in textual criticism, the Revised Version was the only Bible in Smyth's chart that fully integrated textual evidence from the three primary sources ("Manuscripts," "Versions," and "Fathers"); diagonal lines connected these witnesses directly to the Bible of 1881–85.[79]

Evolutionary thinking about the biblical text elevated the process of change to nearly sacramental status and thereby reinvoked the old theme of anti-Catholicism, for Protestants had long stereotyped Catholics as people uncomfortable with change. Puritan theologian William Whitaker, whose anti-Catholic observation appeared as an epigraph in John Eadie's English Bible history, put it clearly:

> The Jesuit reasons thus: if the scriptures should be read by the people in the vulgar tongue, then new versions should be made in every age. . . . [I]t would be absurd that the versions should be so often changed. Therefore the scriptures ought not to be read in the vernacular tongue. I answer, this argument is ridiculous. . . . [N]o inconvenience will follow if interpretations or versions of scripture, when they have become obsolete and ceased to be easily intelligible, be afterwards changed and corrected.[80]

In the end it is legitimate to ask whether Protestants were as open-minded toward change as Whitaker (and Eadie) supposed, for in constant tension with the ideal of a changing Bible was the ideal of the eternal changelessness of God's Word. Captivated by the ideal of biblical immutability—and the alleged permanence of "word" over "image"—a certain segment of Protestants would always resist modification of the inherited version of Scripture. This old-Bible nostalgia was a thorn in the side of textual critics and translators, but it did not prevent the flowering of a full-scale Bible revision movement in the late nineteenth century. The revision movement's first product, the Revised Version, is the subject of the next chapter.

Chapter 2

Coronation of "King Truth"

Bible Revision and the Late-Nineteenth-Century Imagination

✠

*All scripture is given by inspiration of God,
and is profitable for doctrine, for reproof,
for correction, for instruction in righteousness.*

—2 Timothy 3:16 (King James Version, 1611)

*Every scripture inspired of God is also profitable
for teaching, for reproof, for correction,
for instruction which is in righteousness.*

—2 Timothy 3:16 (Revised Version, 1881)

"A New Testament which Needs neither a Glossary nor a Commentary." So proclaimed the New York *Evening Post* on 21 May 1881, in a front-page story announcing the publication of the Revised Version of the Scriptures. The first major English translation since the King James Bible, the Revised New Testament was billed as the most accurate version ever, and the *Post* writer did not hesitate to hyperbolize: the printing of the Revision would probably "rank among the great events of the nineteenth century." Meanwhile, as buyers snatched up the first Testaments in New York, a bigger sensation was building in Chicago. Dubbing the new translation nothing other than "the Bible as it is," the *Chicago Tribune* printed the entire Revised New Testament—from Matthew to Revelation—in its regular Sunday edition. Although the *Tribune* pilfered its scriptural text from the Bible's authorized publishers, the paper lambasted rival *Chicago Times* ("the fraudulent newspaper concern on Wells Street") for printing a "forged" Testament of its own. The unsavory competition in Chicago's Fourth Estate did not deter an eager public, who bought 107,000 copies of the *Tribune*'s Testament alone. Demand for bound editions of the updated Bible was no less intense, with nationwide sales figures quickly surpassing one million.[1]

The consumer frenzy over the Revised New Testament is well known in the annals of publishing, but the Revised Version's significance for American religious history is less recognized. With the publication of the new Bible in 1881, the authority of the Authorized Version was widely questioned for the first time.[2] The language of King James, deeply internalized by many Americans and tacitly assumed to be the very Word of God, began to lose its unchallenged cultural hegemony. More important, however, were the ecumenical consequences of the newly expanded Bible market. As Protestants faced the question, "Authorized or Revised?" they found themselves disagreeing over deeper questions: Is the Bible immutable or subject to revision? Is translation a value-free science, or are translators ideologically driven? Are all Bible translations equally trustworthy as records of Christian history? Disputes over these questions ultimately helped set the tone for the fundamentalist-modernist controversy of the early twentieth century and prefigured Bible battles that have continued down to this day.

In this chapter, I do not fully recount the Revised Bible's creation or attempt a linguistic critique of the translation; both tasks have been discharged adequately elsewhere.[3] The intention here is rather to uncover the motivations of the Bible revisers themselves and to evaluate denominational reactions to their revision. Beginning its work amid a high tide of ecumenical and epistemological optimism, the Revised Bible committee hoped to unite Christians behind the cause of unerring translation—"King Truth" instead of King James, as one denominational newspaper put it. By the early twentieth century, however, the Bible revision movement had accelerated the ideological polarization of American Protestantism. Bible revision had become the bête noir of leading fundamentalists, who suspected ulterior motives on the part of the liberal, ecumenically minded revisers. Fundamentalist champions of biblical inerrancy now suggested that only *some* Scripture—namely, a particular version—was inspired by God.

THE GENESIS AND IDEOLOGY
OF BIBLE REVISION

The Revised Version of the Bible originated as a project of the Church of England, which appointed the initial translation committee in 1870.[4] Though dominated by Anglicans, the sixty-seven-member British committee included Baptists, Congregationalists, Methodists, Presbyterians, and a lone Unitarian. Some of Britain's most prominent scholars and divines were represented, including Edward Harold Browne (chairman of the Old Testament section and bishop of Winchester), Charles John Ellicott (chairman of the New Testament section and bishop of Gloucester and Bristol), Fenton John Anthony Hort (professor at Cambridge), Joseph Barber Lightfoot (bishop of Durham), Richard Chenevix Trench (archbishop of Dublin), and Brooke Foss Westcott (Regius Professor at Cambridge and Lightfoot's successor as bishop of Durham). Also a member was Christian David Ginsburg, a Polish-born Semiticist who had converted from Judaism to Christianity at age sixteen. Ginsburg's inclusion on the committee was as close as the revisers came to non-Protestant representation, although one Catholic, the famous erstwhile Anglican (and later cardinal) John Henry Newman, was invited to participate but declined.

Soon after beginning their work, the British translators asked a group of Americans to join the project. Selected as president of the American committee was Philip Schaff, the Swiss-born, German-educated church historian who had recently left the faculty of the Reformed seminary at Mercersburg, Pennsylvania, to accept a position at Union Seminary in New

York. Schaff assembled an ecumenical committee whose membership roster, like its British counterpart, read like a *Who's Who* of scholars and divines. Representing nine Protestant denominations, Schaff's luminaries included Ezra Abbot (professor at Harvard), Thomas Chase (president of Haverford College), William Henry Green (chairman of the Old Testament section and professor at Princeton Seminary), Charles Porterfield Krauth (professor at the Lutheran seminary in Philadelphia and vice-provost of the University of Pennsylvania), Calvin Ellis Stowe (husband of Harriet Beecher Stowe and professor emeritus at Andover Seminary), and Theodore D. Woolsey (chairman of the New Testament section and former president of Yale). Overwhelmingly from the Northeast and New England, the thirty-four American translators, like their British colleagues, were white male elites committed to the advancement of Anglo-American Protestant scholarship.[5]

American academia, where Schaff and most of his colleagues held forth, was coming into its own in the 1870s and 1880s. Loosely inspired by German models, many American colleges were reconceiving themselves as "research universities" devoted to the impartial pursuit of knowledge. The prototype was the newly established Johns Hopkins University, whose university press also was the first of its kind in the United States. Meanwhile the nondenominational divinity school, introduced when Harvard's seminary severed its Unitarian ties in 1880, was emerging as the new center of scholarship in religion. Biblical scholars, like other academics of the era, increasingly saw themselves as professionals whose work rested on unassailable "scientific" foundations. What historian Gerald Graff has called the "cult of expertise" elevated professional over lay authority, enthroning university professors as the ultimate arbiters of debates ranging from organic chemistry to scriptural exegesis. Academic authority was symbolized by the founding of professional organizations, including the Society of Biblical Literature in 1880, and a spate of new scholarly quarterlies, including the *Journal of Biblical Literature*.[6]

Professionalization in biblical studies went hand in hand with new methods of inquiry, particularly the "higher criticism" imported from Germany to England and America throughout the nineteenth century. New Testament higher criticism emerged during the 1830s in the Tübingen school of Ferdinand Christian Baur and his pupil, David Friedrich Strauss, who interpreted biblical miracle stories as "myths" and construed early Christianity's differentiation from Judaism in terms of Hegelian philosophy. Old

Testament higher criticism took shape under such figures as Julius Wellhausen, professor at Marburg and Göttingen, who argued that the Pentateuch, traditionally attributed to Moses, was the work of multiple unknown authors. After W. Robertson Smith, a Scottish Presbyterian and member of the Revised Version committee, published an article in the *Encyclopedia Britannica* espousing Wellhausen's views, he was expelled in 1881 from his chair at Free Church College, Aberdeen, but later elected a fellow of Christ's College, Cambridge. A similar controversy a decade later surrounded Charles Augustus Briggs, an iconoclastic critic and professor of Hebrew at Union Seminary in New York: it ended when Union retained Briggs and severed its ties to the Presbyterian Church.[7]

Despite Robertson Smith's presence on the Revised Version committee, the translators by and large took a dim view of higher criticism, particularly when applied to the New Testament. Schaff denounced the "radical and destructive" Tübingen school and the "unmerciful assaults" of its "sceptical and infidel critics"; he endorsed instead the "conservative and reconstructive" higher criticism of his own teacher, Johann August Wilhelm Neander, the Berlin professor who penned a lengthy reply to Strauss in 1837. In Schaff's view, the fatal flaw in Baur and Strauss's criticism was its "a priori" rejection of the supernatural, for Jesus himself claimed "superhuman origin and supernatural powers; and to deny them is to make him a liar and impostor." Schaff believed that conservative criticism, in contrast to that of the Tübingen school and its French counterpart in the work of Ernest Renan, would judge Jesus' claims impartially and in the end find them to be true. Schaff summarized the difference between the two schools of criticism in ethnic terms that belied his own Germanic roots: "The German and French mind, like the Athenian, is always bent upon telling and hearing something new, while the Anglo-American mind cares more for what is true, whether it be old or new. And the truth must ultimately prevail."[8]

While Schaff and colleagues distanced themselves from German and French higher criticism, they wholeheartedly embraced "lower" or textual criticism, an enterprise whose rapid maturation during the nineteenth century provided the initial momentum for revision of the King James Bible. Unlike higher-critical questions about sources, authorship, and historical veracity, textual criticism's goal was the reconstruction of ever more accurate or "primitive" Greek and Hebrew texts. New Testament textual criticism in particular had seen tremendous advances in the forty years preceding the Revised Version project. In 1831 the German scholar Karl Lachmann published the first edition of the Greek New Testament not based on the *Textus Receptus,* the long-regnant version modified little since the days of Erasmus. Then between 1844 and 1859, Constantin von Tischendorf, a *Privatdozent* at the University of Leipzig, uncovered a trove of fourth-century biblical manuscripts in the monastery of St. Catherine on Mount Sinai. The collection included the so-called Codex Sinaiticus, the only complete uncial manuscript of the New Testament ever discovered. As Tischendorf compiled a series of Greek New Testament editions based on his manuscript discoveries, the Vatican Library was beginning to allow printed editions of the Codex Vaticanus, another epoch-making fourth-century witness that had been kept under lock and key for centuries.

Vaticanus ("B") and Sinaiticus ("א"), the two most ancient and uncorrupted New Testament codices, ushered in the modern age of Greek textual criticism and made possible a definitive new edition of the Greek Testament by B. F. Westcott and F. J. A. Hort. The two codices became for Westcott and Hort a benchmark amid the daunting task of reconstructing the New Testament text from more than one hundred thousand variant readings occurring in some seventeen hundred Greek manuscript fragments (not to mention attestations in Latin and other sources). As Philip Schaff explained in a preface to the Westcott and Hort text, the agreement of Vaticanus and Sinaiticus "is (with few exceptions) a strong presumptive evidence for the genuineness of a reading, and, when supported by other ante-Nicene testimony, it is conclusive." Using advance proof-sheets of Westcott and Hort's version, Schaff and his translators largely conformed their English revision to the new Greek text, which was published simultaneously with the Revised Version on 17 May 1881. In Schaff's view, 1881 was nothing less than "the year of the republication of the Gospel"—the *annus mirabilis* that brought readers of the Greek and English Testaments closer than ever before to Scripture's long-lost "original autographs."[9]

Apart from the immediate advances in textual criticism, the Revised Version project stemmed from the translators' longstanding theological commitments. These concerns could be divided into three classes: ecumenical, evangelical, and epistemological. First, the translators believed the Bible revision movement heralded the dawn of a new ecumenical era. And no one was more enamored of the movement's ecumenical significance than Philip Schaff. "The Anglo-American Bible Revision movement," Schaff declared, is the "first inter-national and inter-denominational effort in the history of the translation of the Bible."[10] Indeed, Schaff regarded the revision movement as nothing other than "the noblest monument of Christian union and co-operation in this nineteenth century."[11] To Schaff, an ardent believer in the continuity of the universal church throughout the ages, Protestant union was the only alternative to a vulgar sectarianism.[12] Toward the goal of union, Schaff served from 1866 until 1873 as the American secretary of the Evangelical Alliance, a pan-Protestant organization formed in London in 1846. Schaff was a principal organizer of the Alliance's World Conference held in New York in 1873. About the same time, he assumed the presidency of the Bible revision committee, hoping that the work of the translators would help unite Christians everywhere around the cause of an updated Book. Although most Protestants had long been united behind the King James Version, Schaff feared that this unity was dissolving. The American Bible Union, a Baptist organization formed in 1850 in a dispute with the American Bible Society, had recently published its own New Testament (1862–63), which translated the Greek *baptizō* as "immerse." Two other New Testament translations, one by the Unitarian Leicester Sawyer (1858), the other by the Unitarian George Rapall Noyes (1869), also were accused of being theologically biased.[13] To Schaff, no translation produced by a single person or denomination could ever be adequate. He revealed this concern in a letter to W. R. Wittingham, the Episcopal bishop of Baltimore, as he tried in vain to persuade the prelate to join the Revised Bible committee: "We must fall in with this ecumenical revision movement as matters now stand, or run the risk of an indefinite multiplication of sectarian versions, as there are already a Baptist and a Unitarian version."[14]

In contrast to "sectarian" Bible translation efforts, the Anglo-American revision movement was, in Schaff's eyes, an interdenominational endeavor inspired by the very Spirit of God. "A calm retrospect presents the origin of this movement almost in the light of a moral miracle," he wrote. "There is a commonwealth—we may say, an apostolic succession—of Christian life and Christian scholarship which transcends all sectarian boundaries." Schaff knew, of course, that not all American Christians were ecumenically minded and that the Revised Bible would not win immediate acceptance. "Religious prejudices are the deepest of all prejudices, and religious conservatism is the most conservative of all conservatisms." He conceded that it might "take a whole generation to emancipate the mass of the people from the tyranny of ignorance and prejudice." Nevertheless, he believed that unity would one day prevail.[15]

Schaff's beatific ecumenical vision generally reflected the other revisers' opinions. Talbot Chambers, pastor of the Collegiate Dutch Reformed Church in New York City and a member of the American Old Testament committee, exulted in the fact that the revision movement represented, "as far as possible, all bodies of English-speaking Christians."[16] On the British side, Bishop Lightfoot marveled that for the first time, the bishops of the Church of England and the various "Nonconformist divines" were engaged in "a common work of a most sacred kind."[17] Bishop Ellicott echoed Lightfoot, proclaiming with Pauline fervor that in matters of sound scholarship "there is neither High-Church nor Low-Church, neither conformity nor dissent."[18]

The revisers' ecumenism was not boundless, however. Despite the overture to John Henry Newman, the committee retained much of the old Protestant suspicion of Roman Catholicism. Schaff, for example, apparently equated Protestantism with modernity when he contrasted the medieval "church of the Popes" with the "modern church of the Reformers." Elsewhere he observed that although a few Catholics were beginning to practice the science of textual criticism, "the Roman Church cares more for tradition and the living church than for the Bible." Roman Catholics, Schaff asserted, still looked to the Vatican as an infallible oracle, whereas Protestants, "having safely crossed the Red Sea," could not return to "the flesh-pots of the land of bondage." In accepting Scripture as their only oracle, Protestants were united in pursuit of apostolic purity.[19]

Second, the ideology of the revision movement was "evangelical" in the original sense of the word. That is, the revisers believed the new version of the Scriptures would be an indispensable tool in spreading the Gospel among the masses. An updated Bible, the committee members assumed, would pique people's curiosity, thereby prompting more widespread study of God's Word. "It might be well to revise the Bible every fifty years, to induce the people to read it," Schaff speculated.[20] Outside the ranks of the revision committee, other church leaders expressed similar views. Lyman Abbott predicted that the distribution of the Revised New Testament would "stimulate Bible reading such as the age has not seen." Abbott told the *New York Times* that he planned to use the new version in his own parish, and that he would choose for sermon texts the most "sensational" rewordings of King James passages that he could find. Abbott added that James McCosh, president of the College of New Jersey (later Princeton University), planned to use the new version in the college chapel.[21] Meanwhile, Charles E. Robinson, pastor of the Presbyterian Memorial Church in New York City, also saw the Revised New Testament as an effective evangelization tool. Robinson told the *Times* that he had advised the members of his congregation to buy copies of the updated Bible "immediately."[22]

At the same time, Schaff and colleagues recognized that Bible revision was not without limitations as an instrument of evangelization. Some Protestants always would resent any tampering with the Authorized Version, and the revisers did not hide their disdain for such old-Bible nostalgia. The Reverend Howard Crosby, ex-chancellor of the University of the City of New York (later New York University) and member of the New Testament section, observed undiplomatically that the Revised Bible probably would win universal acceptance within a decade or so, after the "old grannies and croakers" were dead. Similarly, Philip Schaff noted that every Bible version in Christian history had been subjected to the "ordeal of martyrdom"—a symbolic crucifixion—before ultimately experiencing resurrection at the hands of the Almighty.[23] Perhaps influenced by Schaff's soteriological speculation, a *New York Tribune* editorialist mused that the Revised Bible might signal the resurrection of religion in general: "Possibly we are on the eve of a great revival of Christianity."[24]

A third facet of the Bible revision movement's ideology may be summed up by the Revised Version's rendering of John 10:38: "that ye may know and understand." The revisers regarded the King James Bible, with its various errors and archaisms, as an epistemological impediment to the true understanding of God's Word. Correction of the King James Version's errors was crucial, lest people lose confidence in the veracity of the Bible. William Henry Green, professor at Princeton Seminary and chairman of the American Old Testament committee, made the point clearly: "There is no surer way of undermining the authority of the Scriptures in the public estimation than, while admitting the existence of inaccuracies, to refuse to allow them to be corrected." Although he was a staunch opponent of higher criticism, Green insisted that knowledge of God required a fully accurate Bible. In an address before the Bible Societies of New Jersey, he exhorted his listeners to support the cause of revision: "Shall we be concerned to have the utmost accuracy in the rendering of Homer, or Plato, or Cicero, or Virgil, and not cherish a similar solicitude in regard to the writings of those holy men, who spake as they were moved by the Holy Ghost?"[25] Similarly, Matthew Brown Riddle, professor at Hartford Seminary and member of the American New Testament committee, argued that linguistic precision was critical for all Christians who valued the Scriptures. Looking back in

1908 on the Bible revision movement, Riddle attacked those who had argued that the Revised Bible, though useful for study, could not replace the King James for devotional purposes. "An intelligent devotion," Riddle insisted, requires "knowledge of the exact sense of scripture."[26]

The desire for a pure, uncorrupted biblical text was not confined to the revisers themselves. Church leaders on both sides of the Atlantic were swept away by the enthusiasm for a "perfect" Bible. F. W. Farrar, canon of Westminster and later dean of Canterbury Cathedral, lamented the fact that some people still preferred the familiar to the correct in choosing a translation of Scripture. "Can it then be said that custom is dearer to us than truth?" Farrar asked. "Do we desire the plain bare facts of that which we call the Word of God, or do we desire melodious glosses and mistaken interpretations?"[27] Among Americans, Henry Ward Beecher praised the Revised Bible project as a positive step toward a more accurate text, adding that he had been "indignant" at the American Bible Society ever since 1858 when, succumbing to conservative pressure, it had canceled a typographically corrected and orthographically updated edition of the King James Bible.[28] David Swing, pastor of Chicago's Central Church and defendant in the celebrated Presbyterian heresy trial of 1874, insisted that because editions of Shakespeare and Dante had been corrected, the Bible deserved the same treatment. Swing's idea of improvement, however, was more radical than most. He suggested that the Old Testament be "condensed" since certain portions, such as the Mosaic Laws, "have no more to do with Christianity than have the Blue Laws of Connecticut." In Swing's estimation, an abridged Old Testament, combined with the existing Revised New Testament, would make for a first-rate book. After all, Swing opined, people deserve "the best of anything, be it food, or clothes, or government, or money, or Bible. What is worth having at all, is worth having well."[29]

Swing's comment undoubtedly embarrassed the revisers, yet it reflected a common objective among the advocates of Bible revision: to extract the kernel of truth from the husk of translated Scripture. Indeed the epistemological aspect of the Bible revision movement had at its heart an almost obsessive concern with historical veracity. In this respect the revisers and their supporters conflated the purposes of historical and textual criticism, for the latter by itself aimed simply to reconstruct the bare text as it appeared to its original audience. The translators' labors often oscillated imperceptibly between textual and historical reconstruction; the textual question (What did it say?) alternated with the historical question (Did this really happen?). Yet the translators seemed oblivious to the instability of their guiding question, taking pains instead to highlight the firm empirical foundation of modern textual and historical investigation. Textual criticism, Schaff wrote, has nothing to do with "hermeneutics and interpretation" or "subjective likes and dislikes, but only with the facts"; similarly, historical criticism has "no other purpose than to ascertain the real facts in the case." Schaff lamented the modern condition—"[n]othing is taken for granted; nothing believed on mere authority; everything must be supported by adequate proof"—yet in the same instance he proclaimed that the reality of miracles and other disputed biblical stories could be corroborated by external and internal evidence: in short, by "the logic of stubborn facts." He reproved Baur and Renan for admitting the apostolicity of only the Apocalypse, Galatians, Romans, and Corinthians; yet he confidently asserted that these books alone were "sufficient to establish the foundation of historical faith" because they confirmed "every important fact" in the Gospels' account of history. Schaff's conclusion was particularly telling, for it implied that textual criticism by itself was a hollow endeavor: "Christianity might live without the letter of the New Testament, but not without the facts and truths which it records and teaches."[30]

This conflation of the textual and historical quests—the inseparability of the letter of the New Testament from the facts it presumably reported—gave Bible revision its explosive potential for controversy but also helped fuel a tremendous consumer demand for "improved" versions of Holy Writ. With all the fin-de-siècle speculation about a Bible that would bring readers as close as they might ever get to the Jesus of history, it is no wonder that millions of Americans and Britons rushed to bookstores for copies of the Revised Version. Here they would find, as Canon Farrar put it, no "melodious glosses and mistaken interpretations" but "plain bare facts."

SENSATIONAL SCRIPTURES: PUBLICATION OF THE REVISED NEW TESTAMENT

The 20th of May 1881—the release date of the Revised New Testament in the United States—was by all accounts a day to remember. At the New York warehouse of Thomas Nelson and Sons, one of the firms authorized to distribute the official edition published by Oxford and Cambridge University Presses, the commotion began at 4:00 a.m. as wagon drivers lined up waiting to load their holy cargo. The drivers, reported the *New York Herald,* "discussed the situation in language that would not have been, it is safe to say, entirely pleasing to the biblical revisers."[31] By 5:30 in the morning, the clamor for copies was well under way at the bookstore of Anson D. F. Randolph and Company. The first buyers, according to the *New York Times,* were clergymen and theological students. As dawn broke, it seemed that a rush for the long-awaited volume had overtaken the whole city. "In fact," observed the *Times,* "no work ever introduced here was bought up with such a degree of avidity, and it is not likely that a larger number of copies of any other book were ever sold in a single day." By 3:00 p.m., Thomas Nelson and Sons had disposed of a quarter of a million Testaments.[32] The books, printed in more than twenty different styles, ranged in price from a quarter to sixteen dollars.

The clamor for the new Bible actually began prior to publication day. One reporter, hoping to secure an advance copy, approached Schaff claiming to be an agent of Oxford University Press who had just arrived on a ship from England. The man asked Schaff if he could borrow a copy of the new version until his own copy, still packed in a trunk, was unloaded from the steamer. Schaff invited the fellow to tea, but the impostor "failed to make his appearance, and left for unknown parts."[33] Meanwhile, Thomas Nelson, the book proprietor, speculated that he could have earned as much as five thousand dollars per book if he had been willing to sell advance copies to eager reporters and publishers.[34]

The most extraordinary scene, however, occurred on publication day near the New York Stock Exchange. As soon as Nelson and Sons released the first copies, a half-dozen street vendors appeared on Wall Street carrying small twenty-five-cent editions and shouting, "Bibles, only a quarter!" Scores of curious brokers and bankers reportedly grabbed up copies. "In fact," observed the *New York Herald,* "the book went off at such a rapid rate as to inspire one with the suspicion that perhaps the brokers were about to get up a 'corner' in the Scriptures." The *Herald* quoted one old gentleman, who marveled at the sight: "I never expected to live to see the Bible sold in Wall Street. They need it here badly enough, Lord knows!"[35]

Sales figures for the Revised Version were phenomenal. In London, two million copies, half of them orders from America, reportedly moved within four days. In the United States, the most active trading occurred in New York, although other northeastern cities saw their share of business. Early sales in Philadelphia topped one hundred thousand. Boston booksellers barely met demand, unloading twenty thousand copies the first day. On the West Coast, the *San Francisco Chronicle* predicted that the Revised Version would "soon come into general use."[36] Even in the South, where Reconstruction had done little to alleviate a severe economic depression, the new Bible sparked interest. The *Richmond Dispatch* reported that a local bookseller had only a limited number of Testaments available.[37]

Sales were not confined to the Bible alone. A variety of "companion" volumes appeared on the market within weeks. To satisfy one's curiosity, one could buy an inexpensive, pocket-size guide listing all the differences between the King James and Revised versions. For citizens of greater means, parallel Bibles, with the old and new versions printed side by side, made a fine addition to any home library.[38] Barely a month after the Revised Version's publication, *Harper's Weekly* advertised a parallel Bible containing the new English translation along with the just-completed Greek Testament of Westcott and Hort.[39] And as in all sectors of publishing, the Bible market was rife with inferior imitations. Although Oxford and Cambridge University Presses were the only official publishers of the new Bible, a lack of American copyright restrictions led to the rapid printing of over thirty Revised Bible editions—some of them more accurate than others. Schaff lamented the inevitable "admixture of the commercial aspect" but expressed gratitude that so many people seemed genuinely interested in the Bible.[40]

In no city was the "commercial aspect" more evident than in Chicago. Sensing a golden opportunity to increase circulation, the *Chicago Tribune* announced plans to print the entire Revised New Testament in its Sunday edition of 22 May. On Saturday, the paper ran on its editorial page a special note to newsdealers stressing the importance of ordering the next day's edition "largely and promptly." Ironically, while advertising its own New Testament section, the paper mocked the Bible bonanza in New York in an editorial. The "idea that the people of that somewhat ungodly city" should scramble so for the Scriptures struck the *Tribune* as "highly amusing": "It is not likely that this tremendous rush is the result of devotion so much as it is of curiosity."[41]

The Sunday *Tribune* of 22 May included the Revised New Testament, along with the translators' preface, in a sixteen-page special section. The newspaper's editors wrote that the *Tribune* was "not inclined to boast of its present achievement," but in the same editorial they bragged that the paper's superior "typographical and mechanical resources" allowed it to print the equivalent of a whole book on just "a day's notice." The *Tribune*, its editors added, "intends always to lead the way and be the first in introducing novelties to the people of this community."

The *Tribune*'s 22 May edition also included the first in a series of polemics against an allegedly bogus New Testament edition published by the "fraudulent newspaper concern on Wells Street"—the Chicago *Times*. For the next several days, the *Tribune* contrasted its accurate New Testament reprint with the "forgeries" perpetrated by the *Times*. Only the *Tribune* printed the Revised New Testament "verbatim et literatim"—a feat that had "never yet been excelled among the many triumphs of modern journalism."[42] The *Tribune*'s New Testament edition was "the most remarkable newspaper ever issued on this continent."[43]

In addition to its New Testament reprint, the *Tribune* ran numerous explanatory articles, including a large excerpt from Alexander Roberts's *Companion to the Revised Version*. The amount of coverage was unprecedented, even for a newspaper that published a religion news section in each day's edition. And when the editors of the *Tribune* sat back and tallied up the results of their media blitz, they liked what they saw. On 26 May the newspaper ran an advertisement headed, "IMMENSE SUCCESS . . . 107,000 Copies Sold in Four Days . . . The Chicago Tribune Edition of the New Testament." Never had a single edition of the paper enjoyed such a huge circulation. If ever there were partisans for the Bible revision movement, they resided on the staff of the *Chicago Tribune*.

TRUTH OR BEAUTY?
NOSTALGIA FOR KING JAMES

Considering all the extravagant claims about the Revised Version's definitive status, it is not surprising that some reviewers thought the updated New Testament was not all it was cracked up to be. Numerous critics, like the celebrated Brooklyn preacher T. DeWitt Talmage, castigated the translators for presuming that they could improve upon the time-honored Authorized Version. Talmage accused the Revised Bible committee of engaging in ecclesiastical "bossism": "D.D. and Ph.D. and LL.D. are often only the heavy baggage of a very slow train."[44] A few months later, the Protestant clergy of New Haven, Connecticut, met in closed session to denounce the Revised Bible as a failure.[45] Like the Revised Version's supporters, the New Haven divines recognized the King James Bible's inaccuracies, but they refused to believe that beauty must be sacrificed for truth.

At least one of the translators themselves held a similar opinion. Charles Porterfield Krauth, a member of the Revised Old Testament section until his death in 1883, lamented the fact that many beauties of the old Bible vanished into the accuracies of the new. If "we cannot have both it is better to have accuracy without beauty," Krauth said. "But is it not possible to have both?"[46] Similarly, the *Evangelical Repository and Bible Teacher,* an organ of the United Presbyterian Church, invoked the judgment of the British preacher Charles Spurgeon, who claimed that the Revised Bible was "strong in Greek, but weak in English." Christians, according to the *Evangelical Repository,* had no obligation to adopt an inferior version of the Scriptures.[47]

The secular press, perhaps emboldened by the perceived conservatism of its readership, also was quick to criticize. The *Washington Post* denounced the "religious barbarism" of the revisers: "Let us say the Lord's Prayer as we are used to say it," the *Post* editorialized, "and keep the Bible that we have."[48] Several months later, the *New York Times* observed that the Revised Bible had not gained a significant popular following.[49] Indeed, most average citizens probably reacted to the new Bible in the way described by one seminary professor: they bought the new Bible "with eagerness; glanced over its pages with interest; and then returned to the Authorized Version, grateful that they had been deprived of so small a portion of their household treasure." In spite of all the scholarly clamor for King Truth, most people still preferred King James.[50]

Official reaction by denominational assemblies was equally indifferent. To Schaff's disappointment, only the American Baptists formally endorsed the Revised New Testament. Schaff's own appeals to the southern and northern Presbyterian assemblies brought no official action on behalf of the new version.[51] Yet Schaff remained confident that Bible revision would win the day: "English readers will not be contented with King James' Version. They know that something better can be made. It is in the interest of loyalty to God's Word that errors should be corrected and a good translation take the place of an inferior one."[52]

CLAMOR FOR CHANGE:
ENSHRINING "KING TRUTH"

Schaff's optimism did not go not unrewarded, for while denominational assemblies proved reluctant to abandon the Authorized Version, numerous denominational periodicals printed editorials recommending the new Bible. The significance of these endorsements by church magazines and newspapers should not be underestimated: denominational editors represented a core constituency of educated elites who would continue in coming decades to rally support for Bible revision and other ecumenical ventures. Yet in the late nineteenth century, the editors' concerns were still less ecumenical than epistemological. Almost without exception, their editorials echoed the translators' own assertions that the Revised New Testament brought readers closer to the unadulterated Word of God—and therefore closer to the splendor of historical truth. Because of its literalness the Revised translation may have lacked beauty, but what, asked the *Unitarian Review,* was more important: truth or beauty?[53] Many Protestant publications, both liberal and conservative, cast their votes for truth. The *Reformed Quarterly Review* conceded that the Revised Bible was not uniformly beautiful but hastened to add that "literary merit is subordinate . . . to fidelity of translation."[54] The *Methodist Quarterly Review* of New York extolled the new Bible as "another step in the march toward an absolutely perfect translation," as if such a thing were possible.[55] Another northern Methodist periodical, the *Christian Advocate,* indulged in a little anti-Catholic polemic, noting that the Revised Bible was a natural outgrowth of Protestantism. "The accuracy of a translation," the *Advocate* editorialized, "is not of primary importance to those who affirm the equal authority of tradition and invest the Pope with infallibility."[56]

Several religious newspapers sought to forestall the criticism that the new Bible eliminated favorite passages. The translation committee had omitted the last part of Romans 8:1 ("who walk not after the flesh, but after the Spirit"), judging the phrase to be a late textual addition. The conservative *Sunday School Times* praised this change: "We may be sorry to miss the last part of [Romans 8:1]; but if Paul did not write it, we do not want it in our Bibles." The newspaper added that average Christians must trust the judgment of the Bible revisers, who alone possessed the necessary expertise in the Greek New Testament manuscripts.[57] The *Evangelical Messenger,* organ of the pietistic Evangelical Association (founded by Jacob Albright in 1800) extolled another omission: the doxology of the Lord's Prayer in Matthew 6:13 ("For thine is the kingdom, and the power, and the glory, for ever. Amen"). The *Messenger* writer, evidently schooled in textual criticism, noted that the "oldest and most reliable manuscripts" lacked the doxology. It should not, therefore, "stand as part of Matthew's text, because the Lord never spoke it."[58]

A few denominational publications praised the Revised Version for its improved clarity. The *Presbyterian Review* of New York likened the King James

Bible to "old pavement, trodden by countless feet into heaving waves of precious mosaic." Yet, asked the writer, shall the Authorized Version "be left to trip the foot of the worshipper as he walks with his eye on the cross? Better surely that the antiquarian be disappointed than that the child or the peasant stumble on the way to the altar."[59] Protestants in predominately white churches were not the only ones who found the Revised New Testament easier to read. The *Christian Recorder,* newspaper of the AME Church, claimed that many King James passages "read as through a glass darkly" while in the Revised Version the same passages appeared "with the light and definiteness of the sun at the meridian." The *Christian Recorder*'s editors urged AME members to take up the Revised Bible for the sake of their "soul's health."[60]

Of all denominational periodicals, perhaps none more dramatically supported the Revised Version than the Dutch Reformed *Christian Intelligencer.* "This is probably the best New Testament . . . anywhere on earth," the *Intelligencer* proclaimed. The Revised Bible, the newspaper added, probably was the last version of the Scriptures that humankind would ever need. Textual critics had collated all the manuscripts and had assimilated all relevant archaeological and linguistic data. "It is difficult to see," the *Intelligencer* concluded, "from what quarter any new light, any additional information can come." As for those Christians who were reluctant to accept the new version, the *Intelligencer* insisted that they had two choices—"King James or King Truth." The question was "not to be settled by our likes and dislikes." Neither could Christians' decisions be affected by "the mist on our grandfather's spectacles as he talks about the old leather-covered book." True Christians must choose Truth—God's Word in pure, unmediated form.[61] Indeed, "King Truth" swayed some influential parish clergymen, who concluded that the Revised New Testament was the most accurate translation ever produced. At the Vermont Avenue Christian Church in Washington, D.C., President James A. Garfield listened as Reverend Fred D. Power declared the new Bible the greatest achievement of Christian scholarship in the nineteenth century.[62]

THE TUMULTUOUS REIGN
OF "KING TRUTH"

By the time the Revised Old Testament was published in 1885, popular interest in new Bibles had abated considerably. Simultaneously, however, changes were occurring in the larger culture that ultimately would summon Protestants to do battle royal over the Scriptures. The fundamentalist movement was beginning to coalesce in response to perceived threats to the intellectual and social order. On the intellectual front, higher criticism and Darwinism seemed to be undermining a biblical view of the universe, while liberal theology and the Social Gospel were downplaying doctrinal orthodoxy in favor of cultural adaptation and ethical responsibility. On the social side, perceived dangers included an influx of "new immigrants" (mostly from southern and eastern Europe and predominantly Catholic), a population explosion in the cities, the rise of big business, an eruption of labor unrest, and the emergence of the women's suffrage movement. War was perhaps fundamentalism's last great catalyst: the Spanish-American War and World War I rounded out a period of extraordinary upheaval in American history.[63]

Amid the shifting sands of early-twentieth-century America, fundamentalism sought solid ground and found it in the idea of an "inerrant" Bible. Quickly adopted as a rallying cry by revivalists of an anti-intellectual bent, the doctrine of inerrancy had been explicated carefully in the late nineteenth century by traditionalist intellectuals at Princeton Theological Seminary. Archibald Alexander Hodge and Benjamin Breckinridge Warfield issued the most famous statement on inerrancy in 1881.[64] Hodge and Warfield challenged higher critics to locate alleged biblical discrepancies and errors in the "original autographs"; the fact that these first manuscripts had long since been lost seemed to erect an impenetrable wall around Scripture's inerrancy.[65] Yet the Princeton position on inerrancy was not as hostile to biblical scholarship as later fundamentalists assumed.[66] Writing in 1893, Warfield distinguished between the "autographic codex," or the long-lost original biblical manuscripts, and the "autographic text," the reconstruction of the original manuscripts through text-critical research. Warfield was confident that textual critics had discerned the "autographic text" almost in its entirety, for "God has not permitted the Bible to become so hopelessly corrupt that its restoration to its original text is impossible."[67] Warfield, like Schaff, thus endorsed the enterprise of lower or textual criticism even while remaining staunchly opposed to higher criticism, which raised fundamental questions about the divine authorship of Scripture.

Warfield's acceptance of lower criticism translated into friendliness toward English Bible revision, and his attitude resembled that of many other evangelicals.[68] Princeton Seminary's William Henry Green, it will be recalled, was intimately involved in the Revised Bible's creation, despite his strong opposition to higher criticism. Equally significant, a number of the authors of *The Fundamentals* (1910–15), the twelve-volume series of booklets that came to symbolize uncompromising orthodoxy, used the Revised Version for biblical citations and thereby tacitly endorsed the work of textual critics.[69]

One contributor to *The Fundamentals* who occasionally cited the Revised Bible was Philip Mauro, a lawyer converted to the gospel of inerrancy in 1903 at age forty-five.[70] Mauro insisted that the Bible is "the only book in the world that is truly 'scientific.'" He further contended that the Bible, unlike human books, is "perfectly" translatable into any language.[71] Yet what, for Mauro, was the one "perfect" English translation? On balance, he seemed to favor the King James, but his occasional quotations of the Revised Version indicated that he saw some merit in the new Bible.

By the 1920s, however, Mauro's unarticulated preference for the King James Bible had become a full-scale attack on the Revised Version. Although not a professional biblical scholar, Mauro became convinced that the underlying Greek text of the Revised New Testament was dangerously flawed. The target of his attack was the "superstitious deference" paid by the revisers to the Greek codices Vaticanus and Sinaiticus. Ostensibly Mauro objected to the assumption that such older manuscripts were necessarily better, yet he harbored deeper suspicions about the origin of Codex Vaticanus itself. Why, he asked, should a manuscript "be carefully treasured in the Vatican, if not for the reason that it contained errors and textual corruptions favorable to the doctrines and practices of Rome?" To Mauro, Roman sympathies were not the only alleged heresies of the "higher critics" who produced the Revised Bible. Mauro also attacked the revisers' belief that certain biblical books were of "composite character," or written by multiple authors. Moreover, he accused the revisers of casting doubt on the authenticity of certain biblical passages by including too many marginal notes with alternate readings.[72]

Mauro was particularly upset by those marginal notes indicating that "some ancient authorities"—typically Vaticanus and Sinaiticus—omitted particular verses. The most contentious instance was the narrative of Jesus' post-Resurrection appearances at the close of Mark (16:9–20), which the revisers set apart, noting in the margin that the "two oldest Greek manuscripts . . . omit from ver. 9 to the end." Textual critics already by 1881 generally agreed that these twelve verses were a later addition to Mark's Gospel, yet Mauro believed that to poke holes in this or any other passage in Scripture's seamless web was to question the veracity of Christianity itself. Mauro also decried the treatment of Luke 23:34 ("Father, forgive them: for they know not what they do"), which the revisers indicated had been omitted by some ancient authorities (most notably in this case Codex Vaticanus). Mauro insisted that Christ's words here were "so divinely gracious" as to be "self-authenticating"—a logic oddly reminiscent of Philip Schaff's argument that to deny Jesus' own claims of superhuman origin was to make him a liar and impostor. Indeed both Schaff and Mauro conflated the purposes of higher and lower criticism in subjecting biblical passages simultaneously to the tests of textual authenticity and of historical accuracy. Although Mauro branded Schaff and colleagues "higher critics" because of their allegedly antisupernaturalist assumptions, the translators were no "higher" than Mauro himself, whose own belief in inerrancy imposed an immense burden of historical proof on Scripture. The difference between Schaff and Mauro was not therefore in method but in conclusion. To Schaff, the textual (lower-critical) rejection of a few passages did not substantially affect the historical (higher-critical) picture: Jesus remained, as Schaff once wrote, "the most certain of all facts." To Mauro, the questioning of even a few biblical facts led Christians down the slippery slope to apostasy.[73]

Mauro peppered his work with citations from the Revised Version's greatest British foe, John William Burgon, dean of Chichester in West Sussex. Burgon's name in the Victorian church was virtually synonymous with conservative polemic. A decade before the Revised New Testament's publication, he penned a fiery vindication of Mark 16:9–20, assailing the authority of Vaticanus and Sinaiticus. After the new Bible's appearance, he defended additional disputed passages in a 549-page series of articles, *The Revision Revised*. Throughout his writings he heaped invective on the "Revisionists" whose New Testament marginal notes were sowing doubts "as to the Truth of Scripture" and "hopelessly unsettling the faith of millions." The revision committee's liberalism, according to Burgon, was partly attributable to the membership of the sole Unitarian, G. Vance Smith, principal of the Presbyterian college in Carmarthen, Wales. Burgon quickly disclaimed personal prejudice—"early in life, I numbered several professing Unitarians among my friends"—but then accused Smith of "ventilat[ing] heresy from within." The heresy for Burgon was historical-critical: Unitarians, more than any other Protestants, lacked compunction about casting disputed Bible verses into history's dustbin. Burgon was not opposed to textual criticism in principle—he endorsed the approach of the revision committee's conservative dissenter, F. H. A. Scrivener, who usually opted for older readings from the *Textus Receptus*—but he objected to any revisions bearing upon the presumed facts of biblical history. The King James Bible was for Burgon a virtual historical textbook, and any revision was a potential affront to the accuracy of the account.[74]

CONSERVATIVE REPUDIATION
OF TEXTUAL CRITICISM

By the 1920s, when Mauro resurrected the late Dean Burgon's arguments for an American audience, an important shift was occurring in the thought of some evangelicals. Hidebound conservatives were turning against not only higher criticism but also lower criticism and, in some cases, *any* revision of the Authorized Version. Mauro feared that modern textual critics and translators had imbibed too much German higher-critical ideology, thereby rendering even well-intended Bible revision subversive of Christian truth. Mauro's suspicion of Bible revisers had been prefigured in the late nineteenth century on the pages of at least one denominational periodical, the *Southern Presbyterian Review.* Theologian Robert Lewis Dabney, a staunch supporter of the Southern cause during the Civil War, seized upon 2 Timothy 3:16, which had been changed from "All scripture is given by inspiration of God, and is profitable" (KJV) to "Every scripture inspired of God is also profitable" (RV). He wrote: "The poisonous suggestion intended is, that among the parts of the 'Scripture,' some are inspired and some are not. Our Bible contains fallible parts! the very doctrine of the Socinian and Rationalist. This treacherous version the Revisers have gratuitously sanctioned!" Dabney conceded that the Revised Version contained some improvements over the old, but he seemed to look askance at the Bible revisers and textual critics in general. The biblical critics who inspired the revision's innovations "are not Popes," Dabney insisted. "The rest of us Bible readers have not lost the right of private judgment."[75]

In attacking the Protestant "Popes," Dabney invoked a theme as old as the English Bible itself: anti-Catholicism. Indeed, many opponents of the Revised Version found sixteenth-century anti-Catholic language polemically useful, for it served the dual purpose of chastening Protestant liberals while reasserting Protestant biblicism in the face of the Romanist menace. Burgon, for example, employed the anti-Catholic trope of idolatry when he selected as an epigraph to his *Revision Revised* the admonition in 1 John 5:21: "Little children, keep yourself from idols." He regarded the idols of Vaticanus and Sinaiticus as scarcely different from the papal idol whose repeated incursions Protestants had shed blood to repel. "The Nemesis of Superstition and Idolatry," he warned, "is ever the same."[76]

The most strikingly anti-Catholic polemic against the Revised Version came fully half a century after its publication in a slender volume, *Our Authorized Bible Vindicated,* by Benjamin G. Wilkinson, dean of the Seventh-day Adventist Washington Missionary College in Takoma Park, Maryland. Wilkinson echoed Mauro when he complained that the Revised Bible had been "built almost entirely on the Vatican Manuscript, kept in the Pope's library, and upon the Sinaiticus, found in a Catholic monastery." Yet he carried the argument a step further, pointing out a number of passages where the Revised Version rendering read like the "Jesuit Bible," that is, the Rheims New Testament of 1582. A particularly grievous parallel for Wilkinson was Luke 2:33, part of the account of the young Jesus in the Jerusalem Temple. Where the Authorized Version read "Joseph and his mother marvelled," the Rheims and Revised versions replaced "Joseph" with "His father," a reading that for Wilkinson impugned the virgin birth of Jesus. Wilkinson failed to explain why sixteenth-century Catholics and nineteenth-century Protestants would have willfully expurgated a doctrine that both held dear.[77]

Wilkinson's allegation of a Rheims-Revised axis was ironic because the influence of Rheims on Protestant translation was at least as clear in the Authorized Version itself. William Fulke's popular 1589 annotated edition of the Rheims New Testament, though intended as an antidote to popery, in reality had served as the vehicle by which some of the Rheimists' Latinisms entered the vocabulary of the King James Bible.[78] But while the Authorized Version remained curiously immune to the charge of Catholic influence, the Revised Version felt the brunt of Wilkinson's nativist suspicions. He drew ammunition from a Catholic journal, the *Dublin Review,* which claimed that the Revised Version sounded the "death-knell of Protestantism" by restoring a more Catholic reading of several key passages. He also quoted Tobias Mullen, the late Catholic bishop of Erie, Pennsylvania, who had triumphantly pointed to the influence of the Rheims version on the Protestant translation tradition.[79] Finally, Wilkinson based his charge of Catholic bias on the reputed sympathy of the translation committee for the high-church Oxford or Tractarian Movement in England, whose leaders John Henry Newman and Edward Bouverie Pusey had been invited to join the revision committee but declined, and the "Romanizing" Mercersburg Theology in America, whose most celebrated figure had been Philip Schaff. In contrast to the Catholic-leaning translators of 1881, Wilkinson declared, the translators of 1611 were "true Protestants."[80]

Wilkinson's hostility toward "Romanizing" tendencies reflected the mutual suspicion between Catholics and Protestants that had festered since the sixteenth century. The terms of the debate remained remarkably consistent over time, as when Bishop Mullen, in polemic reminiscent of Thomas More's 350 years before, criticized the revision committee for preserving the King James reading of "graven image" (as in Exodus 20:4) instead of the less restrictive "graven thing" or "idol." Here was proof, according to Mullen, that the translators' "wicked purpose [was] to convict the down-trodden Catholics of idolatry."[81] Meanwhile the *Dublin Review* exulted in the self-subversive tendency of the revisers, whose rendering of 2 Timothy 3:16 ("Every scripture inspired of God is also profitable") finally destroyed Protestantism's "Bible-only" principle, thus proving that "Scripture is powerless without the Church as the witness to its inspiration."[82]

What had changed since the sixteenth century was not the old debate over church authority but the method of biblical interpretation. The modern critical imperative inexorably directed Bible-reading toward the problem of historical truth, forcing Christians to take sides on the degree of textual correspondence with reality. Ironically, both traditionalist Catholics and fundamentalist Protestants, despite their mutual antipathy, believed in the full correspondence of biblical history and real history. Both therefore opposed lower criticism whenever it appeared to threaten the received text of biblical history. The received text for Catholics meant the Latin Vulgate as translated in Douay-Rheims and revised during the eighteenth century by Bishop Richard Challoner. The received text for Protestants meant the Greek *Textus Receptus* and the Hebrew Massoretic Text as translated in the Authorized Version. Conservatives usually countenanced minor lexical and grammatical refinement of these texts, yet the line separating minor from major changes was as fine as the line separating textual from historical accuracy. Some changes clearly went over the edge: the *Dublin Review* assailed the Revised Version's omission of the Trinitarian proof-text in

1 John 5:7, which translators since the sixteenth century had recognized as a late addition but refused until 1881 to remove from the Bible. The excision of this so-called Comma Johanneum proved to the *Review*'s editors that textual critics were like bookworms: "devoid of light and conscience, following the blind instincts of their nature, they will make holes in the most sacred of books."[83] Years later, Wilkinson opted for a biblical allusion, but his opinion of textual critics was the same:

> The pathetic question of Pilate, "What is Truth," is not more pathetic than the error of those who say that only by balancing one version against another, or by examining the various manuscript readings,—those of apostates as well as those of the faithful,—can we arrive at approximate truth.[84]

Wilkinson charged that the fundamental truths of Jesus' life—his miracle-working, his atonement for human sins, his ascension into heaven, and his promised second coming—were either "changed" or dealt a "deadly blow" by the Revised Version. He seemed oblivious to the possibility that biblical texts might be altered without changing the historical realities they purportedly proved.[85]

Wilkinson's index of "changed" doctrines highlighted a common thread in the writings of Bible revision's opponents and proponents: a preponderant concern for New Testament, rather than Old Testament, translation. Although late-nineteenth and early-twentieth-century debates over evolution constantly underscored the problems of Old Testament exegesis, Bible translation controversies by and large centered on New Testament questions. The reasons were several. First, the discovery of Vaticanus and Sinaiticus during the nineteenth century greatly increased both academic and popular interest in Greek textual criticism. Manuals such as Schaff's *Companion to the Greek Testament* (1883) encouraged Americans to learn about textual variants and dabble in the reconstruction of Christ's original words. Second, in contrast to the vicissitudes of the Greek text's transmission, the Hebrew Scriptures had existed since the tenth century in the relatively stable recension known as the Massoretic Text, which both the revisers and their opponents accepted as authoritative.[86] Finally, and most important, conservatives and liberals alike regarded the Greek New Testament as the fountainhead of Christian "fundamentals" and the sourcebook of the historical Jesus. Even when the Old Testament was drawn into translation battles, the disputed passages very often were alleged prophecies of the life of Christ. Such was the case with Isaiah 7:14, the *cause célèbre* of the RSV controversy of the 1950s, whose treatment in the 1885 Revised Old Testament infuriated Wilkinson (the version retained "virgin" but in the margin included the alternate reading "maiden"). "This change," Wilkinson wrote, "gives room to doubt the virgin birth of Christ."[87]

Wilkinson's indictment of the Revised Version, published nearly a half-century after the translation itself, appeared to beat a dead horse, yet in succeeding decades new Bible battles would lend his work perennial relevance. Indeed, treatises by the Revised Version's most colorful opponents—Burgon, Mauro, and Wilkinson—would enjoy a remarkable shelf-life as late-twentieth-century Protestant conservatives reprinted them as virtual classics.[88] Equally notable was the ecumenical character of opposition to Bible revision. Wilkinson made no reference to his Seventh-day Adventist affiliation in *Our Authorized Bible Vindicated,* concentrating instead on issues of broad evangelical appeal. Mauro, who rejected the Episcopal Church in favor of A. B. Simpson's Christian and Missionary Alliance, cited the Anglican Dean Burgon without compunction, as did Wilkinson. Similarly, David Otis Fuller, a minister in the General Association of Regular Baptists, during the 1970s edited reprints of works by Burgon, Mauro, Wilkinson, and others—all without apparent regard for denominational loyalties.[89]

Such pragmatic alliances among like-minded Protestants would take on additional significance in future Bible battles, for although modern critical consciousness drove conservatives and liberals apart, it also fostered intraconservative and intraliberal cooperation. The legacy of "King Truth" was therefore ambiguous—as relentlessly paradoxical as the legacy of sixteenth-century Protestant-Catholic disputation. The old Reformation debates over authority and interpretation would help set the terms of twentieth-century translation controversies, generating in the process rich rhetorical and ecumenical ironies. In the next chapter, I examine the attempts by members of the RSV committee to wrestle with these multifarious legacies of Reformation and Enlightenment.

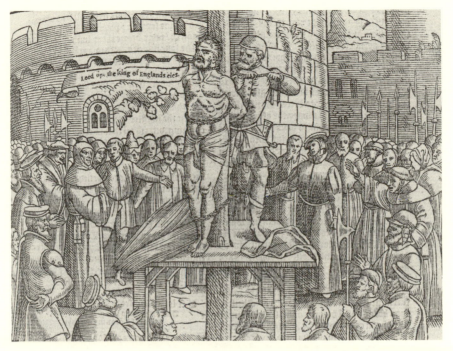

FIGURE 1. *William Tyndale's execution. From John Foxe's* Acts and Monuments *(1563). Courtesy of the Beinecke Rare Book and Manuscript Library, Yale University.*

FIGURE 2. *"Edward VI and the Pope" (1570), artist unknown. Courtesy of the National Portrait Gallery, London.*

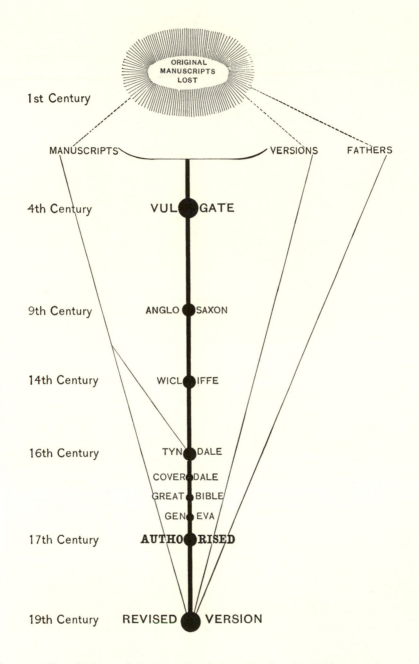

ORIGINAL
MANUSCRIPTS
LOST

1st Century

MANUSCRIPTS   VERSIONS   FATHERS

4th Century   VUL●GATE

9th Century   ANGLO●SAXON

14th Century   WICL●IFFE

16th Century   TYN●DALE

COVER●DALE

GREAT●BIBLE

GEN●EVA

17th Century   **AUTHO●RISED**

19th Century   REVISED●VERSION

FIGURE 3. *Frontispiece to J. Paterson Smyth*. How We Got Our Bible, *new ed. (1899)*.

FIGURE 4. *Philip Schaff, chairman of the American committee for the Revised Version of 1881–85. Courtesy of Union Theological Seminary, New York.*

FIGURE 5. *The RSV committee, Old Testament section, meeting at Yale Divinity School, around 1950. Left to right: George Dahl, James Muilenburg, Julius A. Bewer, J. Philip Hyatt, Fleming James, Luther A. Weigle, Millar Burrows, Harry M. Orlinsky, Herbert G. May, and William A. Irwin. Courtesy of the Princeton Theological Seminary Archives.*

FIGURE 6. *RSV committee chairman Luther A. Weigle presenting the completed Revised Standard Version to President Harry Truman at the White House on September 26, 1952. Courtesy of AP/Wide World Photos.*

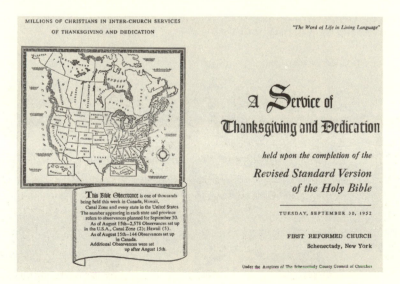

FIGURE 7. *Bulletin cover for the RSV Bible Observance (1952). More than 3,400 services like this one in Schenectady, New York, were orchestrated nationwide on Tuesday evening, September 30, 1952, by the National Council of Churches to mark the RSV's publication. Courtesy of the Princeton Theological Seminary Archives.*

FIGURE 8. *Advertisement for the RSV Bible (1952). The reverse side included a form for ordering copies bound either in buckram ($6) or leather ($10). Courtesy of the Princeton Theological Seminary Archives.*

FIGURE 9. *The Rev. Carl McIntire, chief opponent of the RSV, waves a copy of the new Bible at a December 1952 rally of his American Council of Christian Churches in Denver. Courtesy of AP/Wide World Photos.*

FIGURE 10. *The Rev. Martin Luther Hux, pastor of Temple Baptist Church, Rocky Mount, N.C., preparing to ignite the page from the RSV bearing the disputed verse, Isaiah 7:14. Courtesy of AP/Wide World Photos.*

FIGURE 11. *Luther A. Weigle receiving the Papal Knighthood of St. Gregory the Great under a portrait of St. Thomas More, symbol of Catholic opposition to Protestant Bible translation, on January 27, 1966, in New Haven, Connecticut. From left: Daniel D. Williams, Weigle, Archbishop Henry J. O'Brien of Hartford, Paul S. Minear, and Gerald E. Knoff. Courtesy of Manuscripts and Archives, Yale University Library.*

Chapter 3

Scripture for the Ecumenical Church

The Protestant Establishment and the Making of the RSV Bible

✠

It has been granted to the Americans less than any other nation of the earth to realize on earth the visible unity of the church of God. . . . American Christianity has no central organization, no common creed, no common cultus, no common church history and no common ethical, social or political principles.

—Dietrich Bonhoeffer,
"Protestantism without Reformation" (1939)

THE SIX DECADES from the completion of the Revised Version of the Bible in 1885 to the end of the Second World War significantly diminished the authority of the oldline denominational establishment to speak for all Protestants, much less for Americans as a whole. Currents from within and without eroded the standing of the churches whose financial and cultural capital had sustained the Bible revision movement of the 1870s. Within the Protestant denominations, the crusading evangelical liberals of the Progressive Era felt the stinging polemic of such conservatives as J. Gresham Machen, who having pronounced Christianity and liberalism incompatible, led a secession from Princeton Theological Seminary in 1929 to found Westminster Seminary in Philadelphia.[1] Equally trenchant criticism of theological liberalism came from some erstwhile liberals for whom the ashes of two world wars had vindicated Puritan pessimism about human nature. Neo-orthodox thinkers recognized the evil in humanity, as H. Richard Niebuhr would later recall, "not because we desired to see it, but because it thrust itself upon us."[2]

Even more corrosive than critiques from within were competing forces from outside Protestantism. The apologetic Protestant histories of the English Bible (explored in chapter 1) testified to an ascendant Roman Catholicism sustained by a huge influx of southern and eastern European immigrants between 1880 and the restriction of immigration during the 1920s. Pope Pius X belatedly responded to the American church's changing fortunes by lifting its mission status in 1908, the same year that thirty-three Protestant denominations, perhaps feeling a bit beleaguered, convened to form the Federal Council of Churches.[3] The numerical strength of Catholicism, combined with intractable conservative-liberal tensions within the Protestant denominations, were major factors in what one scholar has famously termed the "second disestablishment" of oldline Protestantism.[4]

In spite of its uncertain fate in a pluralistic world, the Protestant establishment remained remarkably optimistic in the period 1885–1945. Though sometimes viewed by historians as unitive efforts born of common weakness, cooperative ventures such as the Federal Council of Churches evinced a genuine confidence of mission—a new faith in the persuasive power of conciliar Protestantism. In this heyday of ecumenical enthusiasm, the Bible revision movement, as it first did in the 1870s, reemerged as a potential vehicle of unity and evangelism. By the 1920s, as an ever-broadening biblical scholarship was again providing justification for retranslation, leaders of the oldline denominations seized this opportunity to sponsor a new "standard" Bible for the ecumenical church. Yet the partnership between the scholarly and denominational establishments was, from its inception, resented by Protestants outside of the institutional power structures. The idea that any single organization could promulgate a universally definitive edition of Scripture resurrected long-latent Protestant fears of authority. These fears would come to a head in the 1950s, revealing deep ideological fissures within American Protestantism. The visible unity of the church of Christ— a unity premised upon one book—would prove an elusive prize.

THE AMERICAN STANDARD VERSION
AND THE INFRASTRUCTURE OF REVISION

The making of the Revised Version had been a transatlantic affair, yet because of the project's origin in the Church of England, veto power in translation disputes rested with the British committee. Consequently, a list of American textual preferences, mostly minor, was relegated to an appendix in the completed Bible of 1885. The Americans agreed not to publish a rival edition for fourteen years, during which time the university presses of Oxford and Cambridge would hold exclusive rights to the text.

In the fourteen-year interim, an American committee depleted by death—chairman Philip Schaff passed away in 1893—prepared a Yankee revision of the British version, integrating preferences from the 1885 appendix into the text and making spelling and other stylistic changes. Bowing to widespread popular usage, the committee substituted "Jehovah" for "Lord" and "God" (printed in small capitals) in occurrences of the Hebrew Tetragrammaton, YHWH. The committee explained that "a Jewish superstition, which regarded the Divine Name as too sacred to be uttered, ought no longer to dominate in the English or any other version of the Old Testament."[5] Perhaps chastened by conservative criticism of the Revised Version's marginal notes, the Americans also deleted much of the 1885 apparatus, particularly those notes calling attention to variant readings in "some ancient authorities."

The amended Bible appeared in 1901 as the American Standard Version, with the copyright registered to Thomas Nelson and Sons of New York. The minimally revised Scriptures understandably generated little excitement, save for the usual homage from revision-movement partisans. Among the more striking endorsements was that of Princeton Seminary's Benjamin Warfield, an opponent of higher biblical criticism who nevertheless supported text-critical research and ecumenical revision. Warfield praised the ASV as in many respects more judiciously conservative than its British predecessor. He lauded the removal of the "misleading" marginal notes. He commended the restoration of "Jehovah" as "the Lord's *personal* name." Yet, in apparent weariness of the Bible battles of the previous two decades, he cautioned against "hysterical overestimation of minute differences" between different Bible versions, "as if the Word of God were not competently transmitted through the ordinary channels of translation." Warfield's confidence in translated Scripture placed him squarely in line with his Presbyterian forebears, whose Westminster Confession (1648) declared that the biblical text had been "kept pure in all ages" by God's "singular care and providence."[6]

As a translation, the American Standard Version, like its fraternal twin, the Revised Version, was often slavishly literal, and this made it attractive to educators who wanted to place in students' hands a text close to the original Hebrew and Greek. Conservatives such as Wilbert W. White, president of the Bible Teachers Training School in New York and onetime instructor at Moody Bible Institute, publicly endorsed the ASV as the best translation available. Meanwhile, a variety of tracts listed the "great religious denominations" that had adopted the version for their Sunday school curricula.[7] In 1904, the American Bible Society amended its constitution to allow distribution not only of the Authorized Version but also the RV and ASV, thereby conferring the approval of one of America's oldest benevolent organizations upon the Bible revision movement.[8]

With the ASV securing a place for itself in Sunday school classrooms, religious education organizations began to take notice. By 1922, two major Sunday school unions had consolidated to form the International Council of Religious Education, a Chicago-based association that represented at its height some forty Protestant denominations. The ICRE identified as one of the primary objectives of Christian education the "assimilation of the best religious experience of the race, preeminently that recorded in the Bible."[9] The leaders of the ICRE, including General Secretary Hugh S. Magill, a Methodist layman and former Illinois state senator, regarded the council as the logical steward of the ASV text and sponsor of future Bible revision efforts. Accordingly, the ICRE acquired the ASV's copyright in 1929, granting Thomas Nelson and Sons continued publication rights in exchange for yearly payments toward the expenses of a "Standard Bible Committee."[10] Delegates to the ICRE's annual meeting appointed as charter members of the committee Frederick C. Eiselen (president of Garrett Biblical Institute), John R. Sampey (president of Southern Baptist Theological Seminary), and Luther A. Weigle (dean of Yale Divinity School); these three men, in consultation with ICRE officials, selected twelve other scholars for membership on the committee.[11]

The Standard Bible Committee held its first meeting at the Prince George Hotel in New York City on 15 April 1930. First on the agenda was the critical decision of whether to revise the American Standard Version. Three of the committee members, University of Chicago professors Edgar J. Goodspeed and J. M. Powis Smith, and Union Seminary professor James Moffatt, had produced their own modern-language versions of Scripture and thus were well acquainted with the advantages and disadvantages of colloquial translation.[12] Goodspeed, in particular, argued that ancient Greek papyri discovered since the Revised Version's completion in 1885 proved that the New Testament was originally written in a colloquial style and ought to be translated as such.[13] He therefore advocated substantial revision of the American Standard Version, which, though more modern in style than the King James Version, nevertheless had retained the "thee's," "thou's," and other archaic features so familiar to Bible readers. Other committee members, such as Harvard University professor James Hardy Ropes, favored a conservative translation that would revise only those ASV passages shown by recent scholarship to be in error. The committee debated the issue in subsequent meetings, and when it appeared that Goodspeed's view might win the day, Ropes resigned.[14] Privately, Hugh Magill of the ICRE also expressed reservations, writing to Luther Weigle that "there are some things that have come down to us from the past that have inherent worth and carry with them a lofty spirit of beauty and reverence which no modern style can displace." Drawing on an architectural analogy, Magill insisted that the "modernistic" buildings then under construction in Chicago for the 1933 World's Fair could not compare to the classical beauty of Chicago's Field Museum. Similarly, Magill complained of Goodspeed's own "inconsistency" in supporting colloquial translation while at the same time praising the "churchly style" of the University of Chicago's new neo-Gothic Rockefeller Chapel.[15]

In the end, the committee reached something of a compromise, voting for an overhaul of the ASV but in the "Tyndale–King James tradition." Yet the delicate matter of biblical style would soon be the least of the problems

at hand, for the committee's coffers were running low. Though the translators worked without remuneration (save for travel expenses), a major revision would require the appointment of at least two part-time salaried
members if the project were to be completed in a reasonable length of time.
Magill and Weigle approached several donors, including the Rockefeller
family, to no avail: the Great Depression had not only depleted the
churches' financial reserves but also diminished the largesse of the churches'
corporate benefactors. As Weigle steamed homeward aboard the SS
Southern Cross after presiding over the World's Sunday School Association
meeting in Rio de Janeiro, Magill wrote of the "precarious conditions with
respect to income" and suggested that the Standard Bible Committee either
suspend or drastically curtail its work. The committee elected to suspend.[16]

A PROFILE OF THE STANDARD BIBLE COMMITTEE

Plans for Bible revision would lie dormant for the next five years, until Roy
G. Ross, Magill's successor as ICRE general secretary, negotiated a new
deal with Thomas Nelson and Sons that provided thirty-five thousand dollars in advance royalties over seven years for the translators' expenses.
Nelson would for a decade be the exclusive publisher of the new Bible, to
be known as the Revised Standard Version. The committee reconvened in
1937 at New York's Union Seminary, appointing additional members to replace those who had died (including Eiselen and Smith) or resigned. The
membership roster would continue to grow as the project developed.

The committee's demographic profile was thoroughly establishmentarian. All the members were white men, and all were professors at research-
oriented universities or seminaries, save for Walter Russell Bowie, rector of
Grace Church, New York, who later accepted an appointment at Union
Seminary. All were affiliated with eastern or midwestern universities, except for James Muilenburg of the Pacific School of Religion at Berkeley,
California. Although officially the committee members were selected for
their scholarly competencies and not for their religious affiliations, the
scholars represented ten Protestant denominations. From 1929 to 1952,
the thirty-two-member committee included nine Congregationalists, five
Methodists, four Episcopalians, three American Baptists, three Southern
Baptists, two Presbyterians, two members of the United Church of Canada,
one Disciple of Christ, one Quaker, and one Lutheran. In 1945, in a de-

cision that would be denounced by the new Bible's fundamentalist opponents, the committee added a Reform Jew, Harry M. Orlinsky of the Hebrew Union College–Jewish Institute of Religion in New York. The second-youngest member, Orlinsky outlived all his colleagues, all but three of whom had been born in the nineteenth century. In an addition to the thirty-two committee members, several ICRE officials served ex officio, and an advisory board composed of representatives from all the ICRE denominations offered procedural, and occasionally editorial, suggestions. The advisory board included representatives of several African-American denominations.

Like the committee for the Revised Version of 1881–85, the RSV committee's roster read like a *Who's Who* of prominent academicians and churchmen. Of the members active after 1937, five were academic deans or presidents, including Willard L. Sperry, dean of Harvard Divinity School and sometime commentator on American religion, who was one of several people appointed as consultants on literary or educational matters.[17] Among the most famous members was the indomitable Goodspeed, who later would self-assuredly begin his memoir with the observation: "On the night Alexander the Great was born, the temple of Artemis in Ephesus was burned to the ground, and in the very month of my birth, the city of Chicago was reduced to ashes."[18] Another celebrity-scholar was the pugnacious archaeologist, William Foxwell Albright, whose disciples at Johns Hopkins University came to be known as the Baltimore school.[19] Finally, the committee included one Nobel laureate, Harvard professor Henry Joel Cadbury, who accepted the 1947 Nobel Peace Prize on behalf of the American Friends Service Committee, which he had chaired since 1928.[20]

UNITING EDUCATION AND ECUMENISM:
CHAIRMAN LUTHER ALLAN WEIGLE

Holding together the constellation of leading lights on the RSV committee—and placating the potential prima donnas—was the difficult job of chairman Luther Allan Weigle. Born in Littlestown, Pennsylvania, on 11 September 1880, Weigle attended college and seminary at Gettysburg, following his father into the Lutheran ministry. As an undergraduate he took four years of classical Greek, studying Plato and the other philosophers. A biology course introduced him to evolutionary theory, which in turn led

THE STANDARD BIBLE COMMITTEE, 1929–1952

Birth and death dates are listed first, followed by institutional affiliation (at the time of each member's appointment), dates of service on the committee, and denominational affiliation

New Testament Section (*RSV New Testament published 1946*)

1. William P. Armstrong (1874–1944), Princeton Theological Seminary, *1930–1937, Presbyterian*
2. Walter Russell Bowie (1882–1969), Grace Church, New York, *1937–1969, Episcopalian*
3. Henry J. Cadbury (1883–1974), Harvard University, *1930–1974, Quaker*
4. Clarence T. Craig (1895–1953), Oberlin Graduate School of Theology, *1938–1953, Methodist*
5. Edgar J. Goodspeed (1871–1962), University of Chicago, *1930–1962, American Baptist*
6. Frederick C. Grant (1891–1974), President, Seabury-Western Theological Seminary, *1937–1972, Episcopalian*
7. Archibald T. Robertson (1863–1934), Southern Baptist Theological Seminary, *1930–1934, Southern Baptist*
8. James Hardy Ropes (1866–1933), Harvard University, *1930–1932, Congregationalist*
9. Andrew Sledd (1870–1939), Emory University, *1930–1937, Methodist*
10. Abdel R. Wentz (1883–1976), President, Lutheran Theological Seminary, Gettysburg, *1938–1976, Lutheran*

Old Testament Section (*RSV Old Testament published 1952*)

11. William F. Albright (1891–1971), Johns Hopkins University, *1945–1970, Methodist*
12. Julius A. Bewer (1877–1953), Union Theological Seminary, *1930–1951, Congregationalist*
13. George Dahl (1881–1962), Yale University, *1937–1962, Congregationalist*
14. Frederick C. Eiselen (1872–1937), President, Garrett Biblical Institute, *1929–1937, Methodist*
15. Alexander R. Gordon (1872–1930), United Theological College, Montreal, *1930, United Church of Canada*
16. J. Philip Hyatt (1909–1972), Vanderbilt University, *1945–1972, Disciples of Christ*
17. William A. Irwin (1884–1967), University of Chicago, *1937–1967, American Baptist*
18. Fleming James (1877–1959), Dean, University of the South, *1947–1954, Episcopalian*
19. Herbert G. May (1904–1977), Oberlin Graduate School of Theology, *1945–1977, Congregationalist*
20. James A. Montgomery (1866–1949), University of Pennsylvania, *1930–1937, Episcopalian*

21. James Muilenburg (1896–1974), Pacific School of Religion, *1945–1974, Congregationalist*
22. Harry M. Orlinsky (1908–1992), Hebrew Union College–Jewish Institute of Religion, *1945–1992, Jewish*
23. John R. Sampey (1863–1946), President, Southern Baptist Theological Seminary, *1929–1938, Southern Baptist*
24. J. M. Powis Smith (1866–1932), University of Chicago, *1930–1932, American Baptist*
25. Willard L. Sperry (1882–1954), Dean, Harvard University Divinity School, *1937–1954, Congregationalist*
26. William R. Taylor (1882–1951), University of Toronto, *1931–1951, United Church of Canada*
27. Charles C. Torrey (1863–1956), Yale University, *1930–1937, Congregationalist*
28. Leroy Waterman (1875–1972), University of Michigan, *1937–1972, American Baptist*
29. Kyle M. Yates (1895–1975), Southern Baptist Theological Seminary, *1938–1975, Southern Baptist*

Members of Both Sections
30. Millar Burrows (1889–1980), Yale University, *1938–1972, Congregationalist*
31. James Moffatt (1870–1944), Union Theological Seminary, *1930–1944, Presbyterian*
32. Luther A. Weigle (1880–1976), Dean, Yale University Divinity School, *1929–1976, Congregationalist* (Chairman of the Committee, 1930–1966)

him to Spencer and Huxley; he penned his reactions in an essay whose "modest title" (as he later quipped) was "Some Notes on the Genesis of Sin." Having convinced himself of the compatibility of evolution and Christianity, young Weigle enrolled in seminary, where he imbibed "the Christocentric view of the Scriptures that was characteristic of Luther." Weigle's professors "disavowed mechanical theories of inspiration, and taught that the divine revelation is progressive, not because God holds back truth, but because it is relative to occasions and suited to the capacity of man the recipient." Ordained a Lutheran pastor in 1903, Weigle enrolled in graduate school at Yale, where he studied philosophy and worked as a research assistant in experimental psychology. Weigle's dissertation was on Kant, from whom he learned that no reason "based upon facts only can reach incontrovertible conclusions" concerning "the ultimate character of reality."[21]

Weigle spent his early career as a professor of philosophy, and later dean, at Carleton College in Northfield, Minnesota. He built a reputation as the author of a popular textbook for Sunday school teachers, and this led to his appointment in 1916 as the Horace Bushnell Professor of Christian Nurture at Yale Divinity School. The same year he transferred his ministerial standing to the local Congregational association, although he retained his theological affinities for Lutheranism. (He liked to say that he was "in politics a Republican, in theology a Lutheran, and in . . . ecclesiastical connection and ministerial office a Congregationalist.")[22] In 1924 he accepted Yale's Sterling Chair of Religious Education, and in 1928 he became dean of Yale Divinity School, a position he held until his retirement in 1949. Weigle was seventy-two years old when the RSV Bible was completed in 1952; he remained chairman of the Standard Bible Committee until age eighty-six and served as vice chairman until he was ninety.

Weigle's career and writings demonstrated his abiding concern for two of the church's tasks: education and ecumenism. In the field of religious education, he found inspiration in Horace Bushnell's classic, *Christian Nurture* (1847), for which he wrote a new introduction in a centennial reprint. Weigle regarded Bushnell as far ahead of his time in repudiating the crisis conversions and "arbitrary supernaturalism" of old-time revivalism in favor of a more orderly, family-centered approach to Christian socialization. With Bushnell, Weigle believed that children properly reared would never know themselves as anything other than Christian. From the moment of a child's birth, the family would act as a means of grace, a channel of the Holy Spirit. The family also would be a child's first Bible teacher, introducing God's revelation first through story books and then through the Scriptures themselves—preferably in the Standard revision.[23]

Yet the family was not the only locus of a child's education. Weigle devoted much of his career to the professionalization of the Sunday school, an institution he liked to call the "church of tomorrow." For all its great potential as nursery of enlightened piety, the Sunday school was also fraught with peril:

> A common bane of Sunday school teaching has been the haziness of the teacher's own ideas concerning the truths of religion. Too many teachers are just good, well-meaning Christian folk, whose beliefs are rooted in a surface soil of authority or convention and ultimately grounded in a loyal devotion to the right.[24]

The antidote to amateurism was Jesus himself, who heralded neither an imminent apocalypse nor a humanistic utopia but the "educational method": a way of teaching marked by freedom from coercion, fellowship between teacher and pupil, and objectivity in the search for truth.[25] The last of these, objectivity, was particularly important in the teaching of the Bible—the Sunday school's "chief text-book." Individual biblical passages, Weigle believed, must be judged never in isolation but in the larger empirical context of Scripture and church tradition. As he put it, the Bible "is not a collection of dogmas or of proof-texts, in all its parts of equal value"; nor is it "a body of writings and records, each of which carries its own moral and spiritual meaning independent of the rest." The biblical parts have meaning only in light of the whole.[26]

In his quest for a more professional Sunday school, Weigle published scores of articles and a half-dozen books offering practical advice for teachers. Such intimate involvement by a divinity school dean in primary and secondary level religious education would become less common as American universities engaged in ever more specialized, and rarified, research. Yet Weigle lived in an era when the academy optimistically sought to remold the church in its own image. The effort, as Conrad Cherry has argued, often met resistance or indifference at the local level, but the reformers stubbornly pressed on, convinced of the widespread need for their message.[27] Indeed, the educational agenda of Weigle and others transcended the local congregation and even the denomination to envision a pan-Protestant pedagogical reformation. Weigle served for thirty years (1928–58) as chairman of the executive committee of the World's Sunday School Association, an interdenominational organization that advocated under his leadership the modernization of Sunday school curricula. Through the association and other forums, Weigle's writings reached an international audience: although originally commissioned by the Lutheran Publication Society, his book *The Pupil and the Teacher* (1911) appeared under three additional imprints in America and England and was translated into Chinese, Japanese, Portuguese, and Spanish. In all, the book sold well over a million copies.[28]

Weigle's commitment to the World's Sunday School Association reflected his vision of the church's mission as at once educational and ecumenical. Ecumenical cooperation made ambitious (and expensive) educational ventures such as the Revised Standard Version possible. Conversely, educational ventures such as the RSV promoted ecumenism by attempting to unite Protestants in a common biblical vocabulary. To Weigle, then, education and ecumenism always existed in symbiosis. From 1940 to 1942 he served as president of the Federal Council of Churches, and from 1941 to 1950 he chaired the planning committee for its successor, the National Council of the Churches of Christ in the United States of America.[29] He also chaired for twenty years the executive committee of the American Association of Theological Schools.

Weigle and his committee colleagues' participation in the ecumenical movement flowed naturally from the ethos of the research university, which tolerated, even encouraged, a mixture of religious commitments among its faculty. In this context a project such as the RSV was unthinkable without an interdenominational committee of scholars from the "nonsectarian" universities and theological schools. Like other publications by professors, the RSV could not be produced in private: each biblical verse had to withstand peer review by the acknowledged company of experts on the committee.

THE RSV TRANSLATORS AND THE PROBLEM
OF THE VERNACULAR BIBLE

Underlying the translators' debates over individual biblical passages was the less tangible and essentially unending labor of articulating the Standard Bible Committee's operating principles. In this task the Reformation and Enlightenment cast long shadows. The translators of the Revised Version (1881–85) had largely embraced a sixteenth-century sense of vernacular Scripture as a peculiarly Protestant preserve, and adopted a nineteenth-century optimism about translation's role in the historical-critical quest for truth. Yet changing circumstances—an ever-narrowing numerical gap between Catholics and the Protestant majority and ever-increasing polarization among Protestants themselves—meant that for the RSV translators the axioms of the Reformation and Enlightenment operated less as unquestioned presuppositions than as unresolved ambiguities.

The first ambiguity stemmed from the Reformation: What contribution, if any, should Catholics make to Protestant Bible translation? On the one hand it appeared that the RSV translators' answer was none. Typically the translators followed their forebears in equating Protestantism with intellectual freedom and Catholicism with intellectual bondage. Why, so this logic went, would accurately translated Scripture be of any concern in a tradition where the pope ruled on all matters ex cathedra? As Weigle himself once wrote, "Protestantism is democracy in religion" while Catholicism requires the "intermediation of ecclesiastical officialdom." Standard Bible Committee member Herbert Gordon May similarly argued that the English Bible's history was intimately linked to the development of human freedom and that the story of vernacular Scripture was "the story of everyman."[30] Like their late-nineteenth-century counterparts, moreover, the RSV translators venerated William Tyndale as the first great Bible translator and a martyr for the Protestant cause. In their frequent invocations of the "Tyndale–King James tradition," the committee members linked themselves to an unbroken succession of Protestant translation and scriptural authority that obviated the apostolic succession of Roman pontiffs.

Meanwhile, polemics on the other side of the great sixteenth-century divide did little to mitigate traditional Protestant anti-Catholicism. A 1948 tract bearing the imprimatur of the bishop of Fort Wayne, Indiana, insisted that the "sorry spectacle of Protestantism with its hundreds of warring sects" would never have arisen had Protestants accepted the authority of the church to settle disputes of biblical interpretation. The document further upbraided the Protestant tradition of English Bible histories for giving readers the impression that the medieval church withheld Scripture from the people. "Far from being hostile to the Bible," wrote the tract's author, Father J. A. O'Brien, "the Catholic Church is its true Mother" because the church existed prior to the writing of the New Testament.[31] A real estate agent who picked up O'Brien's manifesto in his home parish on Staten Island promptly mailed a copy to Luther Weigle with a note suggesting that he read it before proceeding further on the RSV because it might save the committee "a lot of unnecessary trouble."[32]

Other Catholics claimed that Protestant Bible revision was slowly but surely vindicating the Douay-Rheims translation, which derived from the Latin Vulgate. After the RSV New Testament appeared in 1946, Father Thomas J. Coakley of Sacred Heart Church in Pittsburgh observed from the pulpit that the Standard Bible Committee members "might have saved themselves all this trouble and expense if they had simply used the Catholic Bible, toward which every successive version tends more and more to conform." This prompted a swift rebuttal in the *Pittsburgh Post-Gazette* from J. Carter Swaim, professor at Pittsburgh's Western Theological Seminary, an institution of the Reformed Church in America. Weigle later thanked

Swaim: "You are right, of course; the Revised Standard Version is not a revision in the direction of Roman Catholicism."[33]

Yet such defensiveness on the part of Protestants and Catholics belied a growing openness on both sides toward cooperation in Bible translation. Among Catholics, the 1930s and 1940s had brought a renaissance of biblical scholarship. The Catholic Biblical Association, founded in 1937, played a key role in a 1941 revision of the Douay-Rheims-Challoner New Testament. Officially sponsored by the Confraternity of Christian Doctrine, the new edition remained wedded to the Vulgate but took account of the Greek in the footnotes. Two years later Pope Pius XII issued a major encyclical, *Divino Afflante Spiritu* (1943), fully sanctioning the translation of vernacular Bibles from the original Greek and Hebrew. With this papal blessing, the scholars associated with the Confraternity project launched a new translation of the entire Bible.[34]

Members of the Standard Bible Committee hailed the developments on the Catholic side. Chairman Weigle discerned the hand of Providence in the simultaneous renewal of Bible revision among Catholics and Protestants.[35] W. F. Albright commended *Divino Afflante Spiritu*, noting that while the pope did not hand Catholic biblical scholars a license to employ biblical criticism without restraint, he granted freedom enough:

> [W]hen one seriously examines the enormous mass of subjective speculation . . . which fills most critical libraries in our field, one cannot altogether regret a limitation which prevents Catholic scholars from adding appreciably to the Protestant chaos.[36]

Such self-deprecating endorsements of Catholic scholarship testified to a genuine change in Protestant attitudes, yet cooperation between Catholics and Protestants on Bible translation was still more than a decade away. The sweeping reforms enacted by the Second Vatican Council (1962–65) would clear the way for a variety of ecumenical ventures in translation, but for the years of the RSV project (1937–52), revision in the "Tyndale–King James" lineage remained a Protestant preserve.

Albright's wistfulness about the salutary limits placed on Catholic scholarship was revealing in another respect: it highlighted the ambiguity of authority within Protestantism. For Christians who, in theory at least, claimed the Scriptures as the final court of appeal in all doctrinal disputes, who could adjudicate disputes over the biblical text itself? The four centuries since the Reformation had failed to resolve this issue, for although English-speaking Protestants eventually achieved a remarkable degree of linguistic unity in the King James Bible, the Authorized Version never held sway for all denominations at all times. (One need only recall the various nineteenth-century Baptist versions that substituted "immerse" for "baptize.") Nor were the Greek or Hebrew the final authorities because Protestants continually disagreed over which textual reconstructions came closest to the originals. One could argue, of course, that a single Protestant Bible was unnecessary and even undesirable, yet this transgressed the ecumenical ethos of the RSV translators, who believed that a common book would further the churches' common mission. Weigle, for example, rankled at the suggestion that recent translations such as the RSV were useful for educational purposes but that the King James Bible was preferable for liturgical use. This represented to him the "tacit assumption that truth and understanding are of little consequence in worship."[37] But American Protestants, unlike their Catholic brethren, had no central authority to rule on an acceptable Bible for educational or liturgical use, and it seemed doubtful that endorsement by the International Council of Religious Education would catapult the RSV to instant preeminence among Bibles.

Besides the unresolved problem of authority, the RSV translators faced the unresolved problem of translation's relationship to interpretation. Ever since the Enlightenment and ensuing developments transformed biblical interpretation (both liberal and conservative) into a search for the "real" history beneath the biblical history, accurate translation had been regarded as an essential component of the historical quest. To be reliable as a tool of historical reconstruction, translation had to be absolutely impartial, and the late-nineteenth-century translators of the Revised Version had sanguinely proclaimed the "scientific" foundations of their enterprise.

The RSV translators also seemed to regard translation as impartial, as their correspondence with members of the public revealed. In the years prior to the RSV's publication, chairman Luther Weigle and the Standard Bible Committee received a variety of letters from ordinary Americans suggesting "improvements" on Holy Writ. Some of the suggestions were purely aesthetic, such as the separate proposals by two people to replace "ass" with "donkey" to forestall the inevitable "nudging, whispering, and snickering" among Sunday school students.[38] (In an indication of its stylistic conservatism, the committee retained the traditional "ass.") But other suggestions were transparently doctrinal and arose from correspondents' desire to have the Bible say what they already *knew* it meant. Three people asked Weigle to delete or soften the anti-Jewish passages in the Fourth Gospel. Surely, one woman reasoned, such expressions as "for fear of the Jews" did not reflect the loving spirit that Jesus taught.[39] Another woman, an official with the National Leprosarium in Carville, Louisiana, pleaded for mitigation of the biblical stigma against leprosy.[40] Meanwhile, the secretary of a Women's Christian Temperance Union chapter in California implored the committee to reconsider the use of "wine" in instances such as 1 Timothy 5:23 ("use a little wine for thy stomach's sake"). Undoubtedly, she explained, this referred not to wine in the modern sense but to grape juice, for "St. Paul was the forerunner of modern health enthusiasts who endorse the use of fresh juices."[41]

Theological modification of texts was common among scribes in antiquity, as attested by curse formulas designed to protect against such tampering (e.g., Rev. 22:18–19).[42] Yet the members of the Standard Bible Committee steadfastly refused to make changes that they felt the text itself did not permit, even though the issue of textual warrant was sometimes murky. In their optimism about the unambiguous question of textual emendation, the committee adhered to a nineteenth-century notion of Bible translation as an absolutely impartial science. Thus, for example, committee member Millar Burrows rejected a request to correct the erroneous citation of the prophet Jeremiah in Matthew 27:9, arguing that to make such a change would be "presumptuous and even dishonest" and would give the appearance that the committee was trying to make the Bible seem infallible. No emendation, Burrows explained, "can be made without objective evidence in ancient manuscripts and versions. Once you start making emendations in the text you never know where to draw the line."[43] Similarly, committee member William A. Irwin commented incredulously on the letters from people wanting the translators "to deal a blow to certain antisocial views which unfortunately base themselves on this or that Bible passage." The committee, he insisted, had no authority to "change the Bible."[44] Irwin apparently presupposed the public's ability to distinguish between unjustified "changes" and those alterations of English phraseology that the Greek and Hebrew would allow.

At the same time, however, the RSV committee may not have been quite as idealistic about translation's transparency as Irwin's comment suggested. Elsewhere in their writings the members spoke of translation not as an exact science but as an art. To Weigle, the precise English reproduction of the

Greek and Hebrew was quite elusive and might be "hindered by the temperament, character, and spirit of the translator."[45] Indeed, he believed that literal translation was not only difficult to achieve but even undesirable. Weigle frequently criticized the American Standard Version for being so mechanically literal as to be almost an interlinear edition. Significantly, he also was critical of "ultra-modern" translations that ignored the "Tyndale–King James tradition." Translation for him clearly had a subjective, aesthetic element: the poetry of the original must not be effaced in a quest either for interlinear-like accuracy or contemporary English idiom.[46] For Weigle the crucial test of the RSV would come not in the scrutiny of exacting academicians but in the worship services of the living church. "If men, women, and children are led by [the RSV] to God," he wrote, "and if they find its phrases naturally upon their lips and in their hearts when they pray, it will endure."[47]

For Weigle and his colleagues, therefore, translation was a difficult balance between the scientific impartiality once glorified by the Enlightenment and the artistic subjectivity celebrated by the Enlightenment's discontents. Equally difficult was the balance between the sixteenth-century Protestant ideal of biblical authority and the Catholic ideal of ecclesiastical authority. Arising from the intersection of a powerful tradition of Protestant biblicism with a new movement toward a plenary church organization, the RSV project in some sense straddled the great Reformation divide. The tension between Book and Church—and between an exacting text-critical empiricism and a premodern scriptural aestheticism—would demarcate the RSV's place in American religious history.

THE TRANSLATION AND RECEPTION OF THE RSV NEW TESTAMENT

The RSV committee's New Testament section, whose revision was published six years before the whole Bible, officially convened thirty-one times over 145 days, but much of the hard work of translation occurred between meetings. An initial draft of each New Testament book was prepared by one or two members, typed, and then mimeographed for every scholar in the section. The drafts were then discussed twice by the full section, with the secretary, James Moffatt, both times recording proposed changes and retyping the drafts. Finally, the twice-reviewed New Testament manuscripts were distributed to the members of the Old Testament section. Any deviation from the basic text of the American Standard Version required a two-thirds vote of the entire Standard Bible Committee. (Later, the Old Testament section followed the same arduous but thorough procedure.)[48]

As with most projects of its scope, the RSV's timetable for completion was overly ambitious, and Weigle occasionally had to plead with delinquent members to finish their assigned books. Originally scheduled for completion in 1941, the New Testament did not appear until 1946. Second-guessing of previously approved renderings, particularly in the Old Testament, further slowed the project and exasperated the publisher, Thomas Nelson and Sons; yet in the handling of Holy Writ, excessive scrupulosity usually proved to be a virtue. The fastidiousness of one RSV translator, the Quaker scholar Henry J. Cadbury, acquired the status of legend. Reputedly he sometimes made motions on which everyone would vote in favor—except Cadbury himself, who by then had changed his mind. An inside joke thus arose: "Where's Cadbury? Oh, he's out relining his brakes."[49]

The text of the RSV New Testament drew on ancient manuscripts discovered since the Revised Version's publication in 1881–85, including papyri unearthed in Egypt and acquired by Sir Chester Beatty in 1931. These scrolls dated from the third or even second century, possibly making them more than a hundred years older than the two famous Alexandrian codices Vaticanus and Sinaiticus. Conservative criticism of the Revised Version's reliance on these two codices had nudged the RSV translators toward a more "eclectic" textual method, yet Vaticanus and Sinaiticus, and now Chester Beatty, still carried considerable weight amid the welter of lesser manuscripts. Although the sheer volume of textual evidence had increased considerably since 1881, the RSV translators assured the public that neither the discovery of new manuscripts nor the refinement of text-critical methodology had radically altered the big biblical picture. As one committee member put it, "out of the thousands of variant readings in the manuscripts, none has turned up thus far that requires a revision of Christian doctrine."[50]

Stylistically, the RSV New Testament eliminated much of the obsolete King James terminology that the 1881 revisers had been afraid to touch. Indeed, Chairman Weigle had made it his special project to study biblical words whose usages had changed since 1611.[51] The RSV jettisoned the "thee's" and "thou's," except where the deity was addressed directly. The

"-eth" verb endings disappeared, along with the plural nominative "ye." "Whatsoever" became "whatever"; "insomuch that" became "so that." "Exceeding" was no longer used as an adverb. A few archaic terms that actually had been introduced by the 1881 translators (e.g., 1 Thess. 5:18, "This is the will of God in Christ Jesus to *you-ward*") also were abandoned. Meanwhile, in other cases the RSV adhered to long-cherished King James renderings. Weigle explained that the revisers purposely retained as much as possible of the time-honored wordings in the Lord's Prayer, the Magnificat, the Benedictus, and similar liturgical texts. In all instances the translators strove to make the RSV New Testament easy to read aloud in public worship, and this meant preserving what the translators regarded as the simple but dignified English prose of the "Tyndale tradition."[52]

As publication day for the RSV New Testament approached, the ICRE hired Wertheim Advertising Associates of New York, which made a special effort to arrange coverage in conservative publications such as the *Christian Herald*—support from liberal outlets was assumed—and to secure radio spots by prominent preachers.[53] Yet for the most part, excitement over what was billed as "the most important publication of 1946" did not equal that of 1881, when it had seemed for a fleeting moment that the whole country was enthralled with the prospect of a better Bible. The *Chicago Tribune* abandoned a proposal to print the entire New Testament in a special edition as it had done in 1881, ostensibly because of the wartime rationing of newsprint, though most such restrictions had been lifted by 1946.[54] The actual dedication of the RSV New Testament took place on 11 February 1946, at Central High School, Columbus, Ohio, in conjunction with the ICRE's annual meeting. Harold E. Stassen, former Minnesota governor and the council's president, received the first copy. Among the petitions in the dedicatory litany was a prayer referring to the RSV as "a standard for the Christian Church whereby she may be corrected in error, healed of her divisions, and made One in Christ so that the world may believe."[55]

Public reaction to the new New Testament revealed something of popular Bible-reading practices in America (and to a lesser extent, in England) circa 1946. A significant number of people read the RSV with extreme care, as was indicated by the volume of mail to the committee noting minor typographical errors, textual inconsistencies, or infelicitous renderings. One man, for example, worried that the "swineherds" of Matthew 8:33 could easily be taken to mean the pigs themselves rather than the pigs' keepers.

When the committee incorporated this suggestion, replacing "swineherds" with "herdsmen" in a slightly corrected edition of the New Testament, another man wrote a letter asking if this inconsistency between the first and subsequent printings was intentional. Later, after the publication of the RSV Old Testament, even the Archbishop of Canterbury played the error identification game, notifying Weigle via aerogram of a dittography ("in in") in the Book of Job. "It is always pleasant," commented the Primate of All England, "to find a small blemish in a friend as it increases his excellencies."[56]

Some letter-writers, however, gnashed their teeth at blemishes that did not exist. One man denounced the infelicitous rendering "holy town," which he thought had replaced the Apocalypse's traditional appellation of the New Jerusalem, "holy city." When Weigle informed him that the RSV had in fact retained "holy city," the man apologized profusely.[57] Such misunderstandings were surprisingly common, and would always coexist with the hyper-careful comparisons practiced by some people. Often it seemed that Bible translation battles arose as much from misinformation as from informed judgments, and this made controversies very difficult to contain.

Fortunately for the committee, reaction to the RSV New Testament was generally positive. A correspondent for the standard-bearer of liberal Protestantism, the *Christian Century*, predictably proffered his plaudits, noting in particular the RSV's dignified style and commenting on the suitability of the ICRE to serve as custodian of the Protestant Bible. More surprising, the fundamentalist newspaper *Moody Monthly*, organ of Chicago's Moody Bible Institute, praised the RSV as far better than any previous New Testament translation, even though it was produced by "liberalists, who do not believe in the deity of the Lord Jesus." *Moody Monthly*'s editors particularly liked the RSV's restoration of the old form of 2 Timothy 3:16: "All scripture is inspired by God and profitable." (The American Standard Version had read, "Every scripture inspired of God is also profitable.")[58]

To be sure, not all conservative Protestants liked the RSV. Some criticism stemmed from particular denominational commitments, as when executives at a half-dozen Holiness and Pentecostal publishing concerns announced or threatened boycotts of the RSV if the traditional "sanctify" were not substituted for "consecrate" in familiar passages (e.g., John 17:17, Rom. 15:16, 1 Cor. 1:30, Eph. 5:26).[59] Hoping to avoid further controversy, the committee restored "sanctify" in subsequent printings of the RSV. Indeed, the committee was responsive to criticisms and suggestions both from church leaders and from the general public. Handling all the correspondence became at least a part-time job for Weigle, who dictated responses to nearly every letter while continuing his duties as dean of Yale Divinity School.

Apart from denominationally-motivated objections, conservative criticism of the RSV generally fell into two categories: opposition to Bible revision in general, and opposition to Bible revision by liberals. The former had become almost routine by 1946, as the modern Bible revision movement entered its fourth quarter-century. Echoing the Revised Version's critics of decades before, a contributor to the *Christian Standard* railed against the evolutionist assumptions of textual critics, who regarded the reconstruction of the original Greek as a never-ending ascent toward purity. To this writer, the King James New Testament (as based on the sixteenth-century *Textus Receptus*) was divinely ordained and therefore unsurpassable. As another writer put it: "The King James Version stands on the solid foundation of actual endurance. A thousand versions have fallen at its side."[60]

More troubling to the committee were objections from those who supported Bible revision in principle but who feared that the revisers had a hidden theological agenda. William C. Taylor, a Baptist missionary who would later issue an entire book against the RSV, observed with disdain that the translators all hailed from such "hotbed[s] of modernism" as the theological schools of Chicago, Harvard, Oberlin, and Union (New York). J. Oliver Buswell, former president of Wheaton College (Illinois) and head of the National Bible Institute in New York City, noted in the conservative *Sunday School Times* that apparently no member of the RSV committee believed in Scripture's infallibility: "Oh that the Lord would raise greater facilities for accurate scholarly research among us Bible-believing people!"[61]

Both types of conservative critics—revision's opponents and revision's conditional supporters—tended to reserve their greatest invective for the ICRE. Conservatives typically lumped the council together with the Federal Council of Churches, which they regarded as one step away from a liberal "superchurch." Attacks on the ICRE inevitably were couched in the familiar code words of anti-Catholicism, as in an article by Nashville printer James A. Allen, who predicted that if "overlord" organizations such as the ICRE and the Federal Council won the day, the world-clock would be turned back to "worse than the Dark Ages."[62] Ironically, Allen conducted a latter-day inquisition in good medieval Catholic style. In separate letters, he interrogated all the members of the Standard Bible Committee concerning their beliefs about the "verbal inspiration" of the Scriptures and other cardinal points of fundamentalist orthodoxy. The committee members were relatively unaccustomed to such personal scrutiny, and a number of them refused to respond, while others were quite forthright. Abdel Ross Wentz, president of the Lutheran Theological Seminary at Gettysburg, replied: "I do not believe in what is generally called 'verbal inspiration,' and am ready to give my reasons. You see, Mr. Allen, I am a Lutheran." Wentz did, however, profess his belief in a literal virgin birth, resurrection, and ascension. Weigle took a similar tack, explaining to Allen that "if there is any basic difference between you and me, it is with respect to your phrase 'verbally inspired.' I am not sure what you mean by it." Privately, however, Weigle revealed to a committee colleague his fear that answering critics like Allen could open a Pandora's box of new attacks on the ICRE. "I feel pretty sure," Weigle wrote, "that none of us can in good conscience sign on the dotted line in assent to [Allen's] creed."[63]

Opposition by conservatives to a modernist "superchurch" increased dramatically when the ICRE was absorbed by the National Council of the Churches of Christ in the United States of America, founded at a convention in Cleveland, 28 November to 1 December 1950. Commonly known as the National Council of Churches, it represented twenty-nine Protestant and Eastern Orthodox denominations with a combined membership of thirty-three million. The NCC also served as an umbrella organization for councils of churches in forty states and 875 communities. Under its newly elected president, Henry Knox Sherrill (presiding bishop of the Protestant Episcopal Church), the National Council consisted of a vast bureaucracy with offices scattered throughout seven buildings in New York and one (the former ICRE) in Chicago. Union Seminary president and veteran ecumenist Henry Pitney Van Dusen remarked, with only a hint of hyperbole, that the NCC was "the most complex and intricate piece of ecclesiastical machinery this planet has ever witnessed."[64] This complex machinery subsumed the Standard Bible Committee under the NCC's Division of Christian Education, run by executive secretary Roy G. Ross and four associate executive secretaries, not to mention an executive director of educational promotion, various administrative assistants, and a slate of elected officers (including treasurer and cheddar cheese magnate J. L. Kraft).

The NCC came on the heels of an even larger organization, the World Council of Churches (WCC), constituted in Amsterdam in August 1948. With 147 constituent churches in forty-four countries, the WCC, through its staff in Geneva, would become the mainstay of all future international ecumenism, even though the Vatican, which represents the majority of the world's Christians, has not to this day applied for membership.[65]

The ecumenical *anni mirabiles* of 1948 and 1950 meant that a different kind of exuberance was attendant upon the RSV project than on its nineteenth-century predecessor. Though much was made of ecumenical cooperation in 1881, greater enthusiasm—and controversy—had surrounded the recent revolution in textual criticism. The Revised Version had enjoyed no large ecumenical sponsor, and its progenitor, the Church of England, wielded no authority among Americans. By contrast, the RSV appeared to its translators and supporters to be an element in the imminent consummation of Christian unity. Chairman Weigle, a key player in the National Council's formation, spoke frequently of a "new life astir in the Christian churches."[66] Committee member Clarence Tucker Craig hailed Amsterdam and Cleveland as "bywords" of the ecumenical church. Yet Craig also recognized that the NCC and WCC were mainline organizations, and that over half of American Protestants remained outside their ecumenical umbrella. Many of these Protestants, Craig explained, suspected an ulterior motive among the champions of ecumenism, namely that

> the goal envisaged might be an all-embracing authoritarian organization, a superpapacy which in the end would be as corrupting as that in medieval times. Until this bugaboo is dispelled, distrust and apprehension will cripple the movement.[67]

Craig's observation would prove quite prescient as the RSV project came to full fruition.

AN "EPOCH-MAKING" EVENT: PUBLICATION OF THE COMPLETE RSV BIBLE

As Luther Weigle presented the one-millionth copy of the RSV New Testament to Martin Niemöller, celebrated pastor of the anti-Nazi "Confessing Church" during the Third Reich, the Old Testament section of the Standard Bible Committee was continuing its labor. Translation of the Hebrew Scriptures required forty-two meetings over 352 days, testing the endurance of the section members, most of whom were involved in manifold other projects.

Meanwhile, officials at the newly constituted NCC were making plans for a huge nationwide celebration of the RSV's completion. The Council hired a full-time director of the observance, H. Leroy Brininger, who envisioned an "epoch-making" event for twentieth-century Protestantism. Brininger was assisted by an associate director, an assistant director, and seven steering committees, all of which worked in consultation with the NCC's vast network of state and local councils. Through his "field contacts" across the nation, Brininger set a goal of at least three thousand simultaneous celebrations of the RSV on publication day, 30 September 1952. A target number of observances was established for each state, along with a national speakers' bureau through which communities could reserve a biblical scholar or ecumenical leader for a keynote address on the theme: "The Word of Life in Living Language." All this was undertaken at a cost of five hundred thousand dollars, estimated by *Publishers Weekly* to be the largest promotional budget ever spent on a single book up to that time.[68]

The RSV Bible Observance actually was an eight-day event coinciding with Christian Education Week (28 September to 5 October 1952), World Communion Sunday (5 October), the five-hundredth anniversary of the Gutenberg Bible (celebrated with a special postage stamp), and, though not by design, the publication for Roman Catholics of the first installment of the reconstituted Confraternity of Christian Doctrine translation, the New American Bible. As a prelude to the fanfare, Weigle presented at the White House the first copy of the RSV, a hand-bound edition in red morocco leather, to President Truman, who predicted "peace for all mankind" if only the Bible could make inroads behind the Iron Curtain. Ironically, on the ideologically sensitive issue of Bible revision, Truman was quick to note his own fondness for the King James Version.[69]

A historically unprecedented first printing of nearly a million copies of the RSV preceded the long-awaited official publication day, 30 September 1952. That night 3,418 American communities held Bible observances, officially dubbed "Services of Thanksgiving and Dedication." At Forbes Field in Pittsburgh, an estimated sixteen thousand people gathered for a mass service, while six thousand assembled in Indianapolis; six thousand in Paterson, New Jersey; five thousand in Waterloo, Iowa; and nearly three thousand in Seattle. Larger cities such as New York and Chicago witnessed dozens of simultaneous observances, with total attendance in each city reaching into the tens of thousands. According the program predetermined by the NCC, each ceremony included the presentation of five copies of the

RSV to representative leaders in government, education, business, and family life. A specially commissioned hymn, "The Divine Gift" by Sarah E. Taylor, celebrated the role of Scripture in church life. And as in 1946, a responsive prayer referred to the RSV as "a standard for the Christian Church." Brininger, who worked all night with his staff in Chicago taking telegrams from local councils, was ecstatic: "Never before in Protestant history" he declared in a press release the next morning, "have so many people gathered together in local interchurch services at one time for a single purpose as on Tuesday night, September 30."[70]

In subsequent weeks, Nelson's advertising and the translators themselves pronounced the RSV a "new *authorized* version." Herbert Gordon May exulted that the RSV's authorization came from "probably the largest Protestant Christian group ever to give official support" to a Bible translation.[71] Two other committee members observed that the King James Version, the Revised Version, the ASV, and the RSV stood "in direct succession to the great original translations of the sixteenth century, a stream of tradition so interwoven in our culture as to be considered, in a special way, *the* English Bible."[72] Yet it remained uncertain whether the majority of American Protestants, whose ancestors had rejected the idea of an apostolic succession, would accept a scriptural succession promulgated by the mainline establishment. Already by that day of wonders, 30 September, conservatives were marshaling forces to do battle with the ecumenical Church and its Book.

Chapter 4

The Great RSV Controversy

Bible-Burning, Red-Hunting, and the Strange Specter of Unholy Scripture

✠

The writers of Scripture invariably affirm, where the subject is mentioned by them at all, that the words of their writings are divinely taught. This, of necessity, refers to the original documents, not to translations and versions; but the labours of competent scholars have brought our English versions to a degree of perfection so remarkable that we may confidently rest upon them as authoritative.

—The Scofield Reference Bible (1917),
footnote on 1 Corinthians 2:13

THE REVEREND MARTIN LUTHER HUX, soon-to-be nationwide celebrity, was in many ways a typical country parson. Trained at the Southern Baptist seminary in Wake Forest, North Carolina, he had organized at age twenty-two a new Baptist congregation in Greensboro before eventually winding up as pastor of Temple Baptist Church in Rocky Mount, a manufacturing and distribution center in eastern North Carolina's rural tobacco-growing region. Not unlike other Baptists inclined toward separatism, Luther Hux had gradually become estranged from the North Carolina State Baptist Convention. As a divinity student, he had been dismayed to discover that professors at Southeastern Baptist Theological Seminary were not rock-ribbed fundamentalists but in some cases moderates, even liberals, who sought to adapt the Christian Gospel to contemporary culture. (Hux later claimed that at seminary he was taught that Jesus was the Son of God only in the sense that all men are sons of God.) As a pastor, he had often ran-kled at the "overlordship" of the state convention's theologically moderate leadership, and ultimately he had withdrawn his membership in 1946 to lead the independent Rocky Mount congregation, which he proudly de-scribed as "a missionary Baptist church in the truest sense."

When the Revised Standard Version appeared in September 1952 to the plaudits of prominent men in the state convention, Hux immediately sus-pected a plot to smuggle "modernism" into local churches by way of Holy Scripture. His worst fears were confirmed when he laid hands upon the new Bible and found in the Book of Isaiah a textual emendation that only infi-dels could love: where the prophet had once foretold the birth of Immanuel to a "virgin," the words now prophesied the birth to a mere "young woman." Hux could not take this travesty sitting down. This liberal man-handling of precious biblical testimony would require a dramatic public reprisal.[1]

BACKGROUND TO A BIBLE-BURNING

The completed RSV Bible appeared two months before Advent, a season of immense significance for the Church's understanding of its Book. Although less liturgical Protestants such as Hux and other Baptists did not observe Advent rituals, the four Sundays preceding Christmas were to all Protestants a season of prophecy when Old Testament sages anticipated the New Testament Messiah and thus confirmed the unity of the Christian canon in the person of Jesus Christ.

Of all Old Testament messianic prophecies, Isaiah 7:14 in its King James rendering was exceptional for making an additional claim about the coming Immanuel: that he would be born of a virgin. During the early twentieth century, the dogma of the virgin birth had emerged as one of a half-dozen essential planks in the platform of Protestant fundamentalism. Like the other cardinal doctrines—Christ's miracle-working ministry, his substitutionary atonement, his bodily resurrection, his anticipated second coming, and the attestation of all these in an inerrant, infallible Bible[2]—the claim of the virgin birth spoke to the heart of the fundamentalist conception of Christianity as preeminently supernatural. To conservative Protestants, liberalism had been whittling away for nearly a century the miraculous character of the biblical Christ, leaving instead an admirable but ineffectual sage who announced the ethical precepts of God's kingdom to a recalcitrant world. Jesus was not to Hux and other fundamentalists primarily a teacher (though he surely taught through parable and by example) but the miraculous Redeemer whose significance for humanity rested squarely upon the hard historical certainties of the Incarnation. The miracle of the Incarnation, moreover, was nothing of the kind without the miraculous conception of Christ in the womb of a virgin. As an event of Providence, the virgin birth was foreknown not only by the Godhead but by a Hebrew prophet, Isaiah, who heralded God's plan generations before Jesus' historical birth in Bethlehem. The apostle Matthew recognized the historical truth of Isaiah's prediction when he wrote that Jesus' birth took place "that it might be fulfilled which was spoken of the Lord by the prophet" (Matt. 1:22, KJV).

Real historical events, as accurately predicted by the prophets, were the essence of Christianity, according to the traditionalist Presbyterian J. Gresham Machen, whose monumental study *The Virgin Birth of Christ* (1930) testified to the importance of Isaiah 7:14 in conservative Protestantism.[3] Isaiah's "virgin" symbolized for conservative Protestants not only sexual purity but doctrinal purity—a version of Christianity undefiled by promiscuous liberalism. Indeed, many fundamentalists at midcentury accepted the judgment of another Presbyterian, Cornelius Van Til, whose 1946 book *The New Modernism* contended that even the supposedly trustworthy neo-orthodox theologians were promiscuously drawing upon critical Kantian philosophy to ravish historic Christianity.[4] Theological promiscuity was for fundamentalists perhaps the ultimate sign of an increasingly permissive society in which a "young woman" and a "virgin" were not always one in the same.[5]

The RSV translators did not take virginity lightly, but to them the rendering of the Hebrew *almah* as "young woman" rather than "virgin" was simply a matter of linguistic honesty. The Hebrew language had a specific term for "virgin" (*bethulah*), which appeared elsewhere in Scripture but not in Isaiah 7:14. When Matthew (1:23) cited Isaiah's prediction of the virgin birth, he was quoting the Septuagint, the ancient Greek translation of Hebrew Scripture, which rendered *almah* as *parthenos* (usually translated "virgin"). In using "young woman" in Isaiah 7:14 but "virgin" in Matthew 1:23, the RSV translators insisted that they were not denying the virgin birth in the former instance but simply remaining faithful to the underlying Hebrew. As a nod to tradition, the translators listed "virgin" in a footnote as an alternate reading.[6]

The "young woman" in the main body of the text nevertheless appeared to conservatives to be a denial of the virgin birth and raised the troubling question of the RSV's trustworthiness on other fundamentals of the faith. Although Protestants from the seventeenth-century Westminster divines to the twentieth-century Bible annotator C. I. Scofield typically had professed unswerving trust in translated Scripture, Isaiah 7:14 raised for the first time in American history widespread public doubt about the orthodoxy of a major church-sponsored translation. Whereas the 1881–85 Revised Version had generated a brief flash of intense curiosity only to fall into relative obscurity, the RSV endured wave after wave of popular suspicion as Americans pondered the paradoxical possibility of *unholy* Scripture.

KING JEHOIAKIM, PASTOR HUX, AND OTHER BIBLE-BURNERS

Luther Hux knew full well that the RSV was unholy, and accordingly he announced his intention to burn a copy of the new Bible in his church on Sunday evening, 30 November 1952. The story immediately hit the United and Associated Press wires—"Pastor Plans Public Burning"—and prompted a warning from Rocky Mount fire chief W. B. Parrish about open flames in public buildings. R. A. Ellis, president of the Baptist State Convention, reminded reporters of Hux's denominational independence and denounced his planned protest: "Differences in one's ideas about translation are perfectly legitimate, but the idea of burning God's word is repulsive to every thoughtful Christian." Meanwhile Hux previewed for reporters his sermon topic: "The National Council Bible, the Master Stroke of Satan—One of the Devil's Greatest Hoaxes."

On the night of 30 November Hux delivered a two-hour oration and then led his congregation from the white-frame Temple Baptist Church into the cold autumn air, where every member received a small American flag. Climbing onto the bed of a waiting truck, Hux held aloft a copy of the RSV on which he had written the word "fraud." Instead of burning the whole book, however, he ripped out and ignited the page bearing Isaiah 7:14. "This has been the dream of modernists for centuries," he shouted, "to make Jesus Christ the son of a bad woman." Finally, as if to clarify his protest for the attendant press corps, he added: "I never said I would burn the Bible. I said I would burn a fraud."[7]

Many North Carolinians were unmoved by Hux's claim that he had burned something other than the Bible. Letter-writers to the state's daily newspapers denounced the act as "spiritual indecency" and a "blasphemous stunt." The editorial board of the Raleigh *News and Observer* opined that the "Rev. Mr. Hux is not representative of the people of Rocky Mount any more than he is of the people of North Carolina."[8] Yet despite the vociferous opposition and frequent ridicule, Hux continued his anti-RSV crusade by writing and publishing a tract, *Modernism's Unholy Bible,* denouncing the liberals for "penknifing" God's Word. The allusion was to Jeremiah 36:21–32, the story of the evil Judean king Jehoiakim, who took a penknife and brazenly carved up the scroll of Jeremiah's prophecy before casting it into the fire. For his actions, Jehoiakim incurred divine wrath; yet Hux evidently anticipated no similar consequences for carving up and burning the RSV. In fact, he inspired imitators. On 5 January 1953 Luther Weigle received by registered mail a metal box from Bill Denton, a radio evangelist and pastor of the Furnace Street Mission in Akron, Ohio. Attached to the box was a letter that read in part: "Dear Sir: You will find enclosed the ashes of a book which was once called the Revised Standard Version of the Holy Bible." Soon thereafter came an urgent note from Albert Denton, executive secretary of Akron's Council of Churches, who took pains to disclaim any family relation to the Bible-burning evangelist.[9]

Despite their various attempts to vanquish unholy Scripture by fire, the RSV's opponents engaged mostly in a war of words. New Scripture translations had always suffered a brief initial barrage of unfriendly reviews, but never before had a Bible endured such sustained vilification from the pens of so many and varied critics. Throughout the 1950s, anti-RSV articles appeared in the fundamentalist press, with particularly sensational articles often circulating widely among venues. Meanwhile the publication of anti-RSV tracts became a major cottage industry, as scores of evangelists like Hux issued pronouncements under the imprints of their local printing companies. In some cases, the titles of treatises said it all, as in "The New Per-Version of the Bible"; "The Devil's Masterpiece"; "The Revised Standard Version of the Bible: Posed, Opposed, and Exposed"; and perhaps most ominously, "Whose Unclean Fingers Have Been Tampering with the Holy Bible, God's Pure, Infallible, Verbally Inspired Word?"[10] Other pamphlets were notable not for the idiosyncratic stamp of local evangelists but for their provenance in prominent organizations and institutions of America's fundamentalist subculture, including the Sunday School Times Company, the Bible Institute of Los Angeles ("Biola"), Bob Jones University, and the American Board of Missions to the Jews.[11] Finally, the pamphlet genre proved too limited for a few writers, who penned whole books against the RSV. Volumes ranged from the scholarly treatment by onetime Princeton Seminary professor Oswald T. Allis to the 652-page diatribe published a full two decades after the RSV by fiery Church of Christ preacher Foy E. Wallace, Jr.[12]

The immense volume of polemical literature quickly attracted the attention of the mainstream secular and religious press. Consequently, Americans not privy to the internal literature of the fundamentalist movement could read about the RSV uproar elsewhere. Alongside a flood of stories in local newspapers, exposés of "The Great Bible Controversy" appeared in *Look* and other popular magazines.[13] Liberal interfaith periodicals also weighed in. A writer for *Christianity and Crisis,* eyeing the Rocky Mount Bible-burning, concluded that the RSV affair was a symptom of the more general backwardness of religion in the South, a region that the liberal, predominately northern denominations needed to infiltrate with missionary zeal.[14] (The Rocky Mount incident had prompted joking about the "Bible-*Burning* Belt.")[15]

The magnitude of the RSV affair surprised even members of the Standard Bible Committee, who were by no means unaccustomed to theological disputation. Chairman Luther Weigle had retired in 1949 as dean of Yale Divinity School only to find himself engaging by 1953 in full-time RSV crisis management. Everywhere Weigle went, the controversy dogged him. When he arrived on a nighttime train in Lynchburg, Virginia, to visit his daughter and to address a women's college assembly, reporters were waiting on the railroad platform to question him about a local Baptist minister's attack on the RSV. As was usually his custom, Weigle refused to comment.[16]

Observers of American religion, of course, have not withheld comment on the RSV controversy, although sustained attempts to understand it have been few. The most extensive analysis, written in the midst of the firestorm, was Ralph Lord Roy's *Apostles of Discord* (1953), which devoted a chapter to the RSV conflict and more than a dozen chapters to related right-wing agitation in American Protestantism. Roy's ambitious book, originally his doctoral dissertation at New York's Union Seminary, recounted the Bible-burnings of Luther Hux and Bill Denton and made fascinating reading for mainline ministers and laypeople interested in learning more about the machinations of the Protestant "fringe."[17] An article a decade later by Gerald A. Larue, a former NCC staffer and professor of religion at the University of Southern California, outlined for an academic audience the key points of contention in the RSV controversy, drawing on a survey of more than two hundred anti-RSV pamphlets and articles.[18] More recently, the RSV controversy has taken its place in general textbooks of American religious history, usually as an example of misplaced McCarthyism.[19]

The existing studies suggest at least two interpretations of the RSV controversy. The first is that RSV conflict was the last gasp of the fundamentalist-modernist controversy of the 1920s and was, like the celebrated battle over evolution, a battle featuring a few prima donnas who did not necessarily represent the majority of American Protestants. The other explanation is that the RSV conflict was the peculiar product of the 1950s—the first great Cold War decade and thus a time of high anxiety, when otherwise sensible Americans entertained fantastic conspiracy theories about even that most beloved of institutions, the church. Both of these explanations are true as far as they go, yet to understand the antecedents and enduring consequences of the RSV controversy, one must look behind the 1950s or 1920s or even the twentieth century all the way back to the sixteenth century and the very foundation of Protestantism. In the gradual differentiation of Protestantism from medieval Catholicism, the basic theological problems emerged that would eventuate four centuries later in the battle over the RSV. The first of these problems was authority; the second, interpretation.

IMPRIMATUR: THE PROBLEM OF AUTHORITY

With the appearance of Gutenberg's first printed Bibles in the 1450s, the church suddenly faced the challenge of harnessing the new technology of printing for orthodox ends. England's ecclesiastical hierarchy had already in 1408 imposed strict controls on Scripture's vernacular translation, but in the brave new world of movable type, the regulation and standardization of Holy Writ seemed fraught with new difficulties. Accordingly, when William Tyndale in 1523 sought authorization and patronage from the bishop of London to produce a new English Bible, the prelate's polite refusal was a fateful decision: Tyndale's relocation in Germany led to the exportation of the idea of vernacular Scripture (and the "Lutheran heresy") to England.[20] Tyndale formulated what amounted to the classic Protestant position on Bible translation and publication: that the Scriptures are self-authorizing and therefore need no ecclesiastical license. (Was any other stance possible from a man whose New Testament translation granted Peter authority over a mere "congregation"?)

Yet the solution of scriptural self-authorization was always a precarious one, particularly in nineteenth-century America, where a host of individuals, some eminently qualified and some less so, appointed themselves Bible translators and publishers. Philip Schaff, head of the American wing of the Revised Version committee, was endlessly chagrined by the manifold "sectarian" competitors to the ecumenical Bible of 1881–85. Four decades earlier he had summed up the American situation: "Every theological vagabond and peddler may drive here his bungling trade, without passport or license, and sell his false ware at pleasure."[21] Schaff's vision of an authorized, ecumenical lineage of Bible translation—what he tellingly referred to as an "apostolic succession" of Christian scholarship—carried over into the RSV project, whose participants continually emphasized the unique authority of the National Council of Churches to publish a genuinely pan-Protestant Bible. As late as 1962, promotional literature from the NCC referred to the RSV as the "fifth authorized English Bible" standing in direct succession to the Great Bible of 1539, the Bishops' Bible of 1568, the King James Bible of 1611, and the Revised Version of 1885.[22]

The idea that the National Council could "authorize" any Bible infuriated conservatives, especially those of a separatist bent who regarded the mainline denominations as hopelessly corrupt. Chief of the separatists was Carl McIntire, a renegade Presbyterian minister who built much of his career on opposition to the National Council and the RSV. Born in 1906 in Ypsilanti, Michigan, McIntire grew up in Oklahoma and attended college in Missouri before enrolling at Princeton Theological Seminary in 1927. Two years later, he followed Professor J. Gresham Machen in the schism that would create Westminster Seminary in Philadelphia. The Presbyterian Church in the U.S.A. eventually defrocked Machen and McIntire, just as teacher and pupil were themselves parting ways over biblical interpretation, among other issues. (McIntire, unlike his mentor, supported the dispensationalism popularized by C. I. Scofield, who divided all history into discrete "dispensations" or stages in God's progressive revelation.) In 1937 McIntire and his allies formed the Bible Presbyterian Church, a small denomination with its own ministerial school, Faith Theological Seminary. But McIntire devoted most of his energy to evangelism, first through the *Christian Beacon* newspaper and later through two organizations, the American Council of Christian Churches and the International Council of Christian Churches, that were intended to be rivals to the National Council of Churches and the World Council of Churches.[23]

Shortly after the RSV's appearance, McIntire issued a 24-page pamphlet, *The New Bible, Revised Standard Version: Why Christians Should Not Accept It,* that would become the single most influential publication among opponents of the RSV. Printed by the hundreds of thousands, the pamphlet denounced as heretical the RSV's rendering of Isaiah 7:14 and a few other passages where the King James Version's account of history had been compromised. No less upsetting to McIntire, however, was the claim advanced by RSV publicity that the new Bible was "authorized" by the NCC. "An official Bible is something new in the history of Protestantism," McIntire wrote, "and we have here an effort on the part of the NCC to elevate itself to a position in the Protestant world where it will be 'the authority.'" To say that the Bible needed some authorization was to impugn the self-evident trustworthiness of the Scriptures, and even worse, to raise the specter of Romanism.

> The Roman Catholic Church has, of course, operated on the basis that its Pope and church officials give their imprimatur to its Bibles, but the Protestant world has never had any such practice until this present moment. It is a pretentious, presumptuous claim for the National Council of Churches to do this with the Bible. The Bible belongs to all the people of God. The King James Version has its position in the Christian world simply because it has commended itself universally to Christian people.[24]

Other fundamentalists adopted a similar line. The Baptist radio evangelist and onetime Air Force intelligence officer Edgar Bundy, who assisted McIntire with public relations, decried the National Council's copyright on the RSV: "Copyrighted! Whoever heard of such a thing before in the history of the Bible."[25] Perhaps McIntire and Bundy did not realize that the text of the King James Bible, in England at least, had always been safeguarded by the British crown and its authorized printers and that the 1881–85 Revised Version had been licensed exclusively to the university presses of Oxford and Cambridge. Ultimately, the issue for conservatives was not legal but theological: Does the Bible, as God's infallible Word, need any human imprimatur? Clearly for fundamentalists such as McIntire, the answer was no.

Ironically, McIntire's own ACCC and ICCC belied his railings against the universalistic pretensions of the National Council of Churches. Fundamentalists tended to overlook this contradiction, reserving their invective for the National Council and its Bible. *Moody Monthly,* the organ of Moody Bible Institute, had cautiously endorsed the RSV New Testament in 1946, but when the complete Bible appeared in 1952, the newspaper withdrew its support, citing the National Council's heavy-handed publicity campaign. "Is it that a 'super-church' can dictate what shall be used or not used?" the editors asked.[26] "Superchurch" was by then a familiar epithet in the fundamentalist lexicon for the liberal ecumenical movement.[27] The term bespoke fundamentalist fears that the roads of ecumenism ultimately led to Rome. Yet in a development that would significantly intensify the RSV controversy, this deep-seated fundamentalist anti-Catholicism was soon sublimated into something ostensibly political: anticommunism. The charge of a Red taint upon the RSV project would stick like glue, bedeviling the committee members and stifling constructive debate about genuine problems of Bible translation.

It is impossible to pinpoint a single source of the communism accusation. In 1953 the House Un-American Activities Committee stirred up considerable trouble in fruitless investigations of the RSV translators and Methodist bishop G. Bromley Oxnam, among other church leaders.[28] Wisconsin senator Joseph McCarthy cast additional suspicion on the National Council of Churches, and indirectly on the RSV, after his Senate subcommittee employed J. B. Matthews, a Methodist minister and onetime communist sympathizer (or "fellow traveler") as a professional Redhunter. Matthews had just published an article in the *American Mercury* charging that the Protestant clergy comprised the largest single group of communism's supporters. After protests from the National Council of Churches, the National Conference of Christians and Jews, and even President Eisenhower, McCarthy reluctantly accepted Matthews's resignation after only a few days on the job.[29]

Outside the ranks of government, a major source of the communism accusation was Carl McIntire's ally Verne P. Kaub, a former publicist for the Wisconsin Power and Light Company who organized the American Council of Christian Laymen to root out Reds in the churches. Kaub was largely responsible for a brochure, *How Red Is the Federal (National) Council of Churches?* accusing various Protestant leaders, including NCC executive secretary Samuel McCrea Cavert, of subversive activities. Still more pointed was a second pamphlet, *Thirty of the Ninety-five Men Who Gave Us the Revised Standard Version of the Bible,* issued by the Cincinnati-based Circuit Riders, Inc., a Methodist anticommunist organization led by air-conditioning executive Myers G. Lowman. Lowman's widely distributed booklet alleged that the thirty members cited on the RSV committee and its advisory board were "affiliated with Communist and pro-Communist fronts."[30]

The unseemliness and, in the case of government-sponsored McCarthyism, the unconstitutionality of 1950s Red-hunting would eventually be established by a series of Supreme Court decisions. Yet in the heat of the RSV controversy, Luther Weigle concentrated not on demonstrating the inappropriateness and irrelevance of the communism charges to Bible translation but on exposing the falsity of the accusations. This proved a difficult strategy, for just enough of the translators had supported liberal causes—Henry Joel Cadbury, for example, had chaired the antiwar American Friends Service Committee—to convince Red-hunters that the RSV committee had "subversive" intentions. Weigle recognized this problem, noting in a letter to Cavert that anything short of complete disavowal of all left-wing sympathies would "be seized upon by our enemies and held up to derision as additional evidence that we are a bunch of 'pinks' who are either spineless and weak-minded or subtle and cunning." But Weigle was absolutely loath to "embark upon calling the roll" to determine the patriotism of each committee member and National Council official.[31] Weigle and Cavert consequently rejected a suggestion by committee member William Irwin to invite the FBI to investigate the backgrounds of the translators. "It is probably a new experience for Dr. Irwin to be denounced as a 'subversive,'" Cavert wrote to Weigle, "and I sympathize with his desire to do something about it."[32] Ultimately Cavert issued a pamphlet, *Plain Facts*, answering some of the communism charges, while Weigle responded to selected inquiries from the public and the press. (As evidence of his own patriotism, Weigle unearthed a statement he made in 1941 as president of the Federal Council of Churches criticizing the lack of religious freedom in the Soviet Union.)[33]

To the committee's dismay, Cavert and Weigle's efforts did little to quell fundamentalist suspicions. In fact, the communism charges seemed only to grow more strident. In 1955, Dan Gilbert, a radio evangelist in Claremont, California, published an alleged debate between himself and "Professor George Stevenson," a reputed supporter of the RSV who had supposedly argued that the new Bible was translated so as to be palatable to communists. When the National Council dispatched staffer Gerald Larue to meet with Gilbert, the evangelist was cagey about Professor Stevenson's whereabouts. Eventually the RSV's publisher, Thomas Nelson and Sons, offered a reward of five hundred dollars to anyone who could produce Stevenson, but no one ever stepped forward with any information. A few years later, Gilbert himself was shot dead at an Upland, California, motel by the jealous husband of a former employee with whom the evangelist was having an affair.[34] Thus ended the quest for Professor Stevenson.

The allegations of a "Red Bible" finally came to a head in early 1960 after the U.S. Air Force Reserve published a countersubversion training manual warning recruits to avoid, among other things, the communist-tainted RSV Bible. The manual quoted as authoritative charges made by Billy James Hargis, a fundamentalist evangelist and Red-hunter based in Tulsa, Oklahoma. When National Council executives heard about the manual, they quickly consulted a law firm about possible legal action against the Air Force. Meanwhile the NCC associate general secretary, James Wine, wrote to Defense Secretary Thomas Gates demanding the document's immediate withdrawal. Sensing legal trouble, Gates complied, expressing to Wine his "very deep regret" over the incident.[35] After the scandal hit newspapers, several members of Congress, led by Oregon Democrat Edith Green, took to the House floor to denounce Hargis and defend the RSV. As for the Air Force officials responsible for the manual, Pennsylvania Democrat James Quigley recommended a response in "the true spirit of the Easter season"— that Americans "forgive them because surely they know not what they do."[36]

No denunciation from the halls of Congress would dissuade true believers in conspiracy theories, who continued to entertain suspicions of communism within America's Protestant establishment. Such fears received periodic reconfirmation, as when FBI director J. Edgar Hoover suggested in an October 1960 article series in *Christianity Today* that communists were attempting to co-opt Christian clergy by appealing to their sense of economic justice.[37] Meanwhile fundamentalist literature alleging a "Red" National Council enjoyed a second life throughout the 1960s as "Captain" Edgar Bundy and other doomsayers continued to exploit Americans' Cold War anxieties.[38]

Yet in the final analysis, the rhetoric of fundamentalist anticommunism was remarkable not so much for its longevity but for its resonance with the centuries-old language of anti-Catholicism. In this sense fundamentalist concerns have been more consistent over time than some recent analyses suggest. Sociologist James Davison Hunter, for example, has identified three waves of evangelical political activism in twentieth-century America: the 1920s (characterized by opposition to evolution, alcohol, and Catholicism), the 1950s (characterized by opposition to communism), and the 1980s (characterized by opposition to general moral decline).[39] Hunter encapsulates correctly the prevailing concerns of each period, but it is important also to recognize the subtext of anti-Catholicism running through much fundamentalist literature until fairly recently, when conservative Protestants and Catholics began hazarding uneasy alliances over abortion and homosexuality. The basic ecclesiological premise of fundamentalism has consistently been an iconoclastic rejection of all religious authorities but the Bible, whose legitimacy comes not from the pope or the National Council of Churches but from Almighty God. For fundamentalist combatants in the RSV controversy, the specter of the National Council was scarcely distinguishable from the pope or the Red Menace: all three seemed to reserve the right of censorship over God's Word. Ironically, the National Council was not as authoritarian as fundamentalists assumed, for its "imprimatur" upon the RSV entailed no real editorial jurisdiction. The text of the RSV was dictated by the regnant norms of textual criticism—academic standards that some fundamentalists, in a further irony, banned from their own seminaries in good authoritarian fashion.

Resistance to the type of textual criticism practiced in mainline seminaries was for fundamentalists part of a larger philosophy of separation from the established churches and their corrupting influence. God, fundamentalists believed, required that true Bible-believers separate themselves from all who would exalt any authority other than Scripture. The classic proof-text of this separatism was 2 Corinthians 6:17: "Wherefore come out from among them, and be ye separate, saith the Lord, and touch not the unclean thing; and I will receive you" (KJV). To Carl McIntire, separation was the essence of the sixteenth- and twentieth-century Reformations. In the former, Protestants separated from Catholics, while in the latter (which was still in process), true Protestants were separating from apostate Protestants. True Protestants were those who respected the self-evident and immutable authority of the Holy Scriptures, for "heaven and earth may pass away but the Word of the Lord will endure forever."[40]

NIHIL OBSTAT: THE PROBLEM OF INTERPRETATION

McIntire's vision of the imperishable Word, based on the testimony of Isaiah 40:6–8 and 1 Peter 1:24–25, was shared by conservative and liberal Protestants alike. Yet the Word, once accepted as uniquely authoritative, still had to be interpreted, and therefore interpretation was second only to authority as a basic problem of Protestantism. For the archetypal Protestant biblicist William Tyndale, the Scriptures were self-interpreting: "open places" expounded "dark places," obviating the need for any external commentary.[41] In addition to their optimism about Bible interpretation, early Protestants also evinced great confidence in the essential straightforwardness of Bible translation. The King James Version's translators admitted that the Scriptures contained a few words whose proper rendering was obscure, but such dark places were not to be found "in doctrinal points that concern salvation."[42] When the King James Bible was finally revised in 1881, Philip Schaff exuded no less enthusiasm about the essential unambiguity of the translator's task. Modern Bible-readers, Schaff felt, had been brought "as near to Christ as the Christians of the first generation."[43]

Schaff's optimism, however, belied a widening rift between liberals and conservatives over a handful of key problems in textual criticism and translation. The disagreements were exacerbated by the confusion, prevalent since the Enlightenment and its historical-critical aftermath, of purely textual questions with historical ones. In this respect the battle over Isaiah 7:14 was classically modern. Combatants could not separate the textual question (Does *almah* correspond to "virgin"?) from the historical one (Did "virgin" correspond to Mary's actual state?). The RSV rendering "young woman" seemed to contradict the account of history that conservatives had long presupposed. Despite their opposition to the liberal imprimatur, then, conservatives in the 1950s began to wonder if Bible translations indeed needed some sort of certification that nothing in the text contradicted orthodox doctrine or, in this case, the presupposed account of biblical history. The Catholic solution to this problem was the *nihil obstat,* the official guarantee that "nothing hinders" orthodoxy. The Protestant solution— that the Bible is essentially self-certifying (not to mention self-translating and self-interpreting)—increasingly appeared inadequate to conservatives battling the strange specter of unholy Scripture.

Isaiah 7:14 was not the only passage in the RSV that vexed conservatives, but almost invariably the other disputed verses also were purported references to the historical Jesus. And usually these verses referred not to some mundane aspect of Jesus' life but to his divine status as the Son of God. In other words, almost all the disputed passages (even those from Hebrew Scripture) were ones that were traditionally interpreted christologically.[44] Carl McIntire identified a number of such verses, including Psalm 2:7, which had been changed from "Thou art my Son; this day have I begotten thee" (KJV) to "You are my son, today I have begotten you" (RSV). To McIntire, the substitution of the more contemporary "you" for the grander archaisms "thou" and "thee" implied that God was addressing a mere man rather than the coeternal Son of God. McIntire identified a similar problem in Matthew 16:16, where Peter now confessed to Jesus "You are the Christ" (RSV), rather than "Thou art the Christ" (KJV).[45] The RSV translators explained that they had employed "you" when Jesus was addressed in the course of his earthly life and "thou" when he was addressed in otherworldly contexts. This principle, they felt, did not "in any way impair the truth of our Lord's Deity" and it expressed "the reality of his experience as sharing our humanity."[46]

Yet McIntire pressed the deity issue further. Turning again to Psalm 2, which Christians had long interpreted messianically, he decried the RSV's rendering of the enigmatic verses 11–12: "Serve the Lord with fear, with trembling kiss his feet, lest he be angry." (The King James Bible had translated the disputed passage "Serve the Lord with fear, and rejoice with trembling. Kiss the Son, lest he be angry.") "The new version," McIntire complained, "leaves out all reference to the Son. This removes His deity."[47]

Chairman Weigle explained that the RSV had merely corrected a probable transposition of four Hebrew consonants, which had led the 1611 translators to the unlikely construction "Kiss the Son."[48] But McIntire ruled such textual reconstruction out of order.

In a still more enigmatic passage the issue was the RSV's rearrangement of a single punctuation mark. Greek New Testament manuscripts lacked punctuation, and even spaces between words, so scholars occasionally had to resort to conjecture. In Romans 9:5, the King James translators had punctuated the phrase "God blessed for ever" so as to modify "Christ." ("[w]hose are the fathers, and of whom as concerning the flesh Christ came, who is over all, God blessed for ever. Amen"). After considerable debate, the RSV committee judged the God-reference to be a grammatically independent, and characteristically Pauline, doxology ("to them belong the patriarchs, and of their race, according to the flesh, is the Christ. God who is over all be blessed for ever. Amen"). McIntire seized upon the repositioned period: "The deity of Christ is removed entirely." It was not enough for him that the RSV included a footnote with the King James reading as an alternate. Nor did Weigle help by admitting that either reading was grammatically possible. As Weigle explained, "[m]en equally devout and equally learned are to be found on either side of this question. Fortunately, the proof of the Deity of Christ does not depend upon the way it is decided— that is amply sustained by other unequivocal New Testament texts."[49]

McIntire's index of RSV passages threatening Christ's deity became a virtually canonical starting point for other pamphleteers' attacks on the RSV. Besides the ubiquitous Isaiah 7:14, verses such as Romans 9:5 were so often quoted that they eventually appeared in an unlikely forum: the Michigan legislature. In introducing a resolution protesting the sale and dissemination of the RSV, Republican state senators Alpheus P. Decker and Charles R. Feenstra cited Isaiah 7:14, Psalm 2:11–12, Matthew 16:16, and Romans 9:5, among other verses, as evidence of "the general trend . . . to bring into question the unique Sonship and Deity of the Lord Jesus Christ." "Our national security," the senators continued, "is threatened by the undermining influence of grossly radical and godless ideologies."[50] Rarely in American history—old blasphemy statutes notwithstanding— had Christology become a matter of legislative debate!

In many cases conservatives raised christological objections to the same passages that had caused so much controversy seven decades earlier. The translators of the Revised Version of 1881–85 had omitted or cast doubt on certain verses regarded as late textual corruptions, and when the RSV translators ratified these decisions, fundamentalists were furious. The Revised Version, for example, had set apart with several blank lines the "Longer Ending" of Mark (16:9–20), a passage regarded by most textual critics as spurious. When the RSV translators went one step further and relegated the entire twelve verses—an account of Jesus' post-Resurrection appearances—to a footnote, this looked to South Carolina evangelist Oliver B. Greene like a denial of the Resurrection itself. If Jesus "did not rise from the grave," he reasoned, "then we are a bunch of suckers, fools and nitwits! . . . I believe the old King James Story and shall stand by it as long as the Lord lets me live." Similarly, Baptist evangelist William Carey Taylor rebuked the RSV translators for performing "major surgery" on Mark 16 and then leaving nearly half a page on the operating table.[51]

Another testament to the Resurrection conspicuously absent from main body of the RSV text was Luke 24:6 ("He is not here, but is risen"). The 1881 translators had flagged this verse with a footnote ("Some ancient authorities omit . . . ") but the RSV translators relegated it to the margins. Though many textual critics were convinced of the verse's inauthenticity, conservatives regarded it as an indispensable historical proof-text. Cyril Hutchinson, principal of Berean Bible College in Calgary, Alberta, denounced the "religious vandals" who would lay waste to Christianity's paramount miracle. "Is not this the work of Satan himself?" he asked.[52]

Of course no Bible translation controversy would be complete without consternation over the missing Comma Johanneum, 1 John 5:7, which translators since Erasmus had recognized as inauthentic. "The Unitarian translators," Bible-burner Luther Hux wrote of the RSV committee, "evidently could not stand such plain reading concerning the Triune God." Meanwhile Homer Ritchie, pastor of First Baptist Church in Fort Worth, Texas, pointed out that the RSV translators "omitted the verse without so much as a footnote to acknowledge their crime."[53] In fact, the spuriousness of 1 John 5:7 was such an axiom of textual criticism that even the 1881 translators had felt no need to justify its omission with a footnote. Yet both the nineteenth- and twentieth-century revision committees underestimated conservatives' attachment to the King James Bible's proof-texts of Christ and his position in the Godhead.

Ultimately the christological criticisms of the RSV took a vicious turn as fundamentalists set their sights on Harry Orlinsky, the sole Jewish member of the committee. Orlinsky's appointment in 1945 had been a momentous step. Never before in Anglo-American history had a Jew served on a major Christian Bible translation project[54]—the Revised Version committee had included only the Protestant convert Christian Ginsburg—nor had fundamentalists ever been given such a convenient scapegoat.

Some conservatives confined their criticisms of Orlinsky to the theological realm. Oswald Allis and Columbia Seminary professor William C. Robinson, for example, blamed him for Isaiah 7:14, citing his observation that Aquila, the second-century Jewish Bible translator, had correctly apprehended the meaning of *almah* as "young woman."[55] Allis and Robinson also questioned the legitimacy of allowing a Jew to participate in a Christian translation project.[56] After all, did not the apostle Paul in 2 Corinthians 3:13–16 point out that Jews read the Old Testament with a "veil" upon their hearts? Similarly, Homer Ritchie claimed to oppose Orlinsky not out of anti-Semitism but from a sincere conviction that Christian Bible translation should be undertaken by Christian scholars.[57]

Other fundamentalists were less restrained. Gerald Winrod, a Kansas evangelist and publisher of the anti-Semitic *Defender Magazine,* identified the RSV committee's "modernism" as the "bastard offspring of Talmudism," both of which were "anemic, bloodless" religions that rebelled against the doctrine of Christ's vicarious atonement. Winrod denounced the National Council of Churches for allowing "Jewish rabbis" to participate in projects such as the RSV.[58] Twenty years later, Foy Wallace was still beating the same drum, maligning Orlinsky as a "hostile infidel Jew" who harbored "bitter hatred for Christ and Christians."[59]

Ironically, Orlinsky had been trained by three Christian scholars, RSV committee members William F. Albright, William A. Irwin, and William R. Taylor. He consequently held the Protestant Bible translation tradition in high esteem. When Weigle invited him to join the committee in 1945, he responded that it "is a responsible task to apply modern scientific materials to the Appointed English Version of King James and at the same time to retain the spirit and style of this classic." As a member of the committee, he consistently opposed substantial deviation from the Massoretic Text, the early medieval Hebrew version cherished as a benchmark by Jews and conservative Protestants alike. Most significant, Orlinsky "scrupulously refrained" from voting on passages of Christian doctrinal import, as National Council publicity on the RSV was none too hesitant to point out.[60]

But no attestations of Orlinsky's circumspection were sufficient for fundamentalists who suspected a plot to dethrone the Son of the God, even though Weigle constantly assured inquirers that the RSV committee had "not the slightest intention" to "blur over the deity of our Lord and Savior, Jesus Christ."[61] The RSV translators, like the Revised Version committee of years before, believed that the text-critical alteration or elimination of a few passages did not affect the big biblical picture. Fundamentalists, on the other hand, seemed to take literally the maxim of Deuteronomy 8:3 that "man doth not live by bread only, but by every word that proceedeth out of the mouth of the Lord." No portion of the biblical evidence could be removed without weakening the entire edifice of Christianity. With the Bible's every word assuming importance in their system, fundamentalists not surprisingly seized upon the great shibboleth of "inerrancy" as the final test of the RSV translators' orthodoxy.

The inerrancy question was no simple matter. Fundamentalists had long insisted that the long-lost original biblical manuscripts—what B. B. Warfield referred to as the autographic codex—were without error, but this left ambiguous the status of vernacular translations. Intellectuals such as Warfield saw no inherent contradiction between the immutable autographs and the constantly evolving vernacular Bible. He remained confident that readers of the various versions still had access to God's inerrant words. But on the popular level, many Protestants were wary of the English Bible's evolution, and so they invested the King James Version with de facto inerrancy. This perception of inerrancy was heightened visually by the King James translators' system of italicizing words supplied for clarity but not present in the original Greek and Hebrew. Though the system was notoriously inconsistent, readers of the King James Bible had always lived under the illusion that they could clearly distinguish God's infallible words from mere human interpolations.

When the RSV eliminated the italics, therefore, many conservatives denounced this as subterfuge. Baptist minister H. H. Savage complained in a radio address that the lack of italics left "the average reader with no alternative but to make his own comparisons and discover where 'interpretation' has been substituted for a 'literal translation.'"[62] Weigle tried to explain the problem, telling the *Miami Herald* that the King James system of italics misled readers into thinking that translation is "word-for-word matching."[63] But many fundamentalists insisted that literal translation was not only possible but doctrinally necessary. In some cases, this ironically led to a defense of the RSV's predecessor, the American Standard Version, which had retained the use of italics and which was generally considered a more literal translation than the King James Bible. Dallas evangelist John R. Rice, editor of the widely circulating tabloid the *Sword of the Lord,* lauded the American Standard Version's "holy reverence for the actual wording of the original manuscripts," even though the ASV's copyright was registered to a predecessor organization of the much-despised National Council of Churches.[64] Less than a decade later, the conservative Lockman Foundation, based in La Habra, California, published the first installment of the New American Standard Bible, the product of fifty-eight anonymous scholars who adopted as their model the "Rock of Biblical Honesty," the ASV. Like the ASV, the NASB rendered the Greek and Hebrew rather literally and indicated departures from the original with the all-important italics.[65]

Yet many, if not most, fundamentalists in the fifties and sixties still regarded the King James Version as the only real Bible, save for the autographs themselves. For these Christians, the problem of Bible translation never eclipsed the fundamental question of inerrancy: Is the Bible uniformly true in all matters? To answer in the affirmative, fundamentalists felt, had been the essence of Christian orthodoxy since the Scriptures were first collected. And conservatives strongly suspected that the RSV translators, if compelled to answer yes or no, would to a man answer no.

Some of the RSV translators indeed seemed to have denied biblical inerrancy in their writings. Fundamentalist pamphleteers delighted in ferreting out incriminating statements and then arrogating them to the entire RSV committee. One oft-quoted comment was by Yale professor Millar Burrows:

> Since the only sound criterion for determining whether anything is an authentic revelation is its intrinsic value, and since the contents of the Bible vary greatly in their value even in matters of religious importance, we cannot take the Bible as a whole and in every part as stating with divine authority what we must believe and do.[66]

The closest thing to a confession of faith by the whole committee was the RSV's preface, which conservatives immediately dissected, ultimately seizing upon the statement that the Word of God "must not be disguised in phrases that are no longer clear, or hidden under words that have changed or lost their meaning."[67] Carl McIntire detected in this simple affirmation of ongoing vernacular translation a whiff of heresy: "Here again the neoorthodox position is stated—'hidden under words.' The historic position of the church and the orthodox position is that the language itself *is* the Word of God."[68]

Taking their cue from McIntire, other conservatives rushed to condemn the translators' doctrine of Scripture. But in the process facts were twisted. Illinois radio evangelist E. L. Banta misquoted the RSV preface as stating that "the Word—is hidden under words that have changed or lost their meaning." The RSV translators, he concluded, believe that the Bible merely "contains" the Word of God.[69] A newspaper advertisement placed by the First Baptist Church of Babylon, New York, was even more inaccurate, claiming that the RSV preface "states that [the Bible] contains the Word of God." True Christians, the advertisement insisted, believe that the Bible *is* the Word of God.[70] A concerned supporter of the RSV mailed the clipping to Luther Weigle, who responded that it was the "most malicious" attack he had yet seen. The preface, Weigle noted, "does not anywhere use the expression, 'contains the Word of God.'"[71]

Indeed, the RSV controversy seems to have helped popularize the phrase "contains the Word of God" as the stereotypical liberal doctrine of Scripture. In the process, little light was shed on the translators' actual views of biblical inspiration. Weigle and his colleagues usually were loath to comment directly on the issue, but occasionally an insistent correspondent would elicit a lengthy reply. Such was the case when a woman in Spokane, Washington, inquired of Weigle if any committee member believed in the "plenary verbal inspiration" of the Scriptures. "I am not clear," Weigle replied, "as to just what you mean by the plenary verbal inspiration." If she meant, he said, the doctrine elaborated by the *Formula Consensus Helvetica* (1675)—that the Bible was inspired down to the very diacritical marks, or vowel points, of the Hebrew Massoretic Text—then he was sure that no RSV committee member could concur. If, however, she meant a more general doctrine of inspiration such as that expressed by the Westminster Confession or other "historic creedal statements of the Protestant churches," then he thought that all the committee members could agree.[72]

By singling out the *Formula Consensus Helvetica*, Weigle may have revealed a latent frustration with the ravages of modern, critical Bible interpretation and its relentless obsession with (in)errancy. As Richard Muller has shown, the *Formula* originated toward the end of the period of high Protestant orthodoxy, when Calvinist theology in particular was foreshadowing the debates of a fully critical age.[73] In the Reformed outposts of late-seventeenth-century Europe, precise definitions of the *autographa* were being formulated that would eventuate in nineteenth- and twentieth-century American debates over the inerrancy of the "original autographs." For Weigle, these debates were like the proverbial valley of dry bones: without the living Word of God, they yielded nothing. Yet he remained unsure of how to neutralize the inerrancy question and nudge Protestants toward an unselfconscious appreciation of their Book.

DILEMMAS TO THE LEFT AND TO THE RIGHT

The RSV controversy unearthed a deep vein of Protestant uneasiness on questions of authority and interpretation, and in so doing it saddled both liberals and conservatives with serious dilemmas. The liberal dilemma was whether to respond in a concerted, public way to the manifold conservative criticisms of the RSV. A few months after the version's publication, the fury of conservative opposition already was jeopardizing the committee's dream of a common Protestant Bible, yet Weigle feared that answering Carl McIntire and other critics would "dignify" their charges of heresy and simply increase popular suspicions about the RSV.[74]

By early 1953 Weigle had been persuaded otherwise, so he drafted on the committee's behalf *An Open Letter Concerning the Revised Standard Version of the Bible,* a 24-page pamphlet distributed to clergy in the National Council's member denominations. Weigle began by reminding readers that the King James Version had withstood its own trial by fire and that its translators had endured frequent charges of "blasphemy," "intolerable deceit," and "vile imposture." He went on to defend the RSV point by point against the major textual objections, insisting that the new version clearly affirmed Christ's virgin birth, his deity and incarnation, his redemption of humanity through his blood, his uniqueness as God's only Son, his resurrection and ascension, and his anticipated second coming. He also noted that the RSV affirmed the "inspiration of the Scriptures" through its unimpeachable renderings of 2 Timothy 3:14–17 and 2 Peter 1:20–21. Having dispensed with interpretive issues, he turned to the issue of authority, reiterating earlier publicity that the RSV was the fifth English Bible in the succession of revisions authorized either by the English crown or by the churches. "It is the third revision," he added, "to be made by the full and well-ordered use of the method of face-to-face scholarly conference extending over a period of years, the others using this method being the King James Version and the Revised Version." And, he noted emphatically, the RSV was not the product of some "superchurch." The National Council of Churches "is just what its name implies, a council of churches, associated for the purpose of doing together what can best be done together."[75]

The *Open Letter* inaugurated a series of pamphlets from the National Council's newly formed Committee on the Use and Understanding of the Bible, whose major goal was to solicit and print endorsements of the RSV from prominent Protestant leaders, evidently in the hope of turning the tide of conservative opinion. First to be enlisted was the popular Methodist preacher Clovis Chappell, who testified that the RSV was for him "a genuine joy" because it respected the King James tradition, made the Bible more readable, and most important of all, preserved "every single article of the faith of our fathers."[76]

Another pamphlet was directed specifically at Southern Baptists, whose denomination had attained particular notoriety in the RSV controversy at the hands of schismatic Bible-burner Luther Hux. A. L. Goodrich, editor of the *Baptist Record* in Jackson, Mississippi, described his personal acquaintance with the RSV committee's three Southern Baptists (Kyle M. Yates and the late A. T. Robertson and John R. Sampey), attesting that they had not "one drop of modernistic blood in their veins." The real point of Goodrich's brochure, however, was to defend the "young woman" of Isaiah 7:14 as the only accurate translation of the Hebrew *almah*. "If the translators were trying to deny the Virgin Birth," he added, "they did a poor job, for they used [virgin] in Matthew 1:22–23 and Luke 1:27."[77]

The "young woman" question had become such a *cause célèbre* by 1953 that the RSV translators were determined to stand their ground, lest they lose prestige by appearing indecisive. In a few other instances the RSV committee did resort to minor emendations of the RSV for the sake of public relations. Such was the case with a controversial footnote to Matthew 1:16. The verse itself, which referred to Joseph as "the husband of Mary, of whom Jesus was born," had appeared with no marginal note in the RSV New Testament of 1946. But in the complete Bible of 1952, the translators introduced a footnote: "Other ancient authorities read *Joseph, to whom was betrothed the virgin Mary, was the father of Jesus, who is called Christ*." (The edition of 1952 included some eighty minor emendations of the 1946 New Testament text.)[78] The verse itself had an immensely complicated textual history, and the RSV translators did not lack justification for including one or more variant readings. But to include a variant describing Joseph as Jesus' "father" struck conservatives as yet another denial of Christ's virgin birth. With pamphleteers assailing the footnote, the RSV committee voted on 10 March 1953 to omit it from all future printings. Weigle later confided to a colleague that he was sorry the footnote was ever added since the relevant text-critical problems were too complex to encapsulate in a note anyway.[79]

Another passage modified in response to conservative pressure was the Roman centurion's confession in Matthew 27:54 (compare Mark 15:39), which read in the 1952 edition "Truly this was a son of God." The indefinite article ("a") appeared to conservatives as a denial of Jesus' uniqueness, even though Weigle had explained in the *Open Letter* that the Greek text here lacked the definite article and that the centurion's comment was made from the standpoint of a pagan. When the RSV committee convened in 1959 to review a long list of criticisms and suggestions, it authorized the restoration of the familiar rendering ("the Son of God"), along with about two hundred other changes, mostly involving capitalization and punctuation. The emendations appeared in all printings after 1962.[80]

On the one hand, the RSV committee's willingness to bend on Matthew 1:16 and 27:54 stemmed from at least a tacit recognition of textual criticism's subjectivity. To paraphrase Weigle's earlier remark, well-meaning translators were to be found on both sides of many issues, and the RSV controversy had certainly tempered the inherited nineteenth-century optimism about scientific consensus in Bible translation. On the other hand, the committee's second thoughts on Matthew 1:16 and 27:54 reflected a genuine ambivalence about the RSV's constituency: Could the version, through careful publicity and a few judicious alterations, win the hearts of conservatives as well as liberals? Or were evangelical Protestants the wrong constituency to court? These questions would figure prominently in the committee's deliberations well into the 1970s.

Meanwhile evangelicals were wrestling with the question of whether the RSV could ever be their Bible. To be sure, some conservatives supported the RSV from the beginning, and the committee was more than happy to accept their endorsements. One of the most enthusiastic supporters was a self-described fundamentalist, Henry H. Ness, an Assemblies of God minister and onetime chairman of the Washington State parole board. Ness corresponded extensively with Weigle before publishing in 1953 a 14-page pamphlet refuting a variety of fundamentalist objections to the RSV.

Regarding Isaiah 7:14, he insisted that "young woman" was correct and that God had reserved the full revelation of Mary's virginity for the New Testament. On the disputed article in Matthew 27:54, he maintained that "a Son of God" was simply a literal translation of the original Greek. And as for the charge that the RSV was illegitimately "authorized," he shot back: "The Revised Standard Version is not an authorization of the Word of God but an authorized version of a translation of the Word of God, which is quite different."[81] Ness also took it upon himself to respond directly by letter to some of the RSV's harshest critics, including Michigan pastor David Otis Fuller, who had denounced the "unclean fingers" of the RSV translators. God's infallible Word, Ness told Fuller, "has come down to us [in] its absolute and pure form, not because of, but in spite of, the many 'unclean fingers' it has gone through." The Almighty, he concluded, "does not need our help in preserving His truth."[82]

Another unsolicited conservative endorsement of the RSV came from Methodist minister Clay Sicher, a graduate of two redoubtably fundamentalist schools, Moody Bible Institute and Westminster Seminary. Sicher shared the draft of his article with Weigle before submitting it to the *Christian Herald,* which printed it in March 1953. On the Isaiah 7:14 question, he defended the RSV translation while lamenting that "in our modern and distorted generation" the appellations "young woman" and "young man" did not necessarily indicate virginity. But the crux of his article was his contention that many of the RSV's critics seemed "more interested in discrediting the [National] Council than . . . in safeguarding Holy Writ."[83]

Sicher's defense of the RSV was significant because of its venue. The *Christian Herald* was something of an evangelical flagship, and its editor, Daniel A. Poling, did not take Bible-version endorsements lightly. Though Poling himself had recommended the RSV to *Christian Herald* readers in a 1952 editorial, he later confided to Weigle that the magazine was under increasing criticism from fundamentalist subscribers for the endorsement.[84]

It was a scenario that would be played out time and again: moderate evangelicals feeling pressure from the right to reject the RSV. An especially telling example was the case of Louis Evans, influential pastor of the First Presbyterian Church of Hollywood and "minister-at-large" on behalf of the national Presbyterian Church. Evans had endorsed the RSV shortly after its publication, but in January 1953, as the fundamentalist firestorm raged, he asked the National Council to stop using his name in any RSV publicity because he no longer found himself "in accord with all [the RSV's] interpretations."[85] National Council official Gerald Knoff immediately sent a copy of Evans's letter to Weigle and to Eugene Carson Blake, stated clerk of the Presbyterian Church, urging them to reason with Evans lest his turnabout be used "with disastrous effect" by the RSV's fundamentalist opponents. Weigle promptly wrote to Evans asking if he would please share his specific points of disagreement: "The careful and constructive criticism of a man like yourself will be of real value to the Committee."[86] Yet Evans replied that he was too pressed with other duties to oblige. He insisted that he was "in no way lining up with any critics of this great effort," but neither did he want to remain on board as a supporter. "In this fussy day of hectic Protestant division," he told Weigle, "it is difficult enough to salvage what remains of unity without being 'classified and typed' as belonging to this group and that."[87]

Evans, whose Hollywood church had been the first spiritual home for a young businessman, Bill Bright (founder of Campus Crusade for Christ),[88] evidently felt that the RSV had become a liability in his outreach to conservatives. His reversal revealed how clergy even within the mainline denominations sometimes were indirectly influenced by the RSV's hard-core separatist opponents. Once Isaiah 7:14 became a household word, conservative ministers inclined to support the RSV felt compelled to justify their stance. Since most ministers had forgotten most of whatever Hebrew and Greek they had once learned, they were forced to judge the RSV on other—often political—counts. And it was on the political front that support for the RSV among wavering conservatives usually broke down.

Yet conservatives who had never hesitated to oppose the RSV faced their own dilemma: Should they defend the King James Version as the only true Bible, or should they support some new translation by evangelicals? Many in the McIntire faction such as David Otis Fuller clung tenaciously to the King James Bible and even defended its Greek basis, the sixteenth-century *Textus Receptus,* as virtually infallible.[89] With characteristic bravado, Fuller whipped up the faithful at a 1956 convention of McIntire's American Council of Christian Churches: "Without a moment's hesitation I can say that this 'Revised Standard Version of the Gospel Perverts' is the vilest, boldest, most deliberately devilish attack upon the holy Word of God and the holy Son of God in the past two thousand years." Fuller surveyed the destruction wreaked upon the Bible by modern textual criticism and thanked Carl McIntire for defending Holy Writ from its modernist assailants.[90]

Meanwhile many fundamentalists, even some in McIntire's camp, recognized the scholarly and evangelistic advantages of modern translations and clamored for a viable alternative to the King James Bible and the RSV. These advocates of evangelical translation were beginning to coalesce within two organizations. The first was the National Association of Evangelicals (NAE), an interdenominational alliance founded in 1943 as a rival to the Federal (later National) Council of Churches. (McIntire had already repudiated the NAE as insufficiently separatist, even though his own ACCC had similar pan-denominational ambitions.)[91] The second was the Christian Reformed Church, a denomination of Dutch Calvinist origins whose leaders were well connected to the burgeoning evangelical publishing industry centered in Grand Rapids, Michigan. Out of these institutions would emerge a Bible with an evangelical imprimatur and *nihil obstat*, even as the National Council of Churches secured a different—and heretofore unimaginable—imprimatur and *nihil obstat* for the RSV.

The enduring significance of the RSV battle, then, was only partly visible amid the initial smoke and flames of controversy. Once the Bible-burning and Red-hunting had subsided, it became clear that many conservative Protestants were experiencing a momentous change of mind: although they had deeply internalized the sixteenth-century valuation of Book over Church, prominent conservatives were now joining their liberal counterparts in deeming necessary the ecclesiastical certification of Scripture.

Chapter 5

The Virgin Text

Evangelicals and Liberals in the Quest for an Undefiled Book

✠

[The Protestant Reformers] enthroned the Spirit in place of the Church as the authenticator and interpreter of Scripture; and, since they recognized that the Spirit's testimony to Scripture is given in and through the statements of Scripture itself, they expressed their position by speaking of Scripture as self-authenticating (autopistos was Calvin's word) and self-interpreting.

—J. I. Packer, "Contemporary Views of Revelation," in *Revelation and the Bible*, edited by Carl F. H. Henry (1958)

But when Christians separated from us affirm the divine authority of the sacred Books, they think differently from us—different ones in different ways—about the relationship between the Scriptures and the Church. In the Church, according to Catholic belief, an authentic teaching office plays a special role in the explanation and proclamation of the written word of God.

—Second Vatican Council, Decree on Ecumenism (1964)

THE PROBLEM OF unholy Scripture—a Bible translated by Christians but nevertheless tainted by unorthodoxy—was a sober realization for conservative opponents of the RSV. Yet Protestantism itself did not possess obvious resources for the ecclesiastical regulation of the printed Bible. No American Protestant communion, save for the Episcopal Church, had a code of canon law, and certainly none had ever censored, in theory at least, the text of vernacular Scripture.

In contrast, the Catholic Church since the sixteenth century had claimed two basic rights in the regulation of books: censorship, or the right to amend publications containing doctrinal error; and prohibition, or the right to ban publications judged unredeemably heretical. At the time of the RSV controversy, Canon 1391 of the church's law code (promulgated in 1917) stipulated that vernacular Scriptures could not be printed without papal approval unless prepared under episcopal supervision with annotations taken from the Fathers and other "learned Catholic writers."[1] Meanwhile, evangelical Protestant denominations could, and sometimes did, prohibit the use of particular Bible translations in public worship, but no individual church exercised binding authority for all evangelicals, much less for Protestantism as a whole. Even within denominational contexts, the resolutions passed by churchwide assemblies often went little noticed by people in the pews, who, since Protestantism's foundation, had tended to feel bound chiefly to individual conscience in reading and interpreting Scripture.

The regulation of Holy Writ was therefore a complicated matter for evangelical Protestants. To many, the RSV's failure to meet conservative doctrinal standards suggested the need for an alternative version of the Scriptures that would correct the King James Bible's inaccuracies and archaisms without compromising Christ's virgin birth and other fundamentals of the faith. Yet before embarking on an arduous new translation project, evangelicals needed some way to ensure the forthcoming version's doctrinal acceptability. To secure the necessary proof of orthodoxy, evangelicals borrowed two strategies from the Catholic tradition, an unlikely source, given the long history of Protestant animosity toward Rome.

The first strategy—to seek a de facto imprimatur—had already been tested by liberal Protestants in publishing the RSV under the emblem of the National Council of Churches, which bore the aggregate authority of thirty denominations that, while not uniformly liberal in theology, were all committed to the ecumenical movement. The conservative analogue to the NCC was the National Association of Evangelicals, whose thirty-six member denominations in 1952 ranged from Reformed to Pentecostal and represented not so much a common conciliarism as a shared biblicism.

Just three months after the RSV's publication, the NAE's official organ, *United Evangelical Action,* editorialized on the need for a more conservative translation, without naming the NAE as a possible sponsor.[2] Translating under the NAE banner would necessarily involve exclusion, for the association's officials had already distanced themselves from the thoroughgoing separatists represented by Carl McIntire's American Council of Christian Churches. Stephen W. Paine, president of the NAE, in 1949 had claimed a middle ground between liberals who downplayed denominational differences and strict fundamentalists such as McIntire who remained theologically insular.[3] Outside of McIntire's circle, however, many self-professed fundamentalists regarded the NAE as above reproach. They approved of the NAE constitution's clause on biblical infallibility and preferred the association's uncompromising "scriptural ecumenicity" to the liberals' lowest-common-denominator conciliarism.[4] The final proof of the NAE's reliability was liberal Protestants' distrust of it. Duke University professor H. Shelton Smith articulated the fears of many liberals when he speculated in a 1947 article that the NAE might infiltrate the mainline churches through its policy of opening membership to individuals as well as denominations.[5] The extent of the liberals' worries was revealed at NCC headquarters in 1954 when a lengthy internal memorandum provided background information on all the NAE's member denominations but reminded staffers of the National Council's policy "not to attack any 'anti-ecumenical' groups, even under provocation."[6]

The imprimatur of the NAE could therefore go a long way toward winning conservative supporters for a new Bible. But many advocates of renewed translation felt that, in addition to any de facto imprimatur, a more explicit certification of orthodoxy was needed—namely, a *nihil obstat* in the form of a doctrinal litmus test for the new Bible's translators. This second strategy of certification would occasion bitter debate among both evangelicals and liberals and would raise powerfully disturbing questions about the very nature of Scripture and translation.

CONSERVATIVE PROTESTANTS ON SCRIPTURE'S INERRANT UNITY

Since the beginning of the modern Bible revision movement in the 1870s, most Protestant scholars had regarded translation as an essentially impartial enterprise in the service of truth. Though a certain amount of scholarly subjectivity was taken for granted, at the end of the day Protestants tended to believe that achieving unbiased Bible translation was not only desirable but possible.

The RSV controversy significantly altered the picture. Unlike Bible battles of years past, it summoned Protestants to a sustained conversation—one that continues to this day—about the relationship between translation and theology. Not surprisingly, Isaiah 7:14 quickly emerged as the symbol of the debate. This verse encapsulated several major questions: What is the nature of prophecy and fulfillment? Is the Old Testament a Jewish or Christian text? In what sense are the canons of Old and New Testament a unified whole? The answers to these questions had always been the marrow of theology and historical criticism, but in the 1950s, conservative Protestants increasingly saw them as intimately related to translation.

One of the opening salvos in the debate came from J. Oliver Buswell, Jr., a separatist Presbyterian allied with McIntire who nevertheless moved in wider evangelical circles as president of Wheaton College in Illinois from 1926 to 1940. Although ultimately fired by Wheaton's trustees because of his divisive inclinations, Buswell retained his voice in the evangelical subculture through the *Sunday School Times* and other popular publications. One month after the RSV appeared, he articulated what he regarded as the bias of the new Bible's translators. It was not that they "deliberately introduced false doctrine" or produced translations that were "incapable of some grammatical defense." Rather, the committee's problem, as he saw it, was precisely the opposite: a studied indifference to the doctrinal valences of disputed passages. As he explained, "The liberals' mental process is: 'We must translate what we believe the ancient writer said, regardless of our opinions.'" Such an attitude, Buswell felt, could never result in an acceptable translation because it evinced no "sympathetic understanding" of what certain passages meant in a specifically Christian context. Just what "sympathetic understanding" meant to Buswell was another matter, although it seemed to come down to the belief in biblical inerrancy. Buswell concluded his article with an emphatic appeal for a new translation by scholars "who accept the Bible for what it claims to be, the infallible Word of God, and who accept Christ for what He claims to be, the Eternal Son of God."[7]

The Bible's testimony to its own inspiration had always loomed large in evangelical thought. The cardinal proof-text, so frequently invoked in debates over the 1881 Revised New Testament, was 2 Timothy 3:16 ("All scripture is given by inspiration of God," KJV). In the RSV controversy, however, passages attesting to the inspiration of prophecy assumed even greater importance. One such text was 2 Peter 1:19–21 (KJV):

> We have also a more sure word of prophecy, whereunto ye do well that ye take heed, as unto a light that shineth in a dark place, until the day dawn, and the day star arise in your hearts. Knowing this first, that no prophecy of the scripture is of any private interpretation. For the prophecy came not in old time by the will of man: but holy men of God spake as they were moved by the Holy Ghost.

Scarcely less influential than this passage itself were the glosses on it by fundamentalist interpreters such as C. I. Scofield, who insisted that fulfilled prophecy was a proof of the Bible's inspiration because the "predictions of future events were uttered so long before the events transpired that no merely human sagacity or foresight could have anticipated them."[8] Although evangelicals were far from any consensus on the accuracy of Scofield's dispensationalism, most agreed with his assessment that Old Testament prophecies normally found their fulfillment not in a prophet's own time or even in the immediately succeeding generations but much later during the life of Jesus Christ. Such was the case, according to evangelicals, with Isaiah 7:14: though the birth of Immanuel was purportedly a sign to King Ahaz, its real fulfillment occurred some seven hundred years later in Bethlehem.

Such christological interpretation of Old Testament passages was nothing new. Since the earliest decades of the Common Era, Jews had accused Christian interpreters of twisting the meaning of Isaiah 7:14,[9] while Christian apologists throughout history had vigorously defended the verse as a reference to the virgin birth of Christ. "This passage is obscure," admitted John Calvin, "but the blame lies partly on the Jews, who, by much cavilling, have laboured, as far as lay in their power, to pervert the true exposition." Although Calvin conceded to Jewish interpreters that the Hebrew *almah* technically referred only to the woman's age, he translated it as "virgin" because he felt that no birth to a mere young woman in Ahaz's day could be held out as a special sign.[10] A generation earlier, Luther had given even more credence to Jewish exegetes, translating *almah* as "young woman"—he pointed out that an old woman could be a virgin too—while nevertheless adhering to the traditional christological interpretation.[11]

In America, biblical scholars from an early date regarded the *almah* as "young woman." The Unitarian translator George Rapall Noyes, in reviewing the first volume of Ernst Wilhelm Hengstenberg's *Christologie des Alten Testaments* (1829), strenuously disputed the Berlin professor's contention that Isaiah 7:14 referred to the Virgin Mary rather than to a young woman who gave birth in the days of Ahaz.[12] But few translators were actually willing to substitute "young woman" for "virgin" in the Bible itself. Two exceptions were the Bible of the American Baptist Publication Society (1912), whose translation of Isaiah was completed by University of Chicago president William Rainey Harper,[13] and the American Translation (1931), edited by Edgar J. Goodspeed and J. M. Powis Smith.[14] Relatively few Protestants had actually read these versions, so when the RSV Old Testament appeared in 1952, its rendering of *almah* as "young woman" struck conservatives as an unorthodox innovation and forced them to formulate a general principle concerning the translation of Old Testament prophecies.

One of the first to step into the fray was Donald Grey Barnhouse, editor of the popular evangelical monthly *Eternity*. Though he regarded the RSV as "one of the best translations ever made" and insisted that evangelicals could profit from the new version without thereby endorsing a modernist theological agenda, he lamented the RSV translators' failure to heed 2 Peter 1:21, which proved that Hebrew prophecies such as Isaiah 7:14 were no mere references to mundane Old Testament events but miraculous, Spirit-inspired predictions of Jesus Christ. Correct translation of biblical prophecies meant subordinating the assumptions of secular scholarship to the will of the Holy Spirit.[15]

Barnhouse's article contained the germ of an evangelical philosophy of translation; a more developed statement appeared about the same time in *Bibliotheca Sacra*, the nineteenth-century journal of New England Calvinism acquired in 1933 by Dallas Theological Seminary, a center of thoroughgoing dispensationalism under its president from 1952 to 1986, John F. Walvoord. While the Dallas faculty's detailed schematization of the endtimes was by no means palatable to all evangelicals, its pronouncement on the RSV reflected the feelings of a broad spectrum of conservatives. Of four articles on the RSV in the January 1953 issue of *Bibliotheca Sacra*, an essay by Old Testament professor Merrill F. Unger threw down the gauntlet to the liberals in the translation war. Unger took issue with the RSV committee's claim that there was no place for theology in Bible translation. He pointed to the National Council's introductory booklet on the RSV Old Testament, which noted that "linguistic science knows no theology; those of most contradictory views can meet on common ground devoid of polemic, agreed that Hebrew words mean such and such, and their inflection and syntactical relations imply this or that."[16] To Unger, it was "an extremely subtle and elusive fallacy" for a translator to presume that

> knowledge of words and syntax is all that is necessary if he would adequately perform his task of translation. To capture the spirit and portray the thoughts of the inspired writers, he must comprehend their meaning by enablement of the same Holy Spirit that energized them. As a competent translator he is, of course, not acting in the role of a theologian, nor is he to read his theology into his translation; but he must be aware of the theological implications involved in order to know what rendering to choose when the language itself, as it often does, permits more than one rendering.

Unger insisted that scholars without any theological commitment were unqualified to translate Scripture, regardless of their "purely scientific linguistic talents." Yet what was for him the requisite theology? As with so many conservative Protestants, it seemed to be a commitment to biblical inerrancy, a doctrine corroborated by the Scriptures' own "internal evidence," namely 2 Timothy 3:16–17 and 2 Peter 1:20–21.[17]

A similar statement came from Oswald Allis, no friend of Dallas dispensationalism, in the inaugural volume of the evangelical flagship publication *Christianity Today*. Allis admitted that the *almah* of Isaiah 7:14 "often meant young woman," but he maintained that the committee's refusal to render the term "virgin" indicated a "readiness to find a minimum of truth in a passage instead of a desire to claim the most its language will properly admit."[18] For Allis and other conservatives, a faithful translator would find in Scripture a maximum of truth: two testaments linked by the connective tissue of supernatural prophecy. It was thus becoming clear that any new evangelical Bible—Allis repeated the call for an alternative to the RSV—would carry as its *nihil obstat* an oath of loyalty to the inerrant unity of Scripture.

LIBERALS AND NEO-EVANGELICALS ON TRANSLATION'S IMPARTIALITY

Amid conservative calls for an theologically "sympathetic" Bible, the RSV translators articulated anew their own ideas about Scripture and translation. On the crucial question of Isaiah 7:14, the committee consistently defended "young woman" as the only linguistically admissible translation. William Irwin confessed to the committee's astonishment that Isaiah 7:14 had been "singled out as of prime significance in the translation." As he recalled, the *almah* had occasioned no debate in the committee's sessions because "we all recognized that 'young woman' is the meaning of the Hebrew word."[19] On a more general level, Irwin insisted that "there was no theological bias in the committee's work, but only a sincere effort to tell clearly and fairly what the Biblical writer said." The committee, he explained, remained constantly vigilant of the distinction between translation and interpretation and made sure that the latter was no part of its task.[20] Similarly, Luther Weigle reiterated the claim of colleague Millar Burrows that the committee's only theological assumption was the "firm conviction that taking seriously the belief in divine revelation makes it obligatory to seek only the real meaning of every word and sentence."[21]

Yet the question of "real meaning" was more complicated for the Old Testament than for the New. The RSV translators seemed to believe that Old Testament passages should be translated to make sense within their ancient Jewish context, even if this meant abandoning long-cherished christological renderings of certain Hebrew words. "Old Testament ideas," Irwin explained, "must be understood in and by themselves." He maintained, for example, that the characteristically Christian identification of the Messiah with the Godhead was foreign to ancient Jewish thought. Christian messianism, he believed, had corrupted the translation of such passages as Psalm 45:6 ("Thy throne, O God," KJV), which the RSV rendered as "Your divine throne," thus restoring its original meaning as part of a royal paean not to God but to an Israelite king and his bride.[22]

Luther Weigle also occasionally buttressed purely linguistic arguments with an appeal to the ancient Hebrew context. On the all-consuming Isaiah 7:14, he pointed out that if the prophet had really been referring to the virgin birth of Christ—an event seven hundred years in the future—then he was "trifling" with King Ahaz by falsely promising him an imminent sign.[23] Weigle consistently defended the New Testament doctrine of the virgin birth and seemed to hold out the possibility that Isaiah 7:14 had a second, typological fulfillment in Christ. Yet his argument that Isaiah 7:14 was fulfilled in Ahaz's time implied a view of Old Testament prophecy as essentially self-contained, with meanings and referents existing prior to those identified by New Testament authors.

This conception of the Old Testament's integrity was not without evangelical proponents, particularly among the faculty of Fuller Theological Seminary in Pasadena, California. Founded in 1947 by Charles E. Fuller (host of the immensely popular radio broadcast *The Old Fashioned Revival Hour*) and Harold John Ockenga (pastor of Boston's influential fundamentalist Park Street Congregational Church), Fuller Seminary was intended to recapture the intellectual glory of nineteenth-century Princeton Seminary, the bastion of conservative Protestantism before the fundamentalist-modernist schism there in the late 1920s. As George Marsden has shown, Fuller's faculty "remained loyal to the fundamentals of fundamentalism" but also charted a more scholarly, less separatistic course that came to be known as the new (or neo-) evangelicalism.[24]

With calls mounting in the fifties for a new conservative translation of Scripture, Fuller's faculty stepped in to defend the RSV. George Eldon Ladd critiqued the RSV New Testament for *Christianity Today,* concluding that while the version was not completely adequate, its translators had not misrepresented the Greek original, as many fundamentalists had alleged.[25] But it was the Old Testament that occasioned the most substantial comment from Fuller faculty members. William Sanford LaSor, who had helped oust Carl McIntire from the Presbyterian Church, defended at length the RSV's translation of *almah*, which, he quipped, was now the best known Hebrew word in history. For LaSor, Isaiah 7:14 had both an immediate fulfillment— a child born in the normal biological way to a young woman in Ahaz's day—and a greater, christological fulfillment. LaSor feared that in their rush to preserve the "virgin" of Isaiah's prophecy, conservative Protestants were "about to discard all objective bases of establishing and interpreting" the biblical text. "Objectivity is the only safeguard we have in this world to protect the Word of God which He has committed to our care," LaSor wrote. "Nothing less than the future of evangelical scholarship is at stake."[26]

A still more dramatic statement came from E. J. Carnell, Fuller Seminary's second president, who in 1959 was invited by the liberal Protestant weekly the *Christian Century* to contribute an article to its periodic series "How My Mind Has Changed." Once an unapologetic fundamentalist, Carnell had in fact changed his mind significantly, and the primary catalyst was the RSV controversy. Carnell recalled his shock at being accused of "giving aid and comfort to modernism" for preaching from the RSV, and he decried this "war of nerves" and "unholy crusade" waged by strict separatists. In his view, the obsessive attention to Isaiah 7:14 "betrayed a dreadful confusion in biblical hermeneutics": a tendency to seek such doctrines as the virgin birth in Hebrew Scripture before turning to their real source, the New Testament. Hermeneutical confusion was but one symptom of what Carnell reluctantly concluded was fundamentalism's "serious illness."[27]

Even Carnell's more conservative colleague Harold Lindsell rallied to the RSV's defense, compiling in 1957 a collection of daily Bible readings from the version and then preparing singlehandedly the *Harper Study Bible* (1964), a major annotated edition of the RSV. In a lengthy footnote on Isaiah 7:14, he insisted that Immanuel was born to a young woman in the days of Ahaz and identified the Virgin Mary as the "antitype" of Isaiah's *almah*. Carnell commended Lindsell's study Bible to readers of *Christianity Today*, noting approvingly that its annotations embodied a conception of Scripture as a self-consistent and inerrant body of revelation.[28]

The RSV's supporters at Fuller were vocal enough that Charles Fuller finally ordered a moratorium on all public discussion of the new Bible because his radio ministry was losing valuable fundamentalist contributors.[29] His action highlighted the seminary's awkward relationship with the National Association of Evangelicals, whose leaders and constituents had been among the most ardent advocates of a new conservative Bible translation. The seminary and the association were intimately connected: Harold Ockenga had served as the founding president of both, and both had repudiated the strict separatists led by McIntire. But on the crucial question of whether to support the RSV, the more moderate members of the seminary faculty parted company with NAE leaders such as James DeForest Murch and endorsed the cause of unbiased scholarship that they felt the RSV represented. Meanwhile, the political cost of supporting the "National Council" Bible—a loss of fundamentalist support—proved too high for the NAE and Charles Fuller to pay.[30]

THE DIVIDED MIND OF THE CHRISTIAN REFORMED CHURCH

The evangelical dilemma in Bible translation was nowhere more vivid than in the Christian Reformed Church in North America, a denomination with origins in the Dutch immigration to the midwestern United States during the mid–nineteenth century. With fewer than two hundred thousand baptized members in 1955, the CRC represented a tiny fraction of American Christianity, but its influence would be felt far beyond the ethnic enclave of Dutch Calvinism.[31] Through its principal institutions of higher education, Calvin College and Calvin Theological Seminary (both in Grand Rapids, Michigan), the CRC had long cultivated a rigorous confessionalism centered on the tripartite standard of the Belgic Confession (1561), the Heidelberg Catechism (1562), and the Canons of Dort (1619). The CRC also maintained a system of parochial schools inspired by the theologian Abraham Kuyper (1837–1920), onetime prime minister of the Netherlands, who advocated engagement of the larger social and political spheres from a self-consciously Christian standpoint. These combined tendencies toward intellectualism and cultural activism rendered the CRC's influence far disproportionate to its size. The denomination's impact was especially felt in the realm of biblical scholarship. The CRC's professors took the Bible's claims with the utmost seriousness and therefore devoted immense effort to problems of translation and exegesis. Their work found a natural venue in the publishing firms founded by the Dutch Reformed entrepreneurs William B. Eerdmans and the brothers P. J. and Bernie Zondervan. The Dutch Reformed publishing houses would become standard-bearers for not only ethnic Calvinism but also the wider world of American evangelicalism.[32]

Perhaps to prove its Americanness during the crisis of world war, the CRC became a charter member of the National Association of Evangelicals in 1943. But the alliance was uncomfortable from the beginning because many CRC intellectuals were deeply suspicious of the "Arminian" revivalism so prevalent in the NAE's heavily Methodist, Holiness, and Pentecostal constituency. Fearing the loss of its distinctive Calvinism, the CRC Synod (its highest governing assembly) withdrew the denomination's NAE membership in 1951, even though the CRC and NAE continued to share many concerns, including a firm allegiance to the infallibility of Scripture. Eventually the CRC would rejoin the NAE in 1988, but not before both had pursued different yet intersecting paths in the contentious issue of Bible translation.[33]

Essentially presbyterian in polity, the CRC relied on local consistories, classes (the individual unit was known as a "classis"), and ultimately its annual synods to define and regulate denominational orthodoxy. Soon after the RSV appeared, the various governing bodies naturally took up the matter of the church's stance toward the new Bible. A writer for the CRC magazine, the *Banner,* had already urged readers to avoid the RSV, concluding that "no one can ever expect a really sound, reliable Bible-translation from the pen of liberal scholars."[34] The 1953 Synod appointed four Grand Rapids professors to review the translation, and by the following year they recommended rejection of the version because of its renderings of Isaiah 7:14, Psalm 2:11–12, Matthew 16:16, and other passages made famous in the wider national controversy. The Synod of 1954 in turn voted to prohibit use of the RSV in the public worship of CRC congregations.[35]

Two years later, amid calls from the NAE and elsewhere for an alternative to the RSV, the CRC's Seattle consistory petitioned the 1956 Synod to join other conservative Protestant denominations in producing a more "faithful" translation of the Scriptures. Subsequent synods authorized a special committee to study the Seattle proposal, and by 1965 the committee had helped spearhead an interdenominational conference in Palos Heights, Illinois, to discuss the logistics of a new translation. The Synod of 1966 therefore faced the decision of whether to authorize formal CRC participation in the nascent project.[36]

Shortly before the 1966 Synod, however, one of the study committee's members, Calvin Seminary professor Bastiaan Van Elderen, registered in the *Banner* and elsewhere his strong opposition to a new conservative Bible. Van Elderen objected first of all to the emerging philosophy of evangelical translation, which he insisted would destroy the notion of progressive revelation by illegitimately importing New Testament concepts into Old Testament texts. "The attempt at [biblical] unity through such an artificial procedure," he wrote, "is too great a price to pay at the expense of the more significant organic and progressive unity which the Bible possesses." Second, he feared that the proposed new translation would further isolate evangelical scholars from their mainline counterparts and would increase the "fragmentation of Christendom at an unnecessary and unfortunate level." The past decade of reflection, he believed, had vindicated the objectivity of the RSV translators, who deserved evangelicals' cooperation, not their opposition.[37]

Van Elderen's arguments carried the day. The Synod of 1966 rejected formal CRC involvement in a new translation and appointed instead a six-person panel to recommend improvements in the RSV text. Two years later, the panel submitted to the RSV committee a list of thirty-five textual suggestions. Isaiah 7:14 was not on the list, although the panel did recommend the restoration of a few sensitive passages, including the disputed "Kiss the Son" of Psalm 2:12. Ultimately the committee adopted a few of the CRC suggestions in a second edition of the RSV New Testament (1971), but by then the CRC's 1969 Synod had reversed its 1954 action and approved the RSV for use in the denomination's public worship.[38] Fifteen years of study and debate had convinced the CRC Synod that the RSV was not in fact theologically dangerous. P. J. Zondervan, whose firm was authorized to distribute the RSV, hailed the CRC decision as a "great step forward" and assured a National Council of Churches official that he was already "pushing" the RSV in the Dutch Reformed market.[39]

Yet the CRC would never be of one mind on Scripture or its translation. The interdenominational effort to produce a new conservative Bible had not died when the CRC pulled out in 1966, and a number of leading CRC scholars continued to participate independently in the project. The division among CRC intellectuals reflected the complex interaction of at least two pairs of competing forces: the tug of ethnic confessionalism versus American evangelicalism, and the tug of the mainline academic establishment versus the evangelical academic subculture.

The same tensions bedeviled other conservative ethnic Protestants. A decade before the CRC approved the RSV, a special commission of the Lutheran Church—Missouri Synod concluded that the RSV was, despite a few rough edges, an admirable and decidedly unheretical work of scholarship. Like the CRC panel, the Missouri Synod commission drew up a list of mostly minor textual suggestions, some of which the RSV committee eventually approved.[40] While many Missouri Synod scholars were determined to collaborate rather than compete with mainline translators, however, others charted a separate course. The most prominent of the latter group was Robert Preus, a member of the translation committee for a new evangelical Bible, who helped purge the Missouri Synod seminaries of theological moderates after his brother Jacob's election as president of the denomination in 1969.[41] As other Lutheran denominations moved rapidly toward merger and new status in Protestantism's "mainstream," the Missouri Synod after 1969 stood apart from these ecumenical ventures in a tenacious defense of biblical inerrancy and other dogmas traditionally associated with American fundamentalism.[42] The Missouri Synod also remained aloof from the National Council of Churches, which several other Lutheran groups had joined at its inception. Like their Dutch Reformed counterparts, many Missouri Synod scholars respected the scholarly effort behind the National Council's Bible, but they were deeply skeptical that the RSV could ever be made fully acceptable to conservative Protestants.

THE EVANGELICAL *NIHIL OBSTAT*
AND A MORE RELIABLE BIBLE

Because the evangelical scholarly community retained some respect for the RSV, advocates of a conservative Bible had to make sure that serious collaboration with the RSV committee was out of the question before proceeding with a new translation. As early as April 1953, the Evangelical Theological Society made overtures to the RSV committee about the possibility of effecting conservative revisions in the version. Founded in 1949, the ETS was emerging as the primary representative of what Mark Noll has called critical anti-criticism—biblical scholarship based on the belief that the inerrancy of Scripture is "the epistemological keystone of Christianity itself."[43] Members of the society believed that to question one part of the Bible was to compromise the whole, and therefore most of them could not fully trust the RSV unless certain passages were recast to fit into what one member described as the divinely designed "jigsaw puzzle" of Scripture.[44] Accordingly, the society appointed Baptist New Testament professor Julius Robert Mantey to explore means of cooperation with the liberal translators.

Mantey, who on the whole liked the RSV, inquired of Thomas Nelson and Sons about the possibility of adding several ETS members to the RSV committee to participate in its eventual revision. Nelson forwarded Mantey's letter to Luther Weigle, who replied that a translator's theological or denominational commitments had never been, and could never be, a factor in determining membership on the RSV committee. He suggested that the ETS instead consider appointing several of its members to the RSV's advisory board, which was then composed of representatives from National Council denominations.[45] When Don M. Wagner, principal of the Oak Hills Christian Training School in Bemidji, Minnesota, contacted Weigle with a similar proposal to place evangelicals on the RSV committee, Weigle again rebuffed the suggestion. Wagner replied that "nothing short of an active participation on the part of the large company of protesting evangelicals" would win conservatives over to any future edition of the RSV.[46]

Weigle and his colleagues remained determined not to make theology an official criterion of committee membership, and it soon became clear that evangelicals were equally determined to translate the Bible on their own. Over the next twelve years, two small groups of scholars from the Christian Reformed Church and the National Association of Evangelicals—the latter group included Dallas Seminary president John Walvoord—convened periodically to discuss a new translation of Scripture. Eventually the two groups joined forces, and this led to the 1965 conference at Trinity Christian College in Palos Heights, Illinois, where a project was finally begun that would be known as the New International Version of the Bible.[47]

The Palos Heights assembly included, in addition to translators, representatives of several major Bible publishers. One of these, Oxford University Press Bible editor Wilbur Ruggles, questioned whether enough qualified evangelicals could be assembled to produce a front-rank translation. Some of the scholars themselves shared this concern, which NIV historian Richard Kevin Barnard has called evangelicalism's "ecclesiastical inferiority complex," a malady stemming from evangelicals' familial connection to the much-ridiculed fundamentalists of the 1920s evolution controversy. Ultimately the Palos Heights participants agreed with Calvin Seminary's John Stek that enough competent evangelicals were available, and the conference appointed fifteen scholars to a central committee that would coordinate and edit the work of a larger company of assisting translators.[48]

Yet behind the practical concern about assembling an adequate translation team stood the philosophical issue of what distinguished evangelical from nonevangelical scholars. This identity question came to the fore as the Palos Heights assembly debated the principles that would underlie the new Bible. Evangelical scholars in most cases possessed academic credentials equivalent to those of their nonevangelical counterparts, but evangelicals held a different view of Scripture. Conference participants decided that this difference should be laid out in no uncertain terms.

A logical starting point was the statement of faith adopted by the Evangelical Theological Society, whose clause on Scripture could scarcely have been more emphatic: "The Bible alone, and the Bible in its entirety, is the Word of God written and is therefore inerrant in the autographs." As the touchstone of the society's existence, this formulation of inerrancy had been elaborated over the years in the society's journal by many of the scholars who were now inaugurating the NIV project. The statement's upshot, as Ronald Youngblood later explained, was that nothing in the sixty-six books of Scripture lay outside the pale of God's intended revelation to humanity.[49] To conclude that any portion of Scripture was somehow irrelevant or incorrect was a dangerous human conceit that ignored the possibility of undiscerned divine purpose or undiscovered textual evidence. Evidence of Scripture's truth, moreover, would always be internal to the Bible itself, and must always be accepted on faith. As Robert Preus put it, the Scriptures were "self-authenticating," or certified by the internal testimony of fulfilled prophecy and other interconnections among the biblical books. Christians could claim "no outside criteria for judging the truthfulness or factual content of scriptural assertions." Preus cited modern "scientific historiography" as one example of an illegitimate external criterion.[50] His emphasis on inerrancy, however, presupposed the modern scientific condition that had made Bible translation controversies so explosive. Once the biblical texts had been separated in the popular mind from the facts to which they corresponded, Scripture's inerrancy—or errancy, depending on one's perspective—became an all-consuming passion. And this in turn raised doubts about the sufficiency of Scripture's self-authentication. The example of the RSV made clear to evangelicals that, in the absence of the inerrant autographs, any human version of Scripture would require a very human certification of its trustworthy and orthodox character.

Soon after the Palos Heights conference, therefore, the newly named Committee on Bible Translation adopted a *nihil obstat* for the NIV—a requirement that all its translators accept the ETS statement on inerrancy or some equally high formulation of scriptural authority.[51] As translator Laird Harris later recalled, "all the men working on the NIV believed the Bible to be true in its detail, in its original manuscripts—accurate in science, history, and anything that it touched."[52] Exactly how the committee's allegiance to inerrancy related to translation was never publicly specified, although as the NIV project unfolded, it became evident that the doctrinal test was primarily intended to safeguard the christological link between the Old and New Testaments. The translators' manual stipulated that the NIV should "reflect clearly the unity and harmony of the Spirit-inspired writings" and mandated, for example, that the version capitalize Old Testament references to the Messiah ("Branch," "Root," etc.).[53] Such capitalization had a few precedents in the King James Bible, but it remained to be seen whether the NIV translators would push the principle further.[54] Similar questions remained about how many disputed RSV passages the NIV translators should restore to their traditional form.

The preliminary phase of the NIV project was supervised by Burton L.

Goddard, library director and former dean of Gordon-Conwell Theological Seminary. Early on, Goddard sought the advice of Luther Weigle, thanking him for the high level of scholarship represented by the RSV and noting that "all of us on the Committee on Bible Translation use it a great deal."[55] When the two men met at Weigle's summer home in New Hampshire to discuss translation procedure, Weigle made clear that major conservative theological modifications of the RSV were not on the horizon. As for the matter of English style, Weigle remarked that the RSV had cornered the market on Bible revision in the King James tradition, but he suggested that Goddard's committee might find a niche for a translation in more contemporary language.[56] The Committee on Bible Translation did in fact adopt a somewhat more contemporary style than the RSV, prompted partly by a Christian Reformed Church layman, Howard Long, who had complained about the difficulties that King James English posed for evangelization.[57]

Goddard himself was also convinced of the need for a conservative Bible in truly contemporary idiom, noting that "unless Christian families and churches use the Scriptures in modern English form, more and more of our young people are going to be strangers to the Gospel." Yet he and his colleagues felt that existing contemporary versions were too paraphrastic and informal.[58] One such example was Today's English Version, first published in 1966 as *Good News for Modern Man,* a translation of the New Testament by Robert G. Bratcher of the American Bible Society. The following year, Wheaton, Illinois, translator Kenneth Taylor produced the New Testament installment of the Living Bible, a colloquial paraphrase of the American Standard Version rather than a new translation from the original languages. Decades before, RSV translators Edgar J. Goodspeed and J. M. Powis Smith had helped popularize the contemporary-language genre with their American Translation (1931), but its orthodoxy, like the RSV's, had come under conservative attack. The members of the Committee on Bible Translation therefore believed that the NIV would meet a genuine need for a translation that was contemporary in both language and scholarship yet also self-conscious in its treatment of Scripture as God's inerrant Word.

THE CATHOLIC *IMPRIMATUR* AND THE LIBERAL PROTESTANT QUEST FOR UNITY

Meanwhile, as evangelicals were carving a niche for the NIV, the RSV committee was continuing to convene, and its actions during the years 1952–

65 would further alter the ideological alignments of the American Bible business. The immediate drumbeat in 1952 for a new evangelical translation had frustrated the hopes of RSV promoters for a bipartisan groundswell in favor of the National Council's Bible. Yet with the RSV translators themselves only willing to go so far to satisfy evangelical demands, a common Protestant translation on the order of the King James Bible was clearly a thing of the past.

The first step toward a different kind of common Bible came in October 1952, when the RSV committee responded to a call from the Episcopal Church to translate the Apocrypha, the dozen additional books of the Greek Old Testament (Septuagint) not included in the Hebrew Bible but incorporated into the Vulgate and confirmed as fully canonical for Catholics by the Council of Trent (1546).[59] In English-speaking Protestantism, the apocryphal books had been translated as additions to the Geneva and King James Bibles, and the Church of England and Episcopal Church had always included some apocryphal readings in their lectionaries. Protestants in general, however, associated the books with medieval Catholicism and accepted the verdict of the Westminster Confession (1648) that the Apocrypha was "of no authority in the Church of God."[60] Few American Protestants even knew that a King James Version of the Apocrypha existed because it had rarely been printed as part of the Bible. The RSV Apocrypha project thus seemed destined from the outset to appeal less to evangelical Protestants than to ecumenically minded Catholics.

Indeed, Catholic scholars on the other side of the Atlantic almost immediately took an interest in the RSV Apocrypha, which would be published by Thomas Nelson and Sons in 1957.[61] Ever since the papal encyclical *Divino Afflante Spiritu* (1943), Catholic biblical scholarship had been enjoying a new era of relative freedom. In the British Isles, a major product of this renaissance was *A Catholic Commentary on Holy Scripture*, written over nine years by members of the Catholic Biblical Association of Great Britain and published by Nelson in 1953.[62] The general editor of the commentary, Bernard Orchard, contacted H. Peter Morrison of Nelson in 1953 about the possibility of preparing a Catholic edition of the RSV. With translation of the RSV Apocrypha underway, the full Catholic canon would soon be available in the new version, and Orchard believed that the addition of these deuterocanonical books, along with a few emendations and annotations of existing books, would make the RSV acceptable to the Catholic hierarchy. Although the 1917 code of canon law still technically forbade the general use of non-Catholic Bibles, it permitted their limited use for study purposes.[63] *Divino Afflante Spiritu,* moreover, had implicitly liberalized the church's stance toward Protestant Bibles by allowing translations from the original Greek and Hebrew.

Morrison liked Orchard's idea and contacted Luther Weigle about the possibility of modifying the RSV to satisfy Catholic readers. Morrison explained that although the "tendentious spirit" of Tyndale's day—when translators twisted the meaning of biblical words "to suit pre-conceived theology"—had passed, Catholics and Protestants still naturally entertained a few terminological "prejudices": residual idiosyncrasies requiring a small number of innocuous differences in Bible translation.[64] Morrison felt that a Catholic edition of the Protestant RSV would be a major step toward Christian unity, not to mention a boon for Nelson's list. Weigle agreed, so in July 1954 he and Gerald Knoff, executive secretary of the Division of Christian Education of the National Council of Churches, met in London with officials from Nelson and a subcommittee of the Catholic Biblical Association of Great Britain.[65] The Catholic scholars outlined some of the textual changes they regarded as necessary, including the substitution of "brethren" for Jesus' "brothers" to safeguard, ironically, the perpetual virginity of Mary. The total number of anticipated changes was small, and Weigle signaled the RSV committee's willingness to consider a formal list of emendations.[66]

In June 1955 Weigle distributed the Catholics' list of New Testament preferences, edited by Orchard and his colleague, Reginald C. Fuller, to the members of the RSV committee. Most of the proposed changes involved terminology: "brethren" for "brothers" in more than a dozen places; "full of grace" instead of "favored one" in Luke's annunciation account; and "send her away" rather than "divorce her" in Matthew's narrative of Joseph and Mary. As required by canon law, the Catholic edition of the RSV New Testament would also include endnotes on doctrinal matters still to be determined. The most major changes requested were the restoration of three disputed passages to the main body of the text: (1) the "Longer Ending" of Mark 16:9–20; (2) the *pericope adulterae* of John 7:53–8:11; and (3) a group of less than a dozen verses, mostly in Luke, that the RSV had omitted or replaced with shorter, presumably more authentic readings dubbed "Western non-interpolations" by the nineteenth-century textual critics Westcott and Hort. The most famous "non-interpolation" was Luke 22:19–20 (the account of the Last Supper), where the RSV committee had preserved a shorter reading that included only Christ's institution of the bread, not the wine.

Not surprisingly, some of the proposed changes struck the RSV committee members as uncritical and reactionary. At the same time, the committee was pleasantly surprised that the Catholics were requesting so few alterations—less than fifty in all—and that most of changes were fairly "moderate" and even "reasonable."[67] The translators felt that the emendations could be permitted since an appendix to the new Bible would clearly distinguish them from the original RSV text. Weigle himself confessed to his distaste for the most overtly doctrinal of the proposed alterations, yet he believed that the changes would serve the higher goal of Christian unity. "After all," he told a colleague, "[the Catholics] are making a much greater and more venturesome step than we."[68]

But one RSV committee member, Edgar J. Goodspeed, expressed serious reservations about the plan. Though he strongly opposed on critical grounds the three major textual restorations, his main objection had little to do with textual criticism. Goodspeed feared that the Catholic edition would give "immense ammunition" to the American opponents of the RSV and revive the controversy around allegations of coziness with Rome. "As a matter of sheer expediency," he told Weigle, "I cannot favor the arrangement, flattering as it is. It would do the version more harm than good, corrupting its text to begin with, and weakening its case with American Protestants."[69]

Goodspeed's fears were not unfounded, for many American Protestants at midcentury still harbored a deep-seated fear of "Romanism." Whether emanating from the liberal *Christian Century* or the organ of the National Association of Evangelicals, strident anti-Catholic rhetoric was commonplace. Protestants, as Paul Blanshard did in his *American Freedom and Catholic Power* (1949), popularized the idea of a Catholic fifth column, even as Catholics such as Francis Cardinal Spellman lashed out at the "unhooded Klansmen" who would, among other atrocities, deny Catholic children public transportation to their parochial schools.[70]

Further complicating the situation was the genuine progress that had been made on the scholarly level in American Protestant-Catholic relations. The *Catholic Biblical Quarterly,* founded in 1937, had taken friendly notice of the RSV and had even printed an article by Weigle in 1952.[71] The journal maintained close ties with the Confraternity of Christian Doctrine, which was then publishing the initial installments of its New American

Bible, the first major American Catholic translation based not on the Vulgate but on the original Greek and Hebrew (as sanctioned by *Divino Afflante Spiritu*). When Reginald Fuller contacted Louis Hartman, secretary of the Catholic Biblical Association in the United States, about the possibility of supporting a Catholic edition of the RSV, Hartman bitterly rebuffed the British proposal, noting that it would "stultify" the New American Bible project.[72]

Despite the opposition from various quarters, plans for the newly named RSV Catholic Edition were moving ahead with consideration of the Old Testament and Apocrypha. Though the project's chief patron in the English hierarchy, Bernard Cardinal Griffin, had died an untimely death in 1956 before actually granting the new version his imprimatur, Fuller and Orchard were hopeful that they could secure endorsement from the new archbishop of Westminster, William Cardinal Godfrey. The more conservative Godfrey balked, but the obstacle proved only temporary, for he died in January 1963 and was replaced by the ecumenically minded John Cardinal Heenan.

In the meantime, America had elected a Catholic president, and Pope John XXIII had summoned the Second Vatican Council. These two developments would make it easier for the RSV committee to lend its wholehearted public support to the Catholic Edition. Vatican II, in particular, built upon *Divino Afflante Spiritu* by stating explicitly that "given the opportunity and the approval of the Church hierarchy," Catholics could undertake Bible translations with the "separated brethren." Frederick Grant, RSV committee member and an official Protestant observer to the Council, hailed the "wonderful reawakening" of Catholic biblical scholarship. "What I really wish," Grant wrote, "is that we could all go back to the days of Erasmus and work together in harmony, especially in biblical studies, and forget about all the intervening four centuries of confusion, distrust, and antagonism."[73]

Grant, an Episcopal priest originally trained at the high-church "Anglo-Catholic" seminary at Nashotah, Wisconsin, was perhaps more predisposed than some of his colleagues to view Catholicism favorably. Yet his writings reflected a subtle but important change in attitude among many Protestant biblical scholars during the 1960s. In his 1961 history of the English Bible tradition, Grant contrasted the dynamic biblical aestheticism of the Catholic Middle Ages with the static biblical empiricism of the nineteenth century. He criticized the 1881 Revised Version translators for naively supposing that Bible translation was a scientific, word-for-word enterprise capable of great exactitude and internal consistency.[74] Though Grant was not saying that translation should be blatantly partisan—the RSV committee, after all, had vigorously defended its essential impartiality in the face of evangelical opponents—he did provide tacit justification for projects such as the RSV Catholic Edition, whose textual variants were primarily motivated not by disinterested linguistic considerations but by the doctrinal standards of a living ecclesia.

By late fall of 1963, all that remained for the publication of the RSVCE New Testament was the Catholic hierarchy's official approval. Wary of controverting so soon his recently deceased predecessor, Cardinal Heenan arranged for an imprimatur from Gordon Joseph Gray, archbishop of Saint Andrews and Edinburgh, Scotland, and a *nihil obstat* from Gray's appointed censor, Thomas Hanlon. Heenan also secured the blessing of the Holy Office, the congregation in Rome assigned to safeguard sound doctrine. In America, an additional imprimatur was conferred by Peter W. Bartholome, bishop of St. Cloud, Minnesota. (The Liturgical Press, a publisher in his diocese, was licensed, along with Nelson, to issue the RSVCE.) By then, the *New York Times* had already announced the forthcoming Bible edition on its front page.[75]

The RSVCE New Testament was finally presented to Pope Paul VI at the Vatican on May 22, 1965, by Orchard and Fuller, Christopher Busby of Nelson, and Gerald Knoff of the National Council of Churches. Luther Weigle, by then eighty-four years old, was unable to make the trip. The pope expressed his gratitude, however, by awarding to Weigle and Peter Morrison the papal knighthood of St. Gregory the Great. Weigle's investiture was performed on January 27, 1966, by Henry J. O'Brien, archbishop of Hartford, Connecticut, in St. Thomas More Chapel, the Catholic center at Yale University. The location could not have been more ironic, for Thomas More had been the chief antagonist of William Tyndale, patriarch of the English Bible tradition. In a letter of thanks to the pope, Weigle exulted that "in our time . . . the Bible serves as a bond of Christian unity."[76]

Not everyone was happy with the new version. The most scathing review came from Raymond E. Brown, one of the translators of the New American Bible. Brown objected to the very existence of the RSVCE, which seemed to "imply that Catholics and Protestants have to translate the Bible differently in order to favor their own traditions." Cooperation between Catholics and Protestants in genuine translation projects was to be encouraged, he wrote, but to make cosmetic changes in Scripture to satisfy church dogma was "unscientific" at best. The elimination of the term "divorce" (Matthew 1:19), for example, introduced a blatant anachronism, for the "Catholic Church's opposition to divorce does not change the fact that divorce was accepted by the Jews in Gospel times." Brown insisted, moreover, that the new version's explanatory endnotes often had little factual justification. He singled out the note on Luke's "Infancy Gospel" (1:5–2:52), which suggested that the passage was based on the reminiscences of Mary. This note, Brown wrote, "is so naive that it is embarrassing." Brown feared above all that the RSVCE would "do little to convince Protestants of the ability or objectivity of Catholic biblical scholars."[77]

Brown's review stung Father Fuller, who complained to Gerald Knoff that Brown had misunderstood the intent of the RSVCE. Fuller insisted that the version's purpose was not primarily scholarly but ecumenical. In order to further the cause of Christian unity, he explained, "we had to play down a little the 'pure scholarship' angle." He added that Brown and the other New American Bible translators stood on no firmer ground, critically speaking: "Did they not have to print 'virgin' in Isaiah 7:14 because the bishops wanted it?"[78]

The dissension within Catholic ranks put something of a damper on the 1966 publication of the complete RSVCE, which included the Old Testament along with the deuterocanonicals in their traditional Vulgate order. Partisans for the project, including Boston's Richard Cardinal Cushing, remained effusive in their praise. Cushing's ecumenical enthusiasm led him, paradoxically, to endorse both the RSVCE and the *Oxford Annotated Bible,* wherein the RSV text appeared in its unaltered form. (The Oxford edition did include a handful of Catholic modifications in the footnotes.)[79]

The RSVCE Old Testament contained the obligatory doctrinal notes but no actual textual modifications—not even in Isaiah 7:14. A note on Isaiah's famous prophecy explained that while *almah* did not explicitly mean "virgin," Christ's virgin birth was "unequivocally" stated in Matthew 1:23. Such reassurance of orthodoxy echoed the RSV translators' own affirmations of the virgin birth in the wake of the 1952 Bible-burnings.[80] Indeed, the persistent controversy over the "virgin text" had made clear to both Catholics and Protestants that translated Scripture was not self-evidently pure but rather had to be certified as orthodox.

The RSV Catholic Edition was at once a symbol of unity and discord. On the one hand, it represented a tremendous ecumenical breakthrough, for a Catholic imprimatur upon a Protestant Bible—even a modified one—would have been unthinkable even a few decades earlier. On the other hand, it represented the failure of Protestants (and Catholics) to reach any consensus among themselves in Bible translation. The RSV translators had fairly readily accepted a Catholic corrective for the sake of Christian unity and would by 1968 invite six Catholic scholars, including Orchard and Fuller, to full membership on the committee. But similar collaboration between Protestant liberals and fundamentalists was out of the question for either side. Certain alliances, in other words, were inherently unholy, just as certain texts, lacking the proper imprimatur, were inherently defiled.

Virginity Lost, Virginity Regained?

Translation and Scripturalism since 1965

✠

*I proceed on the conviction that there is genuine continuity
in the language of the Christian church as it readapts itself in every age
to the paradigmatic language of Scripture, particularly to the story
of the gospel and to reading the Old Testament as the "figure"
leading toward fulfillment in that story. I have to go on the
conviction that there is more continuity in the language of the church
and the Scripture than there is in the philosophical languages
and their use of "knowledge," "God," and so on . . .*

—Hans W. Frei, "Response to 'Narrative Theology:
An Evangelical Appraisal'" (1985)

TWO EVENTS IN 1965 marked the end of an era in Bible translation. Among conservative Protestants, the NIV project was born at an interdenominational conference in Palos Heights, Illinois. Among liberal Protestants, the RSV Catholic Edition New Testament helped bridge a centuries-old rift with Rome. Although both endeavors represented important new ecumenical departures, both also signaled the decline of a nineteenth-century ideal of scientific, impartial translation. Though the old rhetoric of impartiality was by no means dead, most scholars had experienced the sober, yet liberating, realization that translation could never be value-free. Translation in this "postmodern" moment involved self-conscious alignment with a particular Christian community, along with all its linguistic and doctrinal norms. Partisan translation was nothing new, but in the modern context it had generally proceeded under the guise of scientific impartiality. Now translators were abandoning the pretense of total objectivity and embracing a brave new world of unapologetically apologetic Bibles.

A striking sign of the times was the presidential address delivered by Kenneth W. Clark at the annual meeting of the Society of Biblical Literature on 30 December 1965 in Nashville, Tennessee. Clark, a professor of New Testament at Duke University, noted the tendency of previous generations of biblical scholars to claim that textual variation had little bearing on theology. He cited RSV translator Frederick Grant's 1946 observation that no variant reading had turned up thus far in the ancient manuscripts that required a revision of Christian doctrine.[1] He also invoked the famous English biblical scholar Sir Frederic Kenyon, who once reassured his readers that they could follow textual criticism "without misgiving" and "without thought of doctrinal consequences." Surely, Clark surmised, scholars of past generations did not really believe that the text critic's work could be separated from theology; nevertheless, they apparently confined any recognition of textual criticism's ideologically fraught character to "a separate compartment of the mind." Clark called on his colleagues to abandon this pretense of objectivity: "Let us no longer implant the belief that Christian doctrine is unaffected by textual emendation, whether for better or worse." The textual tradition of the Greek New Testament, he said, had always been characterized by a great variety of variants, some of them quite doctrinally consequential. He then made a statement that would have struck most nineteenth-century text critics as at least mildly heretical:

> We may well begin to ask if there really was a stable text at the beginning. We talk of recovering the original text, and of course every docu-

ment had such a text. But the earliest witnesses to N[ew] T[estament] text even from the first century already show such variety and freedom that we may well wonder if the text remained stable long enough to hold a priority. Great progress has been achieved in recovering an early form of text, but it may be doubted that there is evidence of one original text to be recovered.

The endless strata of variants meant that the text critic must also be a theologian and a historian, capable of discerning the doctrinal significance of disputed readings in their ancient Near Eastern context. The burden of theology and history fell equally on the translator, who must recognize that every word choice had potential ideological ramifications for the reader. Clark pointed to the RSV controversy and the infant NIV project as proof that translation and textual criticism could never be divorced from contemporary theological concerns, just as the text-copying by ancient scribes could never have occurred in a theological vacuum.[2]

VIRGIN RESTORED: THE NIV AND ITS RECEPTION

Clark's address proved prescient, for the question of theological motivation in translation continued to loom large as the NIV translators finally began their work in 1968. Some evangelicals feared that the committee's allegiance to biblical inerrancy would lead it to impose an artificial unity on Scripture. Stanley E. Hardwick, professor of Old Testament at Bethel Theological Seminary (Baptist General Conference) in St. Paul, argued in *Christianity Today* that the unity of the Old and New Testaments was based on "great over-arching themes" rather than on any "exact equivalence in meaning and translation." He denounced the traditional "virgin" of Isaiah 7:14 as a "travesty" stemming from the forced imposition of the New Testament upon the Old. Because the RSV had corrected this and other mistranslations, he maintained, a new evangelical translation was a waste of time and money.[3] Meanwhile, NIV translator Laird Harris, dean of the faculty and professor of Old Testament at Covenant Theological Seminary (Presbyterian Church in America) in St. Louis, defended the committee's position. He insisted that the RSV had introduced unnecessary conflicts between the testaments and consequently had weakened the "evidential value of Old Testament prediction." That the RSV had diluted scriptural truth was no surprise to Harris since its translators were "modern critical" scholars who did not believe that "truly predictive prophecy is possible."[4]

Such recurring disagreements over translation procedure, however, soon threatened to become moot amid the rising inflation and economic recession of the late sixties and early seventies. In 1966, the NIV translators had secured the sponsorship of the New York Bible Society, but like other established religious institutions, the society was now feeling the effects of America's most serious economic downturn since the 1930s.

Founded in 1809 amid the birth of more than a hundred similar organizations across the early republic, the New York Bible Society became an auxiliary of the newly created American Bible Society in 1816. After a nearly a century as a regional partner in America's benevolent empire, the NYBS declared its independence in 1913, but unlike many former American Bible Society auxiliaries that dissolved or fell into obscurity, the New York organization gradually established itself as an unapologetically conservative presence amid the gathering fundamentalist-modernist storm that would rock American religion in the 1920s. When it seemed in the late fifties that the society might drift into liberalism, an evangelical faction again secured control of the board and in 1963 installed Youngve Kindberg, a minister of the Christian and Missionary Alliance, at the helm.[5] Ironically, Kindberg's eager adoption of the NIV almost spelled the demise of the society, which could barely absorb the project's escalating costs. In the effort to stay afloat, the society sold its New York City headquarters and moved to a cheaper facility in New Jersey. But the monetary woes continued, forcing the translators themselves to spend more time on fundraising lest the NIV project fail.

Crucial support eventually came in the form of advance royalties paid by the Zondervan Corporation, which recognized the NIV's potential appeal to the vast evangelical market and thus negotiated exclusive commercial rights to the new Bible.[6] Chief executive P. J. Zondervan embodied the divided mind of his own denomination, the Christian Reformed Church, in Bible translation: an eager distributor of the RSV, Zondervan also became primary corporate patron of the NIV. Like any publisher, Zondervan's dual loyalties reflected pecuniary as well as theological motives, but such was the pragmatism of the American Bible business.

In addition to Zondervan's backing, the energetic leadership of another CRC stalwart, Edwin W. Palmer, helped bring the NIV project to fruition. Former pastor of the Grandville Avenue Christian Reformed Church in Grand Rapids, Michigan, Palmer was executive secretary of the committee from 1968 until his death in 1980 at age fifty-eight. Converted to conservative Christianity in Harold Ockenga's Park Street Church in Boston, he graduated from Harvard and served as a first lieutenant in the Marine Corps during World War II before earning a bachelor of theology degree from Ockenga's alma mater, Westminster Seminary, in 1949. After completing a doctorate at the Free University of Amsterdam in 1953, he entered the parish ministry of the Christian Reformed Church. Author of a popular study guide on Calvinist theology, Palmer firmly believed that the doctrines of Reformed orthodoxy were simply identical with biblical teachings and therefore had been professed by Christians from the beginning, save for the "long silence of the Middle Ages."[7] A high view of Scripture was for him foundational to all true theology and Bible translation. Upon his appointment as NIV executive secretary, he declared his "strong convictions on the inerrancy of the Scriptures in the original autographs."[8]

The company of translators headed by Palmer was surely one of the largest in the English Bible's history. Each biblical book passed through four tiers of working groups, with veto power residing at the fourth level, the Committee on Bible Translation.[9] More than a hundred biblical scholars, mostly from evangelical colleges and seminaries, participated, along with English stylists and other consultants. The project included a dozen participants from Great Britain, Canada, Australia, and New Zealand; hence the "International" in the new Bible's name.[10] After market-testing the Gospel of John in 1969, the New York Bible Society released the NIV New Testament in the fall of 1973. The society then issued trial runs of Isaiah, Daniel, Proverbs, and Ecclesiastes before releasing the complete NIV on 27 October 1978.[11]

Liberal veterans of the RSV controversy probably were not surprised to find the "virgin" of Isaiah 7:14 restored in the new Bible. Translator and later NIV executive secretary Kenneth L. Barker defended the restoration on the grounds that scholars had not "convincingly demonstrated" that *almah* did *not* mean "virgin."[12] Other disputed passages from the RSV controversy also reappeared in their traditional form. The NIV restored the controverted "Kiss the Son" of Psalm 2:12. The paean in Psalm 45:6 to the "divine throne" of a Jewish king reemerged as an apostrophe to God ("Your throne, O God") in the NIV. In the New Testament, the testimony of Luke 24:6 ("He is not here; he has risen!") was restored. And in Romans 9:5, "God" was again made to modify "Christ."

The NIV translators were not hostile to all judgments of modern textual criticism. Mark 16:9–20, relegated to a footnote in the RSV, was separated by a line from the rest of the NIV text and flagged with a warning that the earliest manuscripts and other ancient witnesses lacked the passage. Meanwhile, the RSV's much-assailed reference to Jesus' "father" (Luke 2:33) also appeared as "father" in the NIV. And the infamous proof-text of the Trinity, the Comma Johanneum of 1 John 5:7, was printed as a footnote in the NIV. The NIV translators did not, therefore, ally themselves with staunch defenders of the sixteenth-century *Textus Receptus* but instead drew eclectically from the "best current printed texts of the Greek New Testament."[13]

In the final analysis, however, the NIV lived up to its billing as a more "evangelical" Bible than the RSV. As expected, the primary instances of conservative influence were Old Testament passages that the translators rendered christologically. While some of these involved problems of semantics (e.g., Isaiah 7:14), others involved problems of capitalization. (Hebrew manuscripts, like Greek, lacked capital letters.) Thus Psalm 2, one of the most frequently cited messianic proof-texts in the Christian tradition, was replete with capitals in the NIV ("Anointed One," 2:2; "One," 2:4; "King," 2:6; "Son," 2:7, 2:12). Similar instances of capitalization occurred in Psalm 16:10 ("Holy One") and Daniel 9:25–26 ("Anointed One").[14] NIV translator Bruce Waltke, professor of Old Testament at Westminster Seminary, explained that though the royal terms in Psalm 2 might have been left uncapitalized on the "historical level," he and his colleagues were more interested in the "canonical level." By their use of capitalization in Psalm 2, Waltke wrote, the NIV translators made plain their "orthodox views not only of inspiration but also of christology."[15]

Although academic reviewers were quick to criticize such christological treatment of the Old Testament, their attitudes toward the new version were generally positive. Critiquing the new Bible for *Christianity Today*, Fuller Seminary's William Sanford LaSor singled out as erroneous the new Bible's rendering of Isaiah 7:14, Psalm 2:12, and Daniel 9:26 but congratulated the translators for producing a generally reliable translation.[16] Similarly, in reviewing the NIV for the *Journal of the Evangelical Theological Society*, Peter C. Craigie noted the "theological assumptions" behind the capitalizations in Psalm 2 and Daniel 9 but praised the new version as a "magnificent monument" to biblical scholarship.[17] And *Good News Bible* translator Robert Bratcher, while lamenting the "Christian bias" in Psalm 2 and elsewhere, nevertheless hailed the NIV as a "significant achievement" and an "occasion for rejoicing." Bratcher put his finger on a significant irony: though advertised as a more contemporary translation than the RSV, the NIV was in fact closest in style to its liberal cousin. The NIV, he observed, "came into being as the result of a repudiation of the RSV by the majority of conservative Protestants in this country, and now that it has appeared it closely resembles the RSV."[18]

Indeed, the differences between the NIV and the RSV were undoubtedly more symbolic than substantive, just as the differences between conservatives and liberals in Bible translation had always been more about Protestant party politics than about Hebrew and Greek philology. The NIV finally offered evangelicals an ideologically safe alternative to the RSV, despite NIV committee members' occasional denials that their translation was specifically "evangelical" rather than simply faithful to the originals.[19] Evangelical consumers, in turn, helped make the NIV an instant commercial success: the initial press run of 1.2 million copies sold out in advance, and by 1996 a phenomenal hundred million copies were in print.[20] Although the NIV project had brought the New York Bible Society to the brink of bankruptcy, the proceeds from sales of the Bible put the society on firm financial footing. The NIV also prompted the NYBS to rechristen itself the New York International Bible Society, and later simply the International Bible Society. The society's new status was symbolized by its 1988 move to Colorado Springs, Colorado, a burgeoning evangelical mecca boasting the headquarters of more than sixty conservative Protestant organizations. A percentage of the royalties from the NIV contributed to the society's extensive missionary efforts, dedicated chiefly to the publication of the Bible in more than five hundred languages.[21]

The NIV's success was therefore a parable of evangelicalism's triumph in postwar America. The liberal Protestant establishment now faced competition from a conservative establishment every bit as powerful as the erstwhile "mainline." The NIV also illustrated conservatives' willingness to unite behind organizations such as the National Association of Evangelicals and the New York Bible Society—at least for the perceived cause of Holy Writ. Even so, evangelicals had never pursued conciliarism for its own sake in quite the same manner as the liberals. The National Council of Churches had hailed the RSV as an instrument of Protestant ecumenism, yet the RSV had now been eclipsed in sales by a Bible whose primary rationale was not the unity of the church but the unity of Scripture. The NIV demonstrated the resilience of "inerrancy" as a rallying cry among American Protestants and proved the marketability of a conservative view of the Old Testament's relationship to the New.

THE CONTEMPORARY BABEL OF BIBLES

Despite the evangelical dominance of the Bible market, officials at the National Council of Churches never completely abandoned the dream of a Bible for all Christians. Two new ecumenical editions of the RSV appeared during the 1970s. The RSV Common Bible (1973) was conceived in part by Lady Priscilla Collins, a convert to Catholicism and wife of Scottish publishing magnate Sir William Collins, who wanted a Bible acceptable to Protestant, Catholic, and Eastern Orthodox Christians.[22] Four years later, an expanded edition of the *Oxford Annotated Bible* improved upon the Common Bible by including 3 and 4 Maccabees and Psalm 151, recognized by most Orthodox communions as authoritative.[23]

Of more lasting consequence was the attempt, prompted by the women's movement of the sixties and seventies, to render the RSV's language gender inclusive. Under chairmen Herbert G. May and then Bruce M. Metzger, the RSV committee identified many references in the version to "man" and "men" that were not supported by the original Hebrew or Greek.[24] In 1974 the committee's membership also became more inclusive with the addition of its first woman, Lucetta Mowry of Wellesley College. Eventually, the committee decided that gender inclusiveness justified a complete overhaul of the RSV, which appeared in 1990 as the New Revised Standard Version. By that time, some fifty-five million copies of the old RSV had been sold, and the National Council of Churches hoped the NRSV would enjoy similar success in the mainline churches.[25] But the NRSV faced a much more crowded Bible market, in which each new version seemed destined to be surpassed within a few years of publication.

Indeed, only five years after the NRSV's release, a separate group of scholars decided that the new Bible had not gone far enough in purging Scripture of exclusive terminology. The editors of *The New Testament and Psalms: An Inclusive Version* took the NRSV text and systematically emended all potentially oppressive language. Whereas for William Tyndale the oppressive word in Matthew 16:18–19 had been "church," for the Inclusive Version editors the oppressive word was "kingdom." In Matthew and all other occurrences of "kingdom," they opted for the purportedly less patriarchal alternative "dominion." Elsewhere, the Inclusive Version changed God the "Father" to "Father-Mother," which, as the translators pointed out, "is not even understandable as a literal statement," thereby emphasizing the metaphorical nature of God-language.[26] Apart from the problem of gender, the editors attempted to mitigate the anti-Jewish tone of the Fourth Gospel by substituting "religious authorities" for John's references to "the Jews."[27]

Many evangelicals were critical of liberal attempts to render Scripture more inclusive. When the NIV committee announced plans in 1997 to introduce in America an inclusive-language edition that had already been tested in Britain, prominent evangelical leaders, including James Dobson and Jerry Falwell, cried foul. Dobson's conservative organization, Focus on the Family, declared that Bible translators "must resist even the subtlest form of language which would serve a particular cultural agenda."[28] After leaders of the Southern Baptist Convention threatened to boycott the proposed version, Zondervan and the International Bible Society abandoned the plan. Yet conservatives' purported concern for "value-free" translation in some cases barely concealed their own commitments to patriarchally encoded biblical language.

Meanwhile, a quick glance through the religion section of any bookstore revealed an array of "study Bibles" catering to particular sexes (*Women's Devotional Bible, Men's Devotional Bible*), particular races (*Original African Heritage Study Bible, African-American Devotional Bible*), particular age groups (*Student Bible, Young Explorer's Bible*), particular denominations (*Wesley Bible, Concordia Reference Bible*), and a variety of other constituencies (*Recovery Devotional Bible, New Believer's Bible*).[29] Most of these Bibles were conservative theologically, and all of them partook of the insight, demonstrated by the Geneva Bible four centuries earlier, that glosses on Scripture could be as influential, and nearly as canonical, as the biblical texts themselves. The explosion in Bible-publishing did not escape the attention of the popular press, which printed endless feature stories on the array of scriptural options. Articles exploring more fundamental issues, particularly during the Christmas season, also were common. *Time* magazine's 18 December 1995 cover story perfectly summarized the dilemma of modern theology: "Is the Bible Fact or Fiction?"

The Reformation's *sola scriptura,* transfigured by the historical-critical revolutions of the eighteenth and nineteenth centuries, had therefore produced by the end of the twentieth century a context in which every word of Scripture had been translated, annotated, and published many times over—all in an incessant quest for the sure foundation of historical fact. Unfortunately, the realities of the critical context meant that even the most uncompromisingly conservative of Bibles would never fully settle the truth-question, for the biblical text would still be evaluated by modern standards of rationality. Fundamentalists who professed unswerving faith in every jot and tittle of Holy Writ still tended to subject the Bible's claims to the scientific criteria of "evidence" and "proof."[30] The very shibboleth of inerrancy presupposed a disjunction between the biblical story and real history. Conservative Bible-readers tended to find complete truth in the text, while liberals tended to find only partial truth; yet for both, history would always exist, to a greater or lesser degree, in discordance with the Scriptures.

THE "VIRGIN TEXT" AS THE CHURCH'S BOOK

It is this truth-obsessed reading of Scripture, not the Babel of Bibles per se, that deserves greater scrutiny. Surely no lover of Scripture can lament the great increase in text-critical knowledge or the accompanying proliferation of translations since the sixteenth century. The sometimes ignoble commercialism of the Bible business should not be allowed to obscure the genuine evangelical zeal of most Bible translators and editors, who, like William Tyndale so long ago, have expended great effort to make Scripture accessible to the average person. The missionary impulse has united even the most theologically opposing translators in a common quest for versions of Scripture that people can, to quote the *Book of Common Prayer,* "read, mark, learn, and inwardly digest."

The inward digestion of Scripture, however, has often proven difficult in a critical context where biblical stories and their translation are endlessly subordinated to the quest for the "real Jesus." The problem of modern Bible-reading is the problem of Isaiah 7:14 writ large—the confusion of textual with historical questions—and this exegetical indigestion is nearly impossible to neutralize, even by so potent a pill as Hans Frei's *Eclipse of Biblical Narrative.* Frei's is nevertheless a powerful case for a more literary, aesthetic reading of Scripture.[31] This method does not exclude truth-questions but brackets them in favor of exegesis that treats the Bible as something like a realistic novel. For Frei, the biblical novel's individual stories are to be read not primarily for their external referents in "real history" but for their internal relations as part of a larger narrative. "Narrative" reading is simultaneously literal and typological: the stories mean what they say, and they relate to each other by providential juxtaposition.[32]

To be sure, the literal sense is not always clear, as Isaiah 7:14 again proves. Some Christians have interpreted the verse as a literal reference to Christ's birth, while others have interpreted it as a typological reference. Yet literal and typological reading, however employed in particular cases, both came naturally in a precritical age. In a critical context, literalism and typology tend to be refracted through the problem of historical truth. The question is one no longer primarily of *internal* reference, whether literal or typological, but of *external* reference to the facts of real history.[33] Frei by no means argued that real historical questions are unimportant, but for him Bible-reading was primarily a matter of discerning Scripture's own internal relations.[34] In Frei's vision, the epic narrative of salvation history was a thing of well-nigh mystical beauty, not unlike the medieval stained-glass windows that Protestant iconoclasts once sought to destroy.

What then becomes of truth-questions? To ignore them completely is to denature the Gospel itself, as reviewers of Frei's "narrative" theological program have never tired of pointing out.[35] But as the story of modern Bible battles has made clear, truth-questions ultimately are settled not by the Book but by the Church. Despite their stated reliance on the Book alone, Protestants in the end have invoked the authority of ecclesiastical (or quasi-ecclesiastical) entities to pass judgment upon particular translations and interpretations of Holy Writ. The Protestant *sola scriptura* inevitably has existed in tension with the linguistic instability of the translated Bible and the legitimate needs of believing communities to limit doctrinal variation.

Bible translation controversies, in other words, always come down to the foundational problem of the Reformation—the choice between Book and Church that redrew the political map of Europe and spilled the blood of William Tyndale. It is fervently to be hoped that future stewards of Book and Church recognize the limitations, as well as the magnificent possibilities, of both.

Notes

Introduction

1. As with all such designations, "conservative" and "liberal" are relative terms; to attempt precise definitions is to invite endless criticism. Nevertheless, I shall use the terms as they are conventionally used in the field of American religious history: "conservative" as shorthand for persons who espouse some doctrine of biblical inerrancy or infallibility, and "liberal" as shorthand for persons who may revere the Bible but who regard it as more or less historically conditioned. On the problems and prospects of "conservative" and "liberal" as analytical categories, see Douglas Jacobsen and William Vance Trollinger, Jr., eds., *Re-Forming the Center: American Protestantism, 1900 to the Present* (Grand Rapids, Mich.: Eerdmans, 1998).

2. On the uniqueness of the Bible's claim to authority, see Erich Auerbach, *Mimesis: The Representation of Reality in Western Literature,* translated by Willard R. Trask (Princeton: Princeton University Press, 1953), 14–16.

3. On notions of image and light in medieval art and theology, see Otto Von Simson, *The Gothic Cathedral: Origins of Gothic Architecture and the Medieval Concept of Order,* 3rd ed., Bollingen Series no. 48 (Princeton: Princeton University Press, 1988), 51–55, 120–22. The phrase "image of the invisible" comes from Pseudo-Dionysius, the sixth-century mystic whose writings profoundly influenced medieval theology and theories of Gothic architecture; see Paul Rorem, *Pseudo-Dionysius: A Commentary on the Texts and an Introduction to Their Influence* (New York: Oxford University Press, 1993), 28. On the didactic function of Gothic art, see Umberto Eco, *Art and Beauty in the Middle Ages,* translated by Hugh Bredin (New Haven: Yale University Press, 1986), 15–16.

4. Eamon Duffy, *The Stripping of the Altars: Traditional Religion in England, 1400–1580* (New Haven: Yale University Press, 1992), 63–68; on the Eucharist and the dramatic importance of the Host, 91, 95–96. On catechesis

in England after the Reformation, see Ian Green, *The Christian's ABC: Catechisms and Catechizing in England c. 1530–1740* (Oxford: Clarendon Press, 1996).

5. The Latin Vulgate's gradual standardization, a process completed only at the Council of Trent, is recounted by Raphael Loewe, "The Medieval History of the Latin Vulgate," in *The Cambridge History of the Bible,* vol. 2, *The West from the Fathers to the Reformation,* edited by P. R. Ackroyd, C. F. Evans, G. W. H. Lampe, and S. L. Greenslade (Cambridge: Cambridge University Press, 1969), 102–54; on medieval iconographic representations of the biblical story, see R. L. P. Milburn, "The 'People's Bible': Artists and Commentators," in the same volume, 280–308.

6. Hans W. Frei, *The Eclipse of Biblical Narrative: A Study in Eighteenth and Nineteenth Century Hermeneutics* (New Haven: Yale University Press, 1974), 1–50. The description of the Middle Ages as a "culture of the Book" is from Norman F. Cantor, *Civilization of the Middle Ages,* rev. ed. (New York: HarperCollins, 1993), 21.

7. Auerbach, *Mimesis,* 74, 15.

8. The standard account of Puritan primitivism, or the repristination of biblical history, is Theodore Dwight Bozeman, *To Live Ancient Lives: The Primitivist Dimension in Puritanism* (Chapel Hill: University of North Carolina Press, 1988).

9. R. G. Collingwood, *An Essay on Metaphysics* (Oxford: Clarendon Press, 1940), 31–32. For a critical assessment of the relation of "absolute presuppositions" to Collingwood's metaphysics, see Alan Donagan, *The Later Philosophy of R. G. Collingwood* (Oxford: Clarendon Press, 1962), 262–307; compare James Patrick, *The Magdalen Metaphysicals: Idealism and Orthodoxy at Oxford, 1901–1945* (Macon, Ga.: Mercer University Press, 1985), 77–108. On the medieval presupposition of the Bible's truth, see also Beryl Smalley, *The Study of the Bible in the Middle Ages,* 3rd ed. (Oxford: Basil Blackwell, 1983), 1, 24. Smalley argues that although medieval scholars might "in rare moments of scepticism" doubt the narrative's "spirit" (its interpretation based on typology, allegory, etc.), they never doubted the narrative's "letter" (its literal-historical sense).

10. Frei, *Eclipse of Biblical Narrative,* 29–30.

11. Compare the extensive typology in the Letter to the Hebrews. On typology within the biblical books themselves, see Thomas M. Davis, "The Traditions of Puritan Typology," in *Typology and Early American Literature,* edited by Sacvan Bercovitch (Amherst: University of Massachusetts Press, 1972), 16.

12. Auerbach, *Mimesis,* 73–74.

13. On the Reformation and typology, see Frei, *Eclipse of Biblical Narrative,* 18–37. On continuities between medieval and Reformation exegesis

broadly considered, see, for example, Alister McGrath, *The Intellectual Origins of the European Reformation* (Oxford: Blackwell, 1987), 122–23, 140–41, 148–49, 201–2; and Roy A. Harrisville and Walter Sundberg, *The Bible in Modern Culture: Theology and Historical-Critical Method from Spinoza to Käsemann* (Minneapolis: Fortress Press, 1995), 14–22.

14. On the seventeenth-century background, an essential supplement to Frei is Klaus Scholder, *The Birth of Modern Critical Theology: Origins and Problems of Biblical Criticism in the Seventeenth Century,* translated by John Bowden (London: SCM Press, 1990). Scholder traces the gradual breakdown of medieval theology under the influence of Copernican cosmology, Cartesian philosophy, and other developments.

15. Frei, *Eclipse of Biblical Narrative,* 42–50. Collins and other English Deists are surveyed in Henning Graf Reventlow, *The Authority of the Bible and the Rise of the Modern World,* translated by John Bowden (Philadelphia: Fortress Press, 1985).

16. Edwards was well aware of Deism, but he encountered it chiefly through Collins and other Old World thinkers; see Kenneth P. Minkema, "The Other Unfinished 'Great Work': Jonathan Edwards, Messianic Prophecy, and 'The Harmony of the Old and New Testament,'" in *Jonathan Edwards's Writings: Text, Context, Interpretation,* edited by Stephen J. Stein (Bloomington: Indiana University Press, 1996), 52–65. On Edwards as a precritical exegete, see the editor's introduction to *The Works of Jonathan Edwards,* vol. 15, *Notes on Scripture,* edited by Stephen J. Stein (New Haven: Yale University Press, 1998), 12–21.

17. Frei, *Eclipse of Biblical Narrative,* 4.

18. The classic account is Henry F. May, *The Enlightenment in America* (New York: Oxford University Press, 1976). See also James Turner, *Without God, Without Creed: The Origins of Unbelief in America* (Baltimore: Johns Hopkins University Press, 1985), especially chapter 1, which is a good introduction to the breakdown of the medieval synthesis in Western thought.

The extent of the Enlightenment's "modernity" has been debated ever since Carl Becker argued that the eighteenth-century philosophers were essentially medieval theologians in disguise. See Carl L. Becker, *The Heavenly City of the Eighteenth-Century Philosophers* (New Haven: Yale University Press, 1932); compare Raymond O. Rockwood, ed., *Carl Becker's Heavenly City Revisited* (Ithaca, N.Y.: Cornell University Press, 1958; reprint, Hamden, Conn.: Archon Books, 1968). Becker's essay is, at the very least, a reminder that the Enlightenment was not the only antecedent of modern historicism.

19. Theodore Dwight Bozeman, *Protestants in an Age of Science: The Baconian Ideal and Antebellum Religious Thought* (Chapel Hill: University of North Carolina Press, 1977), especially 138–43. On the influence of Scottish Common Sense philosophy, see Mark A. Noll, *Princeton and the Republic,*

1768–1822: The Search for a Christian Enlightenment in the Era of Samuel Stanhope Smith (Princeton: Princeton University Press, 1989), especially 36–43, 117–23; and Mark A. Noll, "Common Sense Traditions and American Evangelical Thought," *American Quarterly* 37 (1985): 216–38.

20. Quoted in Bozeman, *Protestants in an Age of Science,* 141.

21. On the influence of Darwinism, see Jon H. Roberts, *Darwinism and the Divine in America: Protestant Intellectuals and Organic Evolution, 1859–1900* (Madison: University of Wisconsin Press, 1988). On Comtean positivism, see Charles D. Cashdollar, *The Transformation of Theology, 1830–1890: Positivism and Protestant Thought in Britain and America* (Princeton: Princeton University Press, 1989).

22. On the meaning of historical consciousness in the American context, see Grant Wacker, "The Demise of Biblical Civilization," in *The Bible in America: Essays in Cultural History,* edited by Nathan O. Hatch and Mark A. Noll (New York: Oxford University Press, 1982), 121–38. For a more general view, see R. G. Collingwood, *The Idea of History* (Oxford: Clarendon Press, 1946). For more on higher (and "lower") biblical criticism, see chapter 2.

23. Frei, *Eclipse of Biblical Narrative,* 7.

24. See ibid., 69, for the critical treatment of Isaiah 7:14 by Anthony Collins; compare the precritical treatment of the same verse by John Calvin, 26. Isaiah 7:14 had been debated since the earliest Christian centuries, especially in the context of Jewish-Christian polemics.

25. Hans W. Frei, *Types of Christian Theology,* edited by George Hunsinger and William C. Placher (New Haven: Yale University Press, 1992), 84.

26. The epistemological kinship of conservatives and liberals has not been fully appreciated by interpreters of American religion. Sociologist James Davison Hunter, for example, claims that conservatives and liberals operate within "two fundamentally different cultural systems" or "two different ways of apprehending reality, of ordering experience." Along similar lines, Kathleen C. Boone incorrectly invokes Frei when she refers to fundamentalist exegesis as "precritical." See James Davison Hunter, *Culture Wars: The Struggle to Define America* (New York: Basic Books, 1991), 43–45, 128–32, 161; and Kathleen C. Boone, *The Bible Tells Them So: The Discourse of Protestant Fundamentalism* (Albany: State University of New York Press, 1989), 46.

27. In the case of the RSV, see, for example, Millar Burrows, *Diligently Compared: The Revised Standard Version and the King James Version of the Old Testament* (New York: Thomas Nelson and Sons, 1964).

28. Several recent works have highlighted various aspects of the diverse American Bible market: Philip L. Barlow, *Mormons and the Bible: The Place of the Latter-day Saints in American Religion* (New York: Oxford University Press, 1991); Paul C. Gutjahr, *An American Bible: A History of the Good Book in the United States, 1777–1880* (Stanford, Calif.: Stanford University Press,

1999); Colleen McDannell, *Material Christianity: Religion and Popular Culture in America* (New Haven: Yale University Press, 1995); Stephen J. Stein, "America's Bibles: Canon, Commentary, and Community," *Church History* 64 (1995): 169–84; and Peter J. Wosh, *Spreading the Word: The Bible Business in Nineteenth-Century America* (Ithaca, N.Y.: Cornell University Press, 1994). The definitive, though unfortunately never updated, catalogue of American Bible versions is Margaret T. Hills, *The English Bible in America: A Bibliography of Editions of the Bible and the New Testament Published in America 1777–1957* (New York: American Bible Society, 1961). See also William J. Chamberlin, *Catalogue of English Bible Translations: A Classified Bibliography of Versions and Editions Including Books, Parts, and Old and New Testament Apocrypha and Apocryphal Books* (Westport, Conn.: Greenwood Press, 1991). For general surveys of Anglo-American Bible translation, see Harry M. Orlinsky and Robert G. Bratcher, *A History of Bible Translation and the North American Contribution* (Atlanta: Scholars Press, 1991); and F. F. Bruce, *History of the Bible in English*, 3rd ed. (Cambridge, England: Lutterworth Press, 1979). For broader cultural perspectives on the Bible in Anglo-American life, see Edwin S. Gaustad and Walter Harrelson, eds., *The Bible in American Culture*, 6 vols. (Philadelphia: Fortress Press, 1982–85); and Hatch and Noll, *The Bible in America*. Finally, for two multivolume attempts to tell the Bible's story from the beginning, see P. R. Ackroyd, C. F. Evans, G. W. H. Lampe, and S. L. Greenslade, eds., *The Cambridge History of the Bible*, 3 vols. (Cambridge: Cambridge University Press, 1963–70); and Charles Kannengiesser, ed., *Bible de tous les temps*, 8 vols. (Paris: Éditions Beauchesne, 1984–85).

29. Becker, *Heavenly City of the Eighteenth-Century Philosophers*, 11–19, especially 16.

Chapter 1

1. Below the mosaic is a reminder of the nationalism that often accompanies biblicism: a bronze shield with the Prussian eagle bearing on his breast the letters "FR" (Fridericus Rex). On the history of the Wittenberg Thesentür, see Helmar Junghans, *Wittenberg als Lutherstadt* (Göttingen: Vandenhoeck and Ruprecht, 1979), 184.

2. German original: "die einige Regel und Richtschnur." "Die Konkordienformel" (Formula of Concord), in Hans Lietzmann, Heinrich Bornkamm, Hans Volz, and Ernst Wolf, eds., *Die Bekenntnisschriften der evangelisch-lutherischen Kirche*, 11th ed. (Göttingen: Vandenhoeck and Ruprecht, 1992), 767. The number of printings of Luther's New Testament is from Lewis W. Spitz, *The Protestant Reformation, 1517–1559* (New York: Harper and Row, 1985), 89.

3. On the inconspicuous place of Lutherans in American religious culture, see Mark A. Noll, "Ethnic, American, or Lutheran? Dilemmas for a Historic Confession in the New World," *Lutheran Theological Seminary Bulletin* [Gettysburg, Pa.] 71, no. 1 (1991): 17–38.

4. Cotton is quoted in Perry Miller, *The New England Mind: The Seventeenth Century* (Cambridge: Harvard University Press, 1939), 468; Alexander Campbell, "A Restoration of the Ancient Order of Things. No. 1," *Christian Baptist* 2 (1825); reprint, Cincinnati: D. S. Burnet and Benjamin Franklin, 1852), 127–28.

5. Bernard M. G. Reardon, *Religious Thought in the Reformation,* 2nd ed. (London: Longman, 1995), 64. Elsewhere Luther wrote that in Christ, "all words form but a single Word" (ibid., 64).

6. "Preface to the New Testament" (1522, revised 1546); English translation in *Martin Luther's Basic Theological Writings,* edited by Timothy F. Lull (Minneapolis: Fortress Press, 1989), 117; Heiko A. Oberman, *Luther: Man between God and the Devil,* translated by Eileen Walliser-Schwarzbart (New York: Image Books, 1992), 173–74, originally published as *Luther: Mensch zwischen Gott und Teufel* (Berlin: Severin und Seidler, 1982). On Luther's view of the primacy of the spoken word over the written, see Willem Jan Kooiman, *Luther and the Bible,* translated by John Schmidt (Philadelphia: Muhlenberg Press, 1961), 200–212, especially 206.

7. Alister McGrath, *The Intellectual Origins of the European Reformation* (Oxford: Blackwell, 1987), 122–23, 140–41, 148–49, 201–2; on Aquinas and Rimini, 122–23, 148–49; compare David C. Steinmetz, *Luther in Context* (Bloomington: Indiana University Press, 1986; reprint, Grand Rapids, Mich.: Baker Books, 1995), especially 47–58.

8. Sermon delivered at Wittenberg, 12 March 1522, in *Luther's Works,* vol. 51, edited and translated by John W. Doberstein (Philadelphia: Muhlenberg Press, 1959), 84–86.

9. For general reflections on sixteenth-century Lutheran iconography, see David Morgan, editor's introduction to *Icons of American Protestantism: The Art of Warner Sallman* (New Haven: Yale University Press, 1996), 6–7. See also Margaret R. Miles, *Image as Insight: Visual Understanding in Western Christianity and Secular Culture* (Boston: Beacon Press, 1985), 114–17.

10. The affinities of the early Reformed tradition with humanism are described in some detail in McGrath, *The Intellectual Origins of the European Reformation,* 43–59; compare 199–200. On Zwingli and Bucer, compare Reardon, *Religious Thought in the Reformation,* 89–92, 33–34, 245–47.

11. Charles Garside, Jr., *Zwingli and the Arts* (New Haven: Yale University Press, 1966), 44.

12. Carlos M. N. Eire, *War Against the Idols: The Reformation of Worship from Erasmus to Calvin* (Cambridge: Cambridge University Press, 1986), 308.

Eire recounts the iconoclasm in Geneva (122–51) and details Calvin's attack on idolatry (195–233). For a different account of Calvin's iconoclasm, see Ann Kibbey, *The Interpretation of Material Shapes in Puritanism: A Study of Rhetoric, Prejudice, and Violence* (Cambridge: Cambridge University Press, 1986), 42–64.

13. Reardon makes this point specifically in reference to Zwingli. See Reardon, *Religious Thought in the Reformation,* 89–92. On the Reformed application of *sola scriptura,* see McGrath, *Intellectual Origins of the European Reformation,* 150.

14. Both the Second Helvetic Confession (1566) and the Westminster Confession (1648) begin with sections on the authority and inspiration of the whole scriptural canon. In contrast, the Lutheran Augsburg Confession (1530) begins with an affirmation of the Nicene Creed and includes no separate section on Scripture. To be sure, seventeenth-century Lutheran orthodoxy was more rigid in its emphasis on scriptural authority, but this should not obscure the fundamental distinction between Lutheran and Reformed biblicism. See *The Book of Confessions* (Louisville, Ky.: Office of the General Assembly of the Presbyterian Church [U.S.A.], 1991), and *The Book of Concord: The Confessions of the Evangelical Lutheran Church,* edited and translated by Theodore Tappert (Philadelphia: Fortress Press, 1959).

15. On Henrician iconoclasm, see John Phillips, *The Reformation of Images: Destruction of Art in England, 1535–1660* (Berkeley: University of California Press, 1973), 61–66, 77–79. Henry's moves toward Protestantism should not be allowed to obscure his abiding opposition to "Lutheran" dissenters and his enforcement of many traditional Catholic doctrines (e.g., transubstantiation). An excellent introduction, with annotated bibliography, to the religious significance of Henry's reign is Clifford S. L. Davies, "Henry VIII," in *The Oxford Encyclopedia of the Reformation,* edited by Hans J. Hillerbrand, vol. 2 (Oxford: Oxford University Press, 1996), 227–33. See also the more detailed study, Richard Rex, *Henry VIII and the English Reformation* (London: Macmillan, 1993). The Henrician injunctions are reprinted in Gerald Bray, ed., *Documents of the English Reformation* (Minneapolis: Fortress Press, 1994), 175–83.

16. On late-medieval English piety, see Eamon Duffy, *The Stripping of the Altars: Traditional Religion in England, 1400–1580* (New Haven: Yale University Press, 1992), 155–69. On the printing revolution and religion, see, for example, Stephen Greenblatt, *Renaissance Self-Fashioning: From More to Shakespeare* (Chicago: University of Chicago Press, 1980), especially chapter 2, "The Word of God in the Age of Mechanical Reproduction," 74–114.

17. Ira Maurice Price, William A. Irwin and Allen P. Wikgren, *The Ancestry of Our English Bible: An Account of Manuscripts, Texts, and Versions of the Bible,* 3rd ed. (New York: Harper and Brothers, 1956), 232–39; compare F. F.

Bruce, *History of the Bible in English,* 3rd ed. (Cambridge, England: Lutter-worth Press, 1978), 12–23. On Wycliffe as "morning star of the Reformation," see P. Marion Simms, *The Bible from the Beginning* (New York: Macmillan, 1929), 163.

18. John Wycliffe, *Tractatus de Officio Pastorali,* excerpted in *Wyclif: Select English Writings,* edited by Herbert E. Winn (London: Oxford University Press, 1929), 19.

19. Details on Tyndale's life are sketchy, but an assiduous recent recon-struction is David Daniell, *William Tyndale: A Biography* (New Haven: Yale University Press, 1994).

20. On the question of Lollardy, see Donald Dean Smeeton, *Lollard Themes in the Reformation Theology of William Tyndale,* Sixteenth Century Essays and Studies, vol. 6 (Kirksville, Mo.: Sixteenth Century Journal Publishers, 1986). On Zwinglian and Puritan parallels, see Leonard J. Trinterud, "The Origins of Puritanism," *Church History* 20 (1950): 37–57, and "A Reappraisal of William Tyndale's Debt to Martin Luther," *Church History* 31 (1962): 24–45; compare A. G. Dickens, *The English Reformation,* 2nd ed. (University Park, Pa.: Pennsylvania State University Press, 1989), 97.

21. Smeeton, *Lollard Themes,* 99–101.

22. In the Vulgate, the edition used by Catholic officialdom, the translation of ἐκκλησία was not an issue since Latin had absorbed into its vocabulary the transliterated Greek word (ecclesia). Modern English Bibles usually translate ἐκκλησία as "church" (cf. Matt. 16:18 in the RSV, NRSV, NIV, NASB, etc.). On the manifold semantic problems surrounding the Greek term, see Karl Ludwig Schmidt, "ἐκκλησία," in *Theological Dictionary of the New Testa-ment,* edited by Gerhard Kittel and translated by Geoffrey W. Bromiley (Grand Rapids, Mich.: Eerdmans, 1965), 3:501–36. On Tyndale's doctrine of the church, and its relation to his translation, see Smeeton, *Lollard Themes,* 159–220. The standard modern-spelling edition of Tyndale's 1534 New Testament is that edited by David Daniell, *Tyndale's New Testament* (New Haven: Yale University Press, 1989), who provides a useful introduction.

23. See 1 Corinthians 5:11 in Daniell, ed., *Tyndale's New Testament,* 248. Erasmus also interpreted εἰδωλολάτρης iconoclastically, rendering it as *simu-lacrorum cultor* (worshipper of images) in his 1519 Latin New Testament. In contrast, εἰδωλολάτρης appeared in Luther's 1545 German Bible as *Ab-göttischer* (idolater) and in the Vulgate as *idolis serviens* (slaves to idols). Modern English Bibles consistently translate εἰδωλολάτρης as "idolater." On the semantic issues involved, see Friedrich Büchsel, "εἰδωλολάτρης," in Kittel and Bromiley, *Theological Dictionary of the New Testament,* 2:375–97.

24. See 1 Corinthians 10:19 in Daniell, ed., *Tyndale's New Testament,* 252. Tyndale may have been influenced by Erasmus, who rendered εἰδωλόθυτόν as *simulacris immolatum* in his 1519 Latin New Testament. Tyndale translated

εἰδωλόθυτόν inconsistently, rendering it as "dedicate unto idols" ("dedicate" used as a noun) in 1 Corinthians 10:28 and "meat dedicate unto idols" in 1 Corinthians 8:4. On εἰδωλόθυτόν, see Kittel and Bromiley, *Theological Dictionary of the New Testament,* 2:378–79; and Walter Bauer, *A Greek-English Lexicon of the New Testament,* translated by William F. Arndt and F. Wilbur Gingrich, 2nd ed. edited by F. Wilbur Gingrich and Frederick W. Danker (Chicago: University of Chicago Press, 1979), 221.

25. William Tyndale, *An Answer to Sir Thomas More's Dialogue,* edited by Henry Walter (Cambridge: Cambridge University Press, 1850), 125.

26. David Daniell samples More's invective in *William Tyndale: A Biography,* 274–80.

27. Thomas More, "Confutation of Tyndale's Answer," in *The Complete Works of St. Thomas More,* edited by Louis A. Schuster, Richard C. Marius, James P. Lusardi and Richard J. Schoeck (New Haven: Yale University Press, 1973), vol. 8, pt. 1, pp. 173–77. I have updated More's orthography.

28. On Foxe's influence, particularly in England, see William Haller, *The Elect Nation: The Meaning and Relevance of Foxe's Book of Martyrs* (New York: Harper and Row, 1963); on Francis Drake and Foxe, see 221.

29. The adoption of Reformation principles by the monarchy was not necessarily accompanied by a popular groundswell in favor of Protestantism, as has traditionally been assumed. Indeed, scholars of the English Reformation disagree on the timing and extent of conversion to Protestantism among the laity. A revisionist account that introduces the issues of the debate is Christopher Haigh, ed., *The English Reformation Revised* (Cambridge: Cambridge University Press, 1987), especially 1–33.

30. On Edwardian iconoclasm, I am indebted to the exceptionally detailed account by Margaret Aston, *England's Iconoclasts,* vol. 1, *Laws Against Images* (Oxford: Clarendon Press, 1988), especially 255–57, 272–77. The Edwardian injunctions are reprinted in Bray, *Documents of the English Reformation,* 247–57. On religious change more generally during the reign of Edward VI, see Dickens, *The English Reformation,* 222–86. On Edward as Protestant icon, see John N. King, *Tudor Royal Iconography: Literature and Art in an Age of Religious Crisis* (Princeton: Princeton University Press, 1989), 90–101.

31. Diarmaid MacCulloch suggests that a coherent "Reformed" stance did not yet exist in this period; he refers instead to Cranmer as a key advocate of the "evangelical stance." See Diarmaid MacCulloch, *Thomas Cranmer: A Life* (New Haven: Yale University Press, 1996), 173. On Cranmer's relationship to Bucer, see Reardon, *Religious Thought in the Reformation,* 228–45; compare John T. McNeill, *The History and Character of Calvinism* (Oxford: Oxford University Press, 1954), 309–13.

The extent of Bucer's influence in England is still debated. See David F.

Wright, "Martin Bucer and England—and Scotland," in *Martin Bucer and Sixteenth Century Europe*, edited by Christian Krieger and Marc Lienhard, vol. 2 (Leiden: Brill, 1993), 523–32; and Basil Hall, "Martin Bucer in England," in *Martin Bucer: Reforming Church and Community* (Cambridge: Cambridge University Press, 1994), 144–60.

32. The "ten commandments" appear in Exodus 20:1–17 and Deuteronomy 5:6–21, but their mode of division into ten separate precepts is not clear. Margaret Aston (*England's Iconoclasts*, 372–92) offers a detailed history of this perennial exegetical problem.

33. Reardon, *Religious Thought in the Reformation*, 242–43; compare Roland H. Bainton, *The Reformation of the Sixteenth Century*, enl. ed. (Boston: Beacon Press, 1985), 202. For a detailed exposition of Cranmer's 1549 and 1552 prayer books, see Horton Davies, *Worship and Theology in England*, vol. 1, *From Cranmer to Hooker, 1534–1603* (Princeton: Princeton University Press, 1970), 173–210. On the evolution of Cranmer's eucharistic doctrine, see MacCulloch, *Thomas Cranmer*, especially 614–17; MacCulloch rejects the view that Cranmer's (or Zwingli's) mature eucharistic doctrine was "mere memorialism," yet he admits that Cranmer, partly under Bucer's influence, gradually abandoned any idea of eucharistic real presence.

34. On Cranmer and the Great Bible, see MacCulloch, *Thomas Cranmer*, 238–40, 258–60. Cranmer's preface is reprinted in Bray, *Documents of the English Reformation*, 233–43.

35. On the Geneva Bible, see P. R. Ackroyd, C. F. Evans, G. W. H. Lampe, and S. L. Greenslade, eds., *The Cambridge History of the Bible*, vol. 3, *The West from the Reformation to the Present Day* (Cambridge: Cambridge University Press, 1963), 155–59; and Christopher Hill, *The English Bible and the Seventeenth-Century Revolution* (London: Penguin Books, 1993), 56–66. The 1560 edition of the Geneva Bible has been reprinted in facsimile (edited, with a useful introduction, by Lloyd Berry) by the University of Wisconsin Press (Madison, 1969); the 1602 Tomson edition has been reprinted in facsimile by Pilgrim Press (Cleveland, 1989).

36. David Daniell, *William Tyndale*, 4, 392 n. 1; J. F. Mozley, *John Foxe and His Book* (London: Society for Promoting Christian Knowledge, 1940), 168. In reviewing Daniell's book, Richard W. Pfaff in effect accused Daniell of producing a Foxe-like hagiography characterized by "assertive partisanship" and "apologetic championship" (*Church History* 65 [1996]: 269–71). I share Pfaff's reservations, while nevertheless saluting Daniell's painstaking attention to detail.

37. Mozley, *John Foxe and His Book*, 155.

38. *The Acts and Monuments of John Foxe*, edited by George Townsend and Stephen Reed Cattley (London, 1838), 5:114–21.

39. Ibid., 127.

40. Ibid., 118.

41. Also in 1582, Martin published *A Discoverie of the Manifold Corruptions of the Holy Scriptures by the Heretikes of Our Daies,* provoking much Protestant hostility. This treatise formed the basis a century later for another Catholic polemic, Thomas Ward's *Errata to the Protestant Bible* (London, 1688), which in turn drew several sharp Protestant responses.

42. Preface to the Rheims New Testament (1582), in Bray, *Documents of the English Reformation,* 367, 374–75, 380–81.

43. Willliam [*sic*] Fulke, *Confutation of the Rhemish Testament, with an Introductory Essay; Including a Biographical Notice of the Author, and a Complete Topical and Textual Index* (New York, 1834). Cartwright apparently started this work, but Fulke completed it; see *Dictionary of National Biography,* vol. 7, s.v. "Fulke, William." (1885–1901; reprint, 66 vols. in 22, London: Oxford University Press, 1949–50).

44. Christopher Hill, *The Century of Revolution, 1603–1714,* Norton Library History of England (New York: Norton, 1961), 97.

45. Harold R. Willoughby, *Soldiers' Bibles through Three Centuries* (Chicago: University of Chicago Press, 1944), 2–5.

46. Horton Davies, *Worship and Theology in England,* vol. 2, *From Andrewes to Baxter and Fox, 1603–1690* (Princeton: Princeton University Press, 1975), 7–13.

47. The Geneva Bible for a time remained the favorite of more separatistic Puritans such as Anne Hutchinson, who recited lengthy Geneva passages from memory during her 1637 heresy trial. See Harry S. Stout, "Word and Order in Colonial New England," in *The Bible in America: Essays in Cultural History,* edited by Nathan O. Hatch and Mark A. Noll (New York: Oxford University Press, 1982), 19–38.

48. Liah Greenfeld, *Nationalism: Five Roads to Modernity* (Cambridge: Harvard University Press, 1992), 52–53. The best overview of the Bible's relation to English nationalism is Hill, *The English Bible and the Seventeenth-Century Revolution,* especially chapter 1, "A Biblical Culture," 3–44.

49. The best study of American Puritan preaching is Harry S. Stout, *The New England Soul: Preaching and Religious Culture in Colonial New England* (New York: Oxford University Press, 1986). On Puritan literacy rates, see Kenneth A. Lockridge, *Literacy in Colonial New England: An Enquiry into the Social Context of Literacy in the Early Modern West* (New York: Norton, 1974).

50. Frye borrows the term from William Blake. See Frye, *The Great Code: The Bible and Literature* (San Diego: Harcourt Brace Jovanovich, 1982), xvi.

51. On Bible-reading in the schools as an aspect of Protestant nativism, see Ray Allen Billington, *The Protestant Crusade, 1800–1860: A Study of the Origins of American Nativism* (New York: Macmillan, 1938; reprint, Chicago:

Quadrangle Books, 1964), 142–65. For Scofield's reading of the Whore of Babylon, see the footnote at Revelation 17 in *The Scofield Reference Bible,* edited by C. I. Scofield et al. (New York: Oxford University Press, 1917), 1010.

52. An excellent example of this tendency is John Lewis, *A Complete History of the Several Translations of the Holy Bible, and New Testament, into English, Both in MS. and in Print: And of the most Remarkable Editions of them since the Invention of Printing,* 2nd ed. (London, 1739), especially the introductory "Dissertation," iii–xvii.

53. For example, J. Paterson Smyth's *How We Got Our Bible* (Philadelphia: Westminster Press), first published in 1886, saw fifteen printings by the turn of the century.

54. H[annah] C[haplin] Conant, *The English Bible: History of the Translation of the Holy Scriptures into the English Tongue: With Specimens of the Old English Versions* (New York: Sheldon, Blakeman, 1856), 15–17; compare 2–3 in updated edition edited by Thomas Jefferson Conant, *The Popular History of the Translation of the Holy Scriptures into the English Tongue* (New York: I. K. Funk, 1881).

55. John W. Lea, *The Book of Books and Its Wonderful Story: A Popular Handbook for Colleges, Bible Classes, Sunday Schools, and Private Students* (Philadelphia: John C. Winston, 1922), 6.

56. Francis Bacon, quoted in John Eadie, *The English Bible: An External and Critical History of the Various English Translations of Scripture,* vol. 1 (London: Macmillan, 1876), first page (not numbered).

57. H. W. Hamilton-Hoare, *The Evolution of the English Bible: An Historical Sketch of the Successive Versions from 1382 to 1885* (London: John Murray, 1901), 18–19.

58. Hugh Pope, *English Versions of the Bible,* edited by Sebastian Bullough (St. Louis: Herder, 1952), 62–69; compare Hugh Pope, *The Catholic Church and the Bible* (New York: Macmillan, 1928).

59. On the Hegelian idea of modernity, see Jürgen Habermas, *The Philosophical Discourse of Modernity,* translated by Frederick G. Lawrence (Cambridge: MIT Press, 1992), 16–17. On modernity's negative self-definition vis-à-vis the Middle Ages, see Brian Stock, *Listening for the Text: On the Uses of the Past* (Baltimore: Johns Hopkins University Press, 1990), 159–60; and Hans Blumenberg, *The Legitimacy of the Modern Age,* translated by Robert M. Wallace (Cambridge: MIT Press, 1983), 77. On Victorian medievalism, see Norman F. Cantor, *Inventing the Middle Ages: The Lives, Works, and Ideas of the Great Medievalists of the Twentieth Century* (New York: Quill, 1991), 28–29.

60. Hamilton-Hoare, *Evolution of the English Bible,* 61, 22.

61. James Baikie, *The English Bible and Its Story: Its Growth, Its Translators and Their Adventures* (Philadelphia: Lippincott, n.d.), 8.

62. John Stoughton, *Our English Bible: Its Translations and Translators* (London: Religious Tract Society, 1878), 2.

63. Christopher Anderson, *The Annals of the English Bible* (London: William Pickering, 1845), 1:xi–xii. On Anderson's career, see *Dictionary of National Biography,* vol. 1, s.v., "Anderson, Christopher."

64. Anderson, *Annals of the English Bible,* 2:568–70.

65. Josiah Strong, *Our Country: Its Possible Future and Its Present Crisis* (New York: Baker and Taylor, 1885); and Theodore Roosevelt, *The Winning of the West,* 4 vols. (New York: Putnam, 1889–96). A provocative recent study of American discourses of "civilization" is Gail Bederman, *Manliness and Civilization: A Cultural History of Gender and Race in the United States, 1880–1917* (Chicago: University of Chicago Press, 1995), especially chapter 5, "Theodore Roosevelt: Manhood, Nation, and 'Civilization.'"

66. On Lutheran glorification of the Luther Bible, see two histories published for its four hundredth anniversary: Johann Michael Reu, *Luther's German Bible: An Historical Presentation Together with a Collection of Sources* (Columbus, Ohio: Lutheran Book Concern, 1934); and P. E. Kretzmann, *The Story of the German Bible: A Contribution to the Quadricentennial of Luther's Translation* (St. Louis: Concordia, 1934). On the Lutheran embrace of Tyndale, see the tract by William Dallmann, *William Tyndale: The Translator of the English Bible* (St. Louis: Concordia, 1904).

67. The term "imagined community" comes from Benedict Anderson, who has noted the power of language (and vernacular Scripture) to increase a sense of nationhood. See chapter 3, "The Origins of National Consciousness," in *Imagined Communities: Reflections on the Origin and Spread of Nationalism,* rev. ed. (London: Verso, 1991), 37–46.

68. Brooke Foss Westcott, *A General View History of the English Bible,* 3rd ed., edited by William Aldis Wright (New York: Macmillan, 1905; originally published in 1868), 7, 25, 51–53, 281–82.

69. See, for example, William Tyndale, *An Answer to Sir Thomas More's Dialogue,* 61.

70. Conant, *Popular History,* 90.

71. James Anthony Froude, *History of England from the Fall of Wolsey to the Defeat of the Spanish Armada,* new ed. (London: Longmans, Green, 1873), 84.

72. Eadie, *The English Bible,* 1:122.

73. John Brown, *The History of the English Bible* (Cambridge: Cambridge University Press, 1911), 52.

74. J. Paterson Smyth, *How We Got Our Bible,* rev. ed. (Philadelphia: Westminster Press, 1889), 97.

75. Froude, *History of England,* 3:84.

76. Westcott, *A General View,* 281.

77. Simms, *The Bible from the Beginning,* 224. The American Standard Version was a slightly amended edition of the Revised Version incorporating mostly minor stylistic variations preferred by the American translators but vetoed by the British committee in 1881–85; see chapter 3.

78. P. Marion Simms, *The Bible in America: Versions That Have Played Their Part in the Making of the Republic* (New York: Wilson-Erickson, 1936), 211.

79. Smyth, *How We Got Our Bible.*

80. Quoted in Eadie, *The English Bible,* vol. 1, n. p.

Chapter 2

1. Quotations from the New York *Evening Post,* 21 May 1881; the *Chicago Tribune,* 20 May 1881; and the *Chicago Tribune,* 23 May 1881. Sales figures are from the *Chicago Tribune,* 26 May 1881; and Philip Schaff, *A Companion to the Greek Testament and English Version* (New York: Harper and Brothers, 1883), 404–5.

2. Although the Revised Version was the first major committee translation since the King James Bible, the idea of Bible revision was not unknown to the public prior to 1881. Throughout the nineteenth century a variety of translations, mainly by individuals, appeared. See Margaret T. Hills, *The English Bible in America: A Bibliography of Editions of the Bible and the New Testament Published in America 1777–1957* (New York: American Bible Society, 1961).

3. On the making of the Revised Version, see Schaff, *A Companion,* 371–494. For a brief evaluation of the version from a text-critical standpoint, see Harry M. Orlinsky and Robert G. Bratcher, *A History of Bible Translation and the North American Contribution* (Atlanta: Scholars Press, 1991), 45–47. From the standpoint of the history of American English, the best critique is Kenneth Cmiel, *Democratic Eloquence: The Fight over Popular Speech in Nineteenth-Century America* (New York: Morrow, 1990), 206–33.

4. Though I make frequent references to the British players in the Revised Version story, it should be remembered that the longer trajectories of Bible revision in Britain and in America are not identical.

5. For a complete list of the American and British committee members, see Schaff, *A Companion,* 571–77.

6. Gerald Graff, *Professing Literature: An Institutional History* (Chicago: University of Chicago Press, 1987), 56–64. On academic professionalism and Americans' selective appropriation of the German model, see Burton J. Bledstein, *The Culture of Professionalism: The Middle Class and the Development of Higher Education in America* (New York: Norton, 1976), especially 318–19. On the rise of divinity schools and "scientific" religious studies, see Conrad

Cherry, *Hurrying toward Zion: Universities, Divinity Schools, and American Protestantism* (Bloomington: Indiana University Press, 1995), especially 14, 24, 91–102. On the organization of modern biblical studies, see Ernest W. Saunders, *Searching the Scriptures: A History of the Society of Biblical Literature, 1880–1980* (Chico, Calif.: Scholars Press, 1982).

7. On New Testament criticism and the related research into the "historical Jesus," the classic study is Albert Schweitzer, *The Quest of the Historical Jesus: A Critical Study of Its Progress from Reimarus to Wrede,* translated by W. Montgomery (New York: Macmillan, 1968), originally published as *Von Reimarus zu Wrede* (1906); compare the critique of Schweitzer and the analysis of Strauss's work in Hans Frei, *The Eclipse of Biblical Narrative: A Study in Eighteenth and Nineteenth Century Hermeneutics* (New Haven: Yale University Press, 1974), 230–44. On the Smith and Briggs cases and American reactions to Old Testament criticism, see Ira V. Brown, "The Higher Criticism Comes to America, 1880–1900," *Journal of Presbyterian History* 38 (1960): 192–212; Lefferts A. Loetscher, *The Broadening Church: A Study of Theological Issues in the Presbyterian Church since 1869* (Philadelphia: University of Pennyslvania Press, 1954), 18–29, 48–62; Mark A. Noll, *Between Faith and Criticism: Evangelicals, Scholarship, and the Bible in America* (San Francisco: Harper and Row, 1986), 11–31; and Ferenc Morton Szasz, *The Divided Mind of Protestant America, 1880–1930* (University: University of Alabama Press, 1982), 15–29.

8. Philip Schaff, *History of the Christian Church,* vol. 1, *Apostolic Christianity* A.D. *1–100,* 3rd ed. (New York: Scribner's, 1891), 207–08, 855, 859, 213.

9. Philip Schaff, introduction to *The New Testament in the Original Greek,* American edition, edited by Brooke Foss Westcott and Fenton John Anthony Hort (New York: Harper and Brothers, 1881), vii, xxvi, lxxxvii. For the history of textual criticism of the New Testament, the standard treatment is Bruce M. Metzger, *The Text of the New Testament: Its Transmission, Corruption, and Restoration,* 3rd enlarged ed. (New York: Oxford University Press, 1992). See also Stephen Neill and Tom Wright, *The Interpretation of the New Testament, 1861–1986,* 2nd ed. (Oxford: Oxford University Press, 1988), especially 35–86.

10. *Anglo-American Bible Revision: Its Necessity and Purpose. By the Members of the American Revision Committee,* rev. ed. (Philadelphia: American Sunday-School Union, 1879), 14.

11. Schaff, *A Companion,* 494.

12. On Schaff's ecumenical vision, particularly as it related to Bible revision, see Stephen R. Graham, *Cosmos in the Chaos: Philip Schaff's Interpretation of Nineteenth-Century American Religion* (Grand Rapids, Mich.: Eerdmans, 1995), 168–75. Other sources on Schaff include James Hastings

Nichols, *Romanticism in American Theology: Nevin and Schaff at Mercersburg* (Chicago: University of Chicago Press, 1961); Klaus Penzel, "Church History and the Ecumenical Quest: A Study of the German Background and Thought of Philip Schaff" (Th.D. diss., Union Theological Seminary, 1962); the editor's introduction to *Philip Schaff: Historian and Ambassador of the Universal Church: Selected Writings,* edited by Klaus Penzel (Macon, Ga.: Mercer University Press, 1991); and George H. Shriver, *Philip Schaff: Christian Scholar and Ecumenical Prophet* (Macon, Ga.: Mercer University Press, 1987).

13. Orlinsky and Bratcher, *A History,* 70–73, 78; on Sawyer, see Cmiel, *Democratic Eloquence,* 97–102.

14. *Documentary History of the American Committee on Revision* (New York, 1885), 66.

15. Schaff, *A Companion,* 380–81, 386, 414.

16. Talbot Chambers, "The Bible as a Classic," in *Anglo-American Bible Revision,* 41.

17. J. B. Lightfoot, "On a Fresh Revision of the English New Testament," in J. B. Lightfoot, Richard Chenevix Trench, and C. J. Ellicott, *The Revision of the English Version of the New Testament* (New York: Harper and Brothers, 1873), 161–62.

18. C. J. Ellicott, "Considerations on the Revision of the English Version of the New Testament," in Lightfoot, Trench, and Ellicott, *The Revision of the English Version,* 160.

19. Schaff, *History of the Christian Church,* 1:16, 854; *A Companion,* 172. Compare Stephen Graham's observation that Schaff distinguished between "Romanism" (or "Popery") and a broad-minded "Catholicism"; see Graham, *Cosmos in the Chaos,* 68.

20. Schaff, *A Companion,* 417.

21. *New York Times,* 20 May 1881.

22. *New York Times,* 21 May 1881.

23. Crosby, as quoted in *New York Times,* 21 May 1881; Schaff, *A Companion,* 287.

24. On the other hand, noted the *Tribune,* the fabulous initial sales of the Revised New Testament might be "nothing more than a passing phenomenon of this doubting, investigating age, which eagerly seizes upon everything that is new, and delights to find imperfections in all that has been regarded in the past as sacred" (22 May 1881).

25. William Henry Green, "The Authorized Version and the Present Revision," *The Wycliffe Semi-Millennial Bible Celebration,* proceedings of the convention of the Bible Societies of New Jersey, Trenton, N.J., 21–22 September 1880, 92–93.

26. Matthew Brown Riddle, *The Story of the Revised New Testament, American Standard Edition* (Philadelphia: Sunday School Times, 1908), 72.

27. F. W. Farrar, "Fidelity and Bias in Versions of the Bible," *Expositor* 3, series 2 (1882): 283.

28. Quoted in *Chicago Tribune*, 23 May 1881. On the Bible Society's ill-fated corrected edition of the King James Bible, see Henry Otis Dwight, *The Centennial History of the American Bible Society* (New York: Macmillan, 1916), 246–53.

29. Quoted in *Chicago Tribune*, 23 May 1881.

30. Schaff, *A Companion*, 171; *History of the Christian Church*, 1:206, 854, 859–61, 863. On the conflation of textual and historical investigation, recall Hans Frei's observation that modern critical Bible scholarship typically amounted to "grammatical and lexical exactness in estimating what the original sense of a text was to its original audience, and the coincidence of the description with how the facts really occurred"; Frei, *Eclipse of Biblical Narrative*, 7.

31. *New York Herald*, 21 May 1881, quoted in Schaff, *A Companion*, 407.

32. *New York Times*, 21 May 1881.

33. Schaff, *A Companion*, 406.

34. As told to the *Chicago Tribune*, 22 May 1881.

35. Quoted in Schaff, *A Companion*, 408.

36. *San Francisco Chronicle*, 24 May 1881.

37. Sales information compiled from Schaff, *A Companion*, 404–5; *Chicago Tribune*, 23 May 1881; and *Richmond Dispatch*, 22 May 1881.

38. Revised Version companion volumes included: *Where the Old and the New Versions Differ: The Actual Changes in the Authorized and Revised New Testament* (New York: Anson D. F. Randolph, 1881); Alexander Roberts, *Companion to the Revised Version of the New Testament, Explaining the Reasons for the Changes Made on the Authorized Version* (New York: I. K. Funk, 1881); and C. J. Vaughan, *Authorized or Revised? Sermons on Some of the Texts in Which the Revised Version Differs from the Authorized* (London, Macmillan, 1882).

39. *Harper's Weekly*, 25 June 1881.

40. Schaff, *A Companion*, 405–6.

41. *Chicago Tribune*, 21 May 1881.

42. *Chicago Tribune*, 23 May 1881.

43. *Chicago Tribune*, 24 May 1881.

44. Quoted in Szasz, *The Divided Mind*, 20. Ironically, Talmage's position differed markedly from that of his denomination's periodical, the *Christian Intelligencer*.

45. *New York Times*, 21 November 1881. Less than two months earlier, the theological faculty of New Haven's Yale College had adopted the Revised Version for use in its chapel services.

46. Quoted in M. Valentine, "The Revised English New Testament," *Lutheran Quarterly*, n.s. 12 (January 1882): 59.

47. *Evangelical Repository and Bible Teacher* 58 (October 1881): 153. Much the same critique was offered by the *Reformed Presbyterian and Covenanter* 19, no. 11 (November 1881): 341–55.

48. *Washington Post,* 23 May 1881.

49. *New York Times,* 13 November 1881.

50. T. Harwood Pattison, *The History of the English Bible* (London: Baptist Tract and Book Society, 1894), 163. By the late 1890s, sales of the Revised Bible were estimated at just 5 to 10 percent of the total Bible market; see Cmiel, *Democratic Eloquence,* 219; compare Szasz, *The Divided Mind,* 20.

51. Shriver, *Philip Schaff,* 77; and David S. Schaff, *The Life of Philip Schaff, In Part Autobiographical* (New York: Scribner's, 1897), 386.

52. Quoted in D. Schaff, *The Life of Philip Schaff,* 386.

53. *Unitarian Review and Religious Magazine* 16 (July 1881): 94.

54. T. Romeyn Beck, "Comparative Merits of the Authorized Version of the English New Testament and the Revised Version as Translations," *Reformed Quarterly Review* 28 (October 1881): 539.

55. H. A. Buttz [president of Drew Theological Seminary], "The Revised Version of the New Testament," *Methodist Quarterly Review* 63 (October 1881): 716.

56. *Christian Advocate* 56, no. 21 (26 May 1881).

57. *Sunday School Times* 23, no. 23 (4 June 1881).

58. A. Huelster, "A Bird's Eye View of the Revised New Testament," *Evangelical Messenger* 34, no. 27 (5 July 1881).

59. Marvin R. Vincent, "Notes on the Revised New Testament," *Presbyterian Review* 2 (1881): 685.

60. *Christian Recorder* 19, no. 22 (2 June 1881).

61. *Christian Intelligencer* 52, no. 21 (25 May 1881); and 52, no. 22 (1 June 1881).

62. *Washington Post,* 30 May 1881.

63. The social and economic side of the upheaval is chronicled in, for example, Nell Irvin Painter, *Standing at Armageddon: The United States, 1877–1919* (New York: Norton, 1987); the religious history of the era is aptly summarized by Martin E. Marty, *Modern American Religion,* vol. 1, *The Irony of It All, 1893–1919* (Chicago: University of Chicago Press, 1986).

64. A. A. Hodge and B. B. Warfield, "Inspiration," *Presbyterian Review* 2 (1881): 225–60. Hodge and Warfield's article inaugurated a three-year debate in the *Presbyterian Review* between supporters and opponents of higher criticism. For an overview of this series, see Loetscher, *The Broadening Church,* 29–39.

65. Ernest Sandeen has argued that Hodge and Warfield's defensive tactic was a theological innovation contradicting the Westminster Confession's assertion that God safeguarded the purity of the biblical text in all ages; see

Sandeen, *The Roots of Fundamentalism: British and American Millenarianism, 1800–1930* (Chicago: University of Chicago Press, 1970), 128–29. Other scholars have viewed the Princeton position as standing in essential continuity with earlier Reformed views of the Bible; see, for example, Randall H. Balmer, "The Princetonians and Scripture: A Reconsideration," *Westminster Theological Journal* 44 (1982), 352–65; and Mark A. Noll, ed., *The Princeton Theology, 1812–1921: Scripture, Science, and Theological Method from Archibald Alexander to Benjamin Warfield* (Grand Rapids, Mich.: Baker Book House, 1983), 218–20.

66. On the differences between the Princeton theology and twentieth-century fundamentalism, see Mark A. Noll, editor's introduction to *The Princeton Defense of Plenary Verbal Inspiration*, Fundamentalism in American Religion Series (New York: Garland, 1988).

67. B. B. Warfield, "The Inerrancy of the Original Autographs," reprinted (with helpful annotations) in Noll, *The Princeton Theology*, 271.

68. Warfield recommended, for example, that the American Bible Society adopt the Revised Version's successor, the American Standard Version (*Presbyterian and Reformed Review* 13 [1902]: 645–48). It should be noted that misgivings about Bible revision were not unheard-of among elder Princetonians. Warfield's mentor Charles Hodge vigorously opposed the Bible Society's attempt in the 1850s to correct the King James text. During the last decade of his life, Hodge was a member of the Revised Bible committee but reportedly never attended any of its meetings. See Archibald Alexander Hodge, *The Life of Charles Hodge D.D. LL.D.* (New York: Scribner's, 1880), 404–6; C. S. Robinson, "The Bible Society and the New Revision," *Scribner's Monthly* (January 1881): 447–56; and Riddle, *The Story of the Revised New Testament*, 17.

69. *The Fundamentals* represented a transitional phase between late-nineteenth-century conservative orthodoxy and modern fundamentalism. For summaries of the issues, see Sandeen, *The Roots of Fundamentalism*, 188–207; Mark A. Noll, *Between Faith and Criticism: Evangelicals, Scholarship, and the Bible in America* (San Francisco: Harper and Row, 1986), 38–47; and George M. Marsden, *Fundamentalism and American Culture: The Shaping of Twentieth-Century Evangelicalism, 1870–1925* (New York: Oxford University Press, 1980), 118–23.

70. Philip Mauro, "A Personal Testimony," in *The Fundamentals: A Testimony to the Truth* (Chicago: Testimony Publishing, 1910–15), 4:105. *The Fundamentals* has been reprinted in facsimile by Garland (New York, 1988), with an introduction by George Marsden.

71. Philip Mauro, "Life in the Word," in *The Fundamentals: A Testimony to the Truth*, 5:31–32.

72. Philip Mauro, *Which Version? Authorized or Revised?* (Boston: Ham-

ilton Bros., Scripture Truth Depot, 1924), 61–64, 103, 96–101. Mauro's volume received an enthusiastic endorsement from the conservative Presbyterian weekly *Herald and Presbyter* 95, no. 29 (16 July 1924). Mauro was a prolific producer of pamphlets and short books. His many works included a treatise against evolutionism, *Evolution at the Bar* (Boston: Hamilton Bros., Scripture Truth Depot, 1917).

73. Mauro, *Which Version?* 76–78, 83; Schaff, *The Person of Christ* (London, 1880), excerpted in Penzel, *Philip Schaff*, 203. For a summary of the textual issues surrounding Mark 16:9–20 and Luke 23:34, see Bruce M. Metzger, *A Textual Commentary on the Greek New Testament* (London: United Bible Societies, 1971), 122–26, 180.

74. John William Burgon, *The Revision Revised: Three Articles Reprinted from the "Quarterly Review"* (London: John Murray, 1883), 115, 504 n. 1, 513. See also John William Burgon, *The Last Twelve Verses of the Gospel According to S. Mark, Vindicated Against Recent Critical Objectors and Established* (Oxford: Parker, 1871). For evaluation of Burgon's criticisms, see F. F. Bruce, *History of the Bible in English,* 3rd ed. (Cambridge, England: Lutterworth Press, 1978), 138–42, 148–52.

75. R. L. Dabney, "The Revised Version of the New Testament," *Southern Presbyterian Review* 32 (July 1881): 582. Mauro also criticized the Revised Version's rendering of 2 Timothy 3:16; see *Which Version?* 93–94.

76. Burgon, *The Revision Revised,* title page, 350.

77. Benjamin G. Wilkinson, *Our Authorized Bible Vindicated* (Washington, D.C., 1930), 255, 92. On Luke 2:33, the Rheims New Testament followed the Vulgate reading ("pater eius"), while the 1881 New Testament followed the equivalent Greek reading in Vaticanus and Sinaiticus (πατὴρ αὐτοῦ). The alternate reading "Joseph" has been regarded by modern scholars as an "orthodox corruption" intended to safeguard the virgin birth of Jesus; see Bart D. Ehrman, *The Orthodox Corruption of Scripture: The Effect of Early Christological Controversies on the Text of the New Testament* (New York: Oxford University Press, 1993), 55–56.

78. P. R. Ackroyd, C. F. Evans, G. W. H. Lampe, and S. L. Greenslade, eds., *The Cambridge History of the Bible,* vol. 3, *The West from the Reformation to the Present Day* (Cambridge: Cambridge University Press, 1963), 162–63; compare Bruce, *History of the Bible in English,* 122.

79. "The Revision of the New Testament," *Dublin Review,* 3rd ser., 6 (July 1881): 136, 143–44 (compare Wilkinson, *Our Authorized Bible Vindicated,* 229–30); Tobias Mullen, *The Canon of the Old Testament* (New York: Frederick Pustet, 1892), 369–70 (compare Wilkinson, *Our Authorized Bible Vindicated,* 229–30). Mullen actually was pointing out the influence of the Rheims-Douay Bible on the King James Version, but Wilkinson incorrectly cited his observation as evidence that the Revised Version was "like the Douay Bible."

80. Wilkinson, *Our Authorized Bible Vindicated*, 147, 256. Wilkinson seemed to equate the Mercersburg Theology and the Oxford Movement, but as Stephen R. Graham notes (*Cosmos in the Chaos*, 58), Schaff could not embrace Tractarianism because it underestimated the "divine significance" of the Reformation.

81. Mullen, *The Canon of the Old Testament*, 319–20; the Douay-Rheims-Challoner Bible rendered the disputed phrase as "graven things."

82. *Dublin Review*, 3rd ser., 6 (July 1881), 144.

83. Ibid., 141. 1 John 5:7 read in Douay-Rheims-Challoner: "And there are Three who give testimony in heaven, the Father, the Word, and the Holy Ghost. And these three are one." (The Authorized Version reading was essentially the same.) For the historical and textual problems surrounding the Comma Johanneum, see Metzger, *A Textual Commentary*, 716–18, and Metzger, *The Text of the New Testament*, 62, 101–2, 290–91, especially 291 n. 2. Ehrman calls this verse "the most obvious instance of a theologically motivated corruption in the entire manuscript tradition of the New Testament" (*The Orthodox Corruption of Scripture*, 45 n. 116).

84. Wilkinson, *Our Authorized Bible Vindicated*, 254.

85. Ibid., 186–87 (on John 2:11), 193 (on 1 Corinthians 5:7), 194–95 (on Matthew 24:3), 201 (on Mark 16:9–20).

86. See the translators' preface to the Revised Old Testament (1885), and Wilkinson, *Our Authorized Bible Vindicated*, 5–6.

87. Wilkinson, *Our Authorized Bible Vindicated*, 192.

88. Burgon's *Revision Revised* is excerpted, and Mauro's *Which Version?* reprinted, in *True or False? The Westcott-Hort Textual Theory Examined*, edited by David Otis Fuller (Grand Rapids, Mich.: Grand Rapids International Publications, 1973). Wilkinson's *Our Authorized Bible Vindicated* is reprinted in *Which Bible?* edited by David Otis Fuller, 3rd ed. (Grand Rapids, Mich.: Grand Rapids International Publications, 1972) and is currently available in another reprint from Leaves Of Autumn Books, a Seventh-day Adventist bookseller and publisher in Payson, Arizona.

89. On Mauro's conversion, see Gordon P. Gardiner, "The Story of Philip Mauro," in Fuller, *True or False?* 46–55; compare Marsden, *Fundamentalism and American Culture*, 121. David Otis Fuller was unrelated to Charles E. Fuller, cofounder of Fuller Seminary; see the brief mention in George Marsden, *Reforming Fundamentalism: Fuller Seminary and the New Evangelicalism* (Grand Rapids, Mich.: Eerdmans, 1987), 136.

Chapter 3

1. J. Gresham Machen, *Christianity and Liberalism* (New York: Macmillan, 1929); on the argument and import of this volume, see D. G. Hart,

Defending the Faith: J. Gresham Machen and the Crisis of Conservative Protestantism in Modern America (Baltimore: Johns Hopkins University Press, 1994), 59–83. On the Princeton-Westminster schism, see Bradley J. Longfield, *The Presbyterian Controversy: Fundamentalists, Modernists, and Moderates* (New York: Oxford University Press, 1991), 162–80.

2. H. Richard Niebuhr, "The Anachronism of Jonathan Edwards" (1958), in *H. Richard Niebuhr: Theology, History, and Culture: Major Unpublished Writings,* edited by William Stacy Johnson (New Haven: Yale University Press, 1996), 133.

3. On the ironic dual significance of 1908, see John F. Wilson, *Public Religion in American Culture* (Philadelphia: Temple University Press, 1979), 14. On the Protestant church unity movement, see Robert Lee, *The Social Sources of Church Unity: An Interpretation of Unitive Movements in American Protestantism* (New York: Abingdon Press, 1960).

4. Robert T. Handy, *A Christian America: Protestant Hopes and Historical Realities,* 2nd ed. (New York: Oxford University Press, 1984), 159–84; compare Robert T. Handy, *Undermined Establishment: Church-State Relations in America, 1880–1920* (Princeton: Princeton University Press, 1991), 30–48.

5. Preface to the Old Testament, American Standard Version (New York: Thomas Nelson and Sons, 1901).

6. Benjamin B. Warfield, review of the American Standard Version, *Presbyterian and Reformed Review* 13 (1902): 645–48; Westminster Confession of Faith, chapter 1, no. 8, in *The Book of Confessions* (Louisville, Ky.: Office of the General Assembly, Presbyterian Church [U.S.A.], 1991), n. p. On the history and features of the ASV, see Jack P. Lewis, *The English Bible from KJV to NIV: A History and Evaluation,* 2nd ed. (Grand Rapids, Mich.: Baker Book House, 1991), 69–105; and Harry M. Orlinsky and Robert G. Bratcher, *A History of Bible Translation and the North American Contribution* (Atlanta: Scholars Press, 1991), 106–10.

7. See two undated tracts, *The Wonderful Story of How the Bible Came down through the Ages,* with a preface by W. W. White (circa 1920) and *The Passing of the Old Revised Bible of 1611, commonly Known as the King James Bible,* by John Clark Hill (circa 1912), both in Speer Library, Princeton Theological Seminary. On White, see Virginia Lieson Brereton, *Training God's Army: The American Bible School, 1880–1940* (Bloomington: Indiana University Press, 1990), 91–95.

8. *Eighty-eighth Annual Report of the American Bible Society* (New York, 1904), 5–6. Subsequent ABS annual reports carried advertisements for various editions of the ASV Bible.

9. *Christian Education Today: A Statement of Basic Philosophy* (Chicago: International Council of Religious Education, 1940), 17. On the earlier history of Sunday school organizations, see Anne M. Boylan, *Sunday School: The*

Formation of an American Institution (New Haven: Yale University Press, 1988), 60–100.

10. Standard Bible Committee was the official name; I shall use it interchangeably with "RSV committee."

11. On the agreement between the ICRE and Nelson, see "A Proposal for Protecting the Integrity and Purity of the Text of the American Standard Edition of the Revised Bible" (statement adopted by the ICRE, 1929), RSV Committee Papers.

12. James Moffatt, *The New Testament: A New Translation* (New York: Hodder and Stoughton, 1913), and *The Old Testament: A New Translation* (New York: George H. Doran, 1924–25); Edgar J. Goodspeed, *The New Testament: An American Translation* (Chicago: University of Chicago Press, 1923), and J. M. Powis Smith, ed., *The Old Testament: An American Translation* (Chicago: University of Chicago Press, 1927), published together in revised form as *The Bible: An American Translation* (Chicago: University of Chicago Press, 1931). Two of Goodspeed and Smith's collaborators, Alexander R. Gordon and Leroy Waterman, also were members of the RSV committee; however, Gordon died soon after his appointment in 1930, and Waterman was not appointed until 1937.

13. Edgar J. Goodspeed, *The Making of the English New Testament* (Chicago: University of Chicago Press, 1925), 116–17.

14. Ropes to Weigle, 21 November 1931, RSV Committee Papers. Ropes wrote in part: "It isn't the 'thee' and 'thou' question that troubles and deters me; it is the whole idea of making any changes in the version except those absolutely required for tolerable intelligibility, and for accuracy in those few cases where greater accuracy is of any importance."

15. Magill to Weigle, 10 December 1931, RSV Committee Papers.

16. Magill to Weigle, 25 August 1932, RSV Committee Papers. On the early history of the Standard Bible Committee, see the firsthand account by Weigle, "The Making of the Revised Standard Version of the New Testament," *Religion in Life* 15 (1946): 163–73.

17. See Willard L. Sperry, *Religion in America* (New York: Macmillan, 1946); on Sperry's theological views, see William L. Fox, *Willard L. Sperry: The Quandaries of a Liberal Protestant Mind, 1914–1939* (New York: Lang, 1991).

18. Edgar J. Goodspeed, *As I Remember* (New York: Harper and Brothers, 1953), 11.

19. Albright's most famous work was *From the Stone Age to Christianity: Monotheism and the Historical Process*, 2nd ed. (Garden City, N.Y.: Doubleday, 1957); on his career and influence, see the two recent works Burke O. Long, *Planting and Reaping Albright: Politics, Ideology, and Interpreting the Bible* (University Park: Pennsylvania State University Press, 1997), and Bruce

Kuklick, *Puritans in Babylon: The Ancient Near East and American Intellectual Life, 1880–1930* (Princeton: Princeton University Press, 1996), 185–93.

20. On Cadbury, the AFSC, and the Nobel Prize, see Margaret Hope Bacon, *Let This Life Speak: The Legacy of Henry Joel Cadbury* (Philadelphia: University of Pennsylvania Press, 1987), 147–51.

21. Luther Allan Weigle, "The Religious Education of a Protestant," first published in *Contemporary American Theology: Theological Autobiographies,* edited by Vergilius Ferm (New York: Round Table Press, 1932), and reprinted in *The Glory Days: From the Life of Luther Allan Weigle,* edited by Richard D. Weigle (New York: Friendship Press, 1976), 8–26; compare the biographical sketches in *Current Biography* (1946), 632–34; and *The National Cyclopaedia of American Biography,* vol. F (1939–42), 142.

22. See, for example, Weigle to Theophil A. Goebel, 31 December 1952, RSV Committee Papers.

23. On the family as a means of grace, see Weigle's introduction to Horace Bushnell, *Christian Nurture* (1847; reprint, New Haven: Yale University Press, 1947), xxxiv–xxxv; on family Bible-reading, see Luther A. Weigle, *The Training of Children in the Christian Family* (Boston: Pilgrim Press, 1922), 200–201.

24. Luther A. Weigle, *Talks to Sunday-School Teachers* (New York: Richard R. Smith, 1930), 109.

25. Luther A. Weigle, *Jesus and the Educational Method* (New York: Abingdon Press, 1939), 67, 105.

26. Luther A. Weigle, *The Pupil and the Teacher* (New York: Hodder and Stoughton, 1911), 102–3, 107.

27. Conrad Cherry, *Hurrying toward Zion: Universities, Divinity Schools, and American Protestantism* (Bloomington: Indiana University Press, 1995), 43–45; on the effort to professionalize Sunday schools, compare Robert W. Lynn and Elliott Wright, *The Big Little School: Two Hundred Years of the Sunday School* (Birmingham, Ala.: Religious Education Press, 1980), 131.

28. See Weigle, *The Glory Days,* 28–29, 116. The World's Sunday School Association was later renamed the World Council of Christian Education.

29. On the Federal Council, see Robert A. Schneider, "Voice of Many Waters: Church Federation in the Twentieth Century," in *Between the Times: The Travail of the Protestant Establishment in America, 1900–1960,* edited by William R. Hutchison (Cambridge: Cambridge University Press, 1989), 95–121.

30. Luther A. Weigle, "The Religious Education of a Protestant," 24–25; Herbert Gordon May, *Our English Bible in the Making: The Word of Life in Living Language* (Philadelphia: Westminster Press, 1952), 7–8.

31. J. A. O'Brien, *The Church: The Interpreter of the Bible* (Huntington, Ind.: Our Sunday Visitor Press, 1948), 1–3, 25–26, 30–31, RSV Committee Papers.

32. M. James Hughes to Weigle, 25 January 1950, RSV Committee Papers.

33. "Coakley Lauds Bible Revision," *Pittsburgh Post-Gazette,* 18 February 1946; letter to the editor from J. Carter Swaim, unidentified clipping (presumably from the *Pittsburgh Post-Gazette*), 25 February 1946, RSV Committee Papers; Weigle to Swaim, 27 February 1946, RSV Committee Papers.

34. For the English text of *Divino Afflante Spiritu* ("Inspired by the Divine Spirit"), see Claudia Carlen, ed., *The Papal Encyclicals, 1939–1958* (Wilmington, N.C.: Consortium, McGrath Publishing Co., 1981), 4:65–79, especially 70; on the Confraternity translation and *Divino Afflante Spiritu,* see Gerald P. Fogarty, *American Catholic Biblical Scholarship: A History from the Early Republic to Vatican II* (San Francisco: Harper and Row, 1989), 199–221.

35. Luther A. Weigle, *The English New Testament from Tyndale to the Revised Standard Version* (New York: Abingdon-Cokesbury Press, 1949), 139–41.

36. W. F. Albright, "The War in Europe and the Future of Biblical Studies," in *The Study of the Bible Today and Tomorrow,* edited by Harold R. Willoughby (Chicago: University of Chicago Press, 1947), 168.

37. Quoted in a news release from the Yale University News Bureau, 29 September 1952, RSV Committee Papers; compare Weigle, *The English New Testament,* 143.

38. Herbert S. Magney to Weigle, 22 November 1938; compare "An Interested Person" to Weigle, 8 October 1943; RSV Committee Papers.

39. Mrs. Edgar Heermance to Weigle, 25 February 1939; compare A. Gerber to Weigle, no date (probably 1938); and Lewis Mills to Weigle, 1 January 1939; RSV Committee Papers.

40. Maude Thomas to Willard L. Sperry (forwarded to Weigle), 6 August 1939, RSV Committee Papers.

41. Mrs. A. W. Barker to Weigle, 10 March 1939, RSV Committee Papers.

42. See Bart D. Ehrman, *The Orthodox Corruption of Scripture: The Effect of Early Christological Controversies on the Text of the New Testament* (New York: Oxford University Press, 1993), 26–31.

43. Burrows to George P. Magruder, 14 October 1942, RSV Committee Papers; the reference to Jeremiah's prophecy in Matthew 27:9 is actually a loose quotation of Zechariah 11:13. On textual emendation, compare the similar view in Weigle to Mrs. Edgar Heermance, 28 February 1939, RSV Committee Papers.

44. William A. Irwin, "Method and Procedure of the Revision," in *An Introduction to the Revised Standard Version of the Old Testament* (New York: Thomas Nelson and Sons, 1952), 14.

45. Weigle, *The English New Testament,* 12.

46. Luther Weigle, "The Revision of the English Bible," news release, 30

September 1941; Weigle to William Curtis White, 12 January 1939; Weigle to John L. Cheek, 25 October 1947; RSV Committee Papers.

47. Weigle, *The English New Testament*, 126.

48. On committee procedures, see Weigle, "The Making of the Revised Standard Version of the New Testament," 166–67, 170.

49. Goodspeed, *As I Remember*, 75; Bacon, *Let This Life Speak*, 144.

50. Frederick C. Grant, "The Greek Text of the New Testament," in *An Introduction to the Revised Standard Version of the New Testament* (New York: International Council of Religious Education, 1946), 37–42; on the significance of the Chester Beatty papyri, see Stephen Neill and Tom Wright, *The Interpretation of the New Testament, 1881–1986*, 2nd ed. (Oxford: Oxford University Press, 1988), 81–84.

51. Weigle's study, with the help of a collaborator, eventuated in a substantial book; see Ronald Bridges and Luther A. Weigle, *The Bible Word Book, Concerning Obsolete or Archaic Words in the King James Version of the Bible* (New York: Thomas Nelson and Sons, 1960).

52. This summary of stylistic changes relies heavily on Weigle, "The Making of the Revised Version of the New Testament," 168–72; and Weigle, *The English New Testament*, 132–38.

53. Edward L. Wertheim to Philip C. Landers, 9 December 1945, 27 December 1945, RSV Committee Papers.

54. Telegram from John Evans (*Tribune* religion editor) to Luther Weigle, no date; Roy Ross to Weigle, 3 January 1946; RSV Committee Papers.

55. Theodore S. Liefeld, "New Testament Revised Version Will Make Debut Here Monday," *Columbus Sunday Dispatch*, 10 February 1946; program from the RSV presentation ceremony, 11 February 1946; RSV Committee Papers.

56. J. Guy Saunders to Thomas Nelson and Sons (forwarded to Weigle), 3 March 1947; John W. Meloy to ICRE (forwarded to Weigle), 4 March 1950; Archbishop Fisher to Weigle, 16 October 1956; RSV Committee Papers.

57. A. Johanson to Weigle, 10 May 1949; Weigle to A. Johanson, 16 May 1949; RSV Committee Papers.

58. W. E. Garrison, "A New New Testament—Coming," and "The New New Testament—Here!" *Christian Century* 63 (6 February and 13 February 1946), 171–72, 202–4; and "The Revised Standard Version of the New Testament: Editorial Book Review," *Moody Monthly* (June 1946), 592, 643, 646.

59. Weigle and the ICRE received letters from the E. V. Publishing House (Brethren in Christ Church), 22 July 1947; the *Church Herald and Holiness Banner* (Church of God [Holiness]), 23 July 1947; the Gospel Publishing House (Assemblies of God), 24 July 1947; and the Church of God Publishing House (Church of God [Cleveland, Tenn.]), 25 July 1947; RSV Committee Papers. A

variety of articles appeared in Holiness publications, including J. Ward Seberry, "What about the New Translation?" *Free Methodist,* 14 June 1946, RSV Committee Papers.

60. Rupert C. Foster, "The Revised Standard Version," *Christian Standard* 23 February 1946, 6, 16; Bob Shuler, "Conditioning Bible Readers," *Reading (Pa.) Shopping Bulletin,* 17 April 1952 (reprinted from *Methodist Challenge*); RSV Committee Papers.

61. W. C. Taylor, "The New Bible," *Baptist and Reflector,* 14 March 1946, 5; J. Oliver Buswell, Jr., "The New Revised Version of the New Testament," *Sunday School Times,* 16 March 1946, 227–29. On Buswell, see the biographical sketch by Joel A. Carpenter in *Dictionary of Christianity in America,* edited by Daniel G. Reid et al. (Downers Grove, Ill.: InterVarsity Press, 1990), 203–4; compare George Marsden, *Reforming Fundamentalism: Fuller Seminary and the New Evangelicalism* (Grand Rapids, Mich.: Eerdmans, 1987), 43–46.

62. [James A. Allen], "Disappointed in the New Version," *Apostolic Times* 15 (June 1946): 136–37. The "superchurch" epithet appears in, among others, a pamphlet by R. C. Foster, *The Revised Standard Version of the New Testament: An Appraisal* (Cincinnati: Standard, 1946), RSV Committee Papers.

63. Allen to Weigle (with copies to the other committee members), 25 March 1946; Wentz to Allen, 22 April 1946; Weigle to Allen, 3 April 1946; Weigle to Henry J. Cadbury, 3 April 1946; RSV Committee Papers. Allen's inquiry was not the only one of its kind; see, for example, S. S. Lappin to Weigle, 21 March 1946, RSV Committee Papers.

64. Quoted in Samuel McCrea Cavert, *The American Churches in the Ecumenical Movement, 1900–1968* (New York: Association Press, 1968), 210; for details of the NCC's formation and early administrative structure, see 203–11. Compare H. George Anderson, "Ecumenical Movements," in *Altered Landscapes: Christianity in America, 1935–1985,* edited by David W. Lotz, Donald W. Shriver, Jr., and John F. Wilson (Grand Rapids, Mich.: Eerdmans, 1989), 94–97.

65. For background, see Willem Adolf Visser 't Hooft, "The Genesis of the World Council of Churches," in *A History of the Ecumenical Movement, 1517–1948,* edited by Ruth Rouse and Stephen Charles Neill, 3rd ed. (Geneva: World Council of Churches, 1986), 697–724.

66. Weigle, *Jesus and the Educational Method,* 117; compare the ICRE statement, "Christian Education Today" (primarily authored by Weigle), 10.

67. Clarence Tucker Craig, *The One Church in the Light of the New Testament* (New York: Abingdon-Cokesbury Press, 1951), 113, 122.

68. "Record Budget Planned to Back Revised Standard Version," *Publishers Weekly,* 16 February 1952; on planning for the RSV Bible observance,

see the *Observer* (the official observance newsletter) 1, no. 1 (January 1951), and 2, no. 1 (February 1952); and Brininger to Weigle, 25 May 1951; RSV Committee Papers.

69. "Truman Gets First Copy of Newest Bible," *Washington Post,* 27 September 1952; "Truman Gets First Revised Bible," *New York Herald Tribune,* 27 September 1952.

70. NCC news releases, 1 October and 7 October 1952; *Observer,* final issue (November 1952); program for "A Service of Thanksgiving and Dedication"; RSV Committee Papers.

71. May, *Our English Bible in the Making,* 53.

72. See the third revised edition of Ira Maurice Price, *The Ancestry of Our English Bible: An Account of Manuscripts, Texts, and Versions of the Bible* as updated by RSV committee members William A. Irwin and Allen P. Wikgren (Wikgren joined the committee in 1953) (New York: Harper and Brothers, 1956), 4.

Chapter 4

1. Account of Martin Luther Hux compiled from Burke Davis, "Pastor Burns Single Page of Revised Bible Edition," *Greensboro (N.C.) Daily News,* 1 December 1952; "Rocky Mount Pastor Burns Page of Revised Bible," *(Raleigh, N.C.) News and Observer,* 1 December 1952; and various Associated Press reports.

2. Historians have been quick to note that accounts of fundamentalism's "fundamentals" varied and that fundamentalists were never doctrinally united. Nevertheless, certain dogmas enjoyed broad acceptance. On the disputed historiography of the "fundamentals," see Ernest R. Sandeen, *The Roots of Fundamentalism: British and American Millenarianism, 1800–1930* (Chicago: University of Chicago Press, 1970), xiv–xv; and George M. Marsden, *Fundamentalism and American Culture: The Shaping of Twentieth-Century Evangelicalism, 1870–1925* (New York: Oxford University Press, 1980), 117.

3. J. Gresham Machen, *The Virgin Birth of Christ* (New York: Harper and Brothers, 1930), especially 287–297. Regarding Machen's view of Christianity's historical character, see D. G. Hart, *Defending the Faith: J. Gresham Machen and the Crisis of Conservative Protestantism in Modern America* (Baltimore: Johns Hopkins University Press, 1994), 88–90. For a broader view of debates over the virgin birth in American religious history, see Robert Bruce Mullin, *Miracles and the Modern Religious Imagination* (New Haven: Yale University Press, 1996), 152–59, 165–73, 224–37.

4. Cornelius Van Til, *The New Modernism: An Appraisal of the Theology of Barth and Brunner* (Philadelphia: Presbyterian and Reformed Publishing,

1946); on the influence of this text among fundamentalists, see George M. Marsden, *Reforming Fundamentalism: Fuller Seminary and the New Evangelicalism* (Grand Rapids, Mich.: Eerdmans, 1987), 101.

5. On fundamentalist concerns about maintaining the sexual order in the 1950s, see Margaret Lamberts Bendroth, *Fundamentalism and Gender, 1875 to the Present* (New Haven: Yale University Press, 1993), 113–17; compare the treatment of earlier fundamentalist views of sexuality in Betty A. DeBerg, *Ungodly Women: Gender and the First Wave of American Fundamentalism* (Minneapolis: Fortress Press, 1990), especially 99–117.

6. RSV Chairman Luther Weigle explained the translators' position on Isaiah 7:14 in *An Open Letter Concerning the Revised Standard Version of the Bible* (New York: National Council of the Churches of Christ in the United States of America, n.d.), 8–9. This pamphlet is treated in greater detail hereafter. For an excellent brief discussion of the lexical issues surrounding Isaiah 7:14, see Lloyd R. Bailey, Sr., "A Comparison of Versions" (appendix 2) in *The Word of God: A Guide to English Versions of the Bible,* edited by Bailey (Atlanta: John Knox Press, 1982), 200–201.

7. Narrative of Hux's Bible-burning compiled from reports in the *Greensboro Daily News* and *(Raleigh) News and Observer.*

8. Roby C. Leonard to the *Greensboro Daily News,* 4 December 1952; Charles J. Tilley to *(Raleigh) News and Observer,* 2 December 1952; editorial in *(Raleigh) News and Observer,* 2 December 1952.

9. Bill Denton to Weigle, 2 January 1953; Albert Denton to Weigle, 22 January 1953; RSV Committee Papers.

10. All filed in the RSV Committee Papers: Edgar Bundy, *Communism Invading the Churches: The New Per-Version of the Bible* (Lockland, Ohio: Lockland Baptist Church, n.d.); James Cowan, *The Revised Standard Version: The Devil's Masterpiece: The Reasons Why I Reject It* (Prince Albert, Saskatchewan, n.d.); Nevin L. Seibert, *The Revised Standard Version of the Bible, Posed, Opposed, and Exposed* (New Cumberland, Pa., n.d.); and David Otis Fuller, *Whose Unclean Fingers Have Been Tampering with the Holy Bible, God's Pure, Infallible, Verbally Inspired Word?* (Grand Rapids, Mich.: Wealthy Street Baptist Church, n.d.).

11. All filed in the RSV Committee Papers: G. Douglas Young and J. Oliver Buswell, Jr., *Reviews of the Revised Standard Version of the Bible* (Philadelphia: Sunday School Times, 1952); Charles Lee Feinberg, *The Revised Standard Version: What Kind of Translation?* (Los Angeles: Bible Institute of Los Angeles, n.d.); J. Barton Payne, *A Criticism of the Revised Standard Version of the Bible* (Greenville, S.C.: Bob Jones University, n.d.); and Joseph Hoffman Cohn, *The Revised Standard Version—A Sad Travesty* (New York: American Board of Missions to the Jews, 1952).

12. Oswald T. Allis, *Revised Version or Revised Bible? A Critique of the*

Revised Standard Version of the Old Testament (Philadelphia: Presbyterian and Reformed Publishing, 1953); and Foy E. Wallace, Jr., *A Review of the New Versions: Consisting of an Exposure of the Multiple New Translations* (Fort Worth, Tex.: Foy E. Wallace Jr. Publications, 1973). Wallace attacked other modern Bible translations but devoted nearly three hundred pages to the RSV. See also the anti-RSV book by William Carey Taylor, *The New Bible: Pro and Con* (New York: Vantage Press, 1955).

13. Peter Chew, "The Great Bible Controversy," *Look,* 2 November 1952, 97–98; this and dozens of other newspaper and magazine clippings are filed in the RSV Committee Papers.

14. Charles Drake, "The Battle on the Revised Standard Version," *Christianity and Crisis* 13 (22 June 1953): 90–92.

15. For example, Dale Moody (of the Southern Baptist Theological Seminary, Louisville) to Luther Weigle, 5 December 1952, RSV Committee Papers.

16. Margaret Weigle Quillian, letter to the author, 14 July 1997.

17. Ralph Lord Roy, *Apostles of Discord: A Study of Organized Bigotry and Disruption on the Fringes of Protestantism,* Beacon Studies in Church and State (Boston: Beacon Press, 1953), especially chapter 9, "'Modernism'—and the 'Battle of the Bible.'"

18. Gerald A. Larue, "Another Chapter in the History of Bible Translation: The Attacks upon the Revised Standard Version," *Journal of Bible and Religion* 31 (1963): 301–10.

19. For example, Martin E. Marty, *Modern American Religion,* vol. 3, *Under God, Indivisible, 1941–1960* (Chicago: University of Chicago Press, 1996), 367–72.

20. David Daniell, *William Tyndale: A Biography* (New Haven: Yale University Press, 1994), 83–87.

21. Philip Schaff, *The Principle of Protestantism* (1844), quoted as an epigraph to Nathan O. Hatch, *The Democratization of American Christianity* (New Haven: Yale University Press, 1989), vii.

22. *Come and Worship: Celebrating the Enrichment Brought to the Church through the Revised Standard Version of the Holy Bible* (New York: National Council of the Churches of Christ in the United States of America, n.d.), a pamphlet with special orders of worship to commemorate the RSV's tenth anniversary.

23. On McIntire's career, see the helpful summary and bibliography by Shelley Baranowski, "Carl McIntire," in *Twentieth-Century Shapers of American Popular Religion,* edited by Charles H. Lippy (Westport, Conn.: Greenwood Press, 1989), 256–63; see also Marsden, *Reforming Fundamentalism,* 43–46; and Gary K. Clabaugh, *Thunder on the Right: The Protestant Fundamentalists* (Chicago: Nelson-Hall, 1974), 69–97. The sole book-length study is Jutta Reich, *Amerikanischer Fundamentalismus: Geschichte*

und Erscheinung der Bewegung um Carl McIntire, 2nd ed. (Hildesheim: Dr. H. A. Gerstenberg, 1972).

24. Carl McIntire, *The New Bible, Revised Standard Version: Why Christians Should Not Accept It* (Collingswood, N.J.: Christian Beacon, n.d.), 13–14, RSV Committee Papers.

25. Bundy, *Communism Invading the Churches;* on Bundy's career, see Arnold Forster and Benjamin R. Epstein, *Danger on the Right* (New York: Random House, 1964), 144–50.

26. "Launching the New Version," *Moody Monthly* (November 1952): 179, RSV Committee Papers.

27. See the observation on this point by RSV committee member Clarence Tucker Craig (previous chapter); compare also Louis Gasper, *The Fundamentalist Movement, 1930–1956* (The Hague: Mouton, 1963; reprint, Grand Rapids: Baker Book House, 1981), 40–74.

28. "Information from the Files of the Committee on Un-American Activities" (U.S. House of Representatives, 6 January 1953), RSV Committee Papers.

29. J. B. Matthews, "Reds and Our Churches," *American Mercury* (July 1953): 3–13; compare his related article, "Red Infiltration of Theological Seminaries" *American Mercury* (November 1953): 31–36, RSV Committee Papers. See also Samuel McCrea Cavert, "Memorandum on the Protestant Clergy and the McCarthy-Matthews Episode" (National Council of Churches, July 1953), RSV Committee Papers; Marty, *Modern American Religion,* 3:359–60; Richard M. Fried, *Nightmare in Red: The McCarthy Era in Perspective* (New York: Oxford University Press, 1990), 136–37; and Ellen Schrecker, *The Age of McCarthyism: A Brief History with Documents* (Boston: Bedford Books, 1994), 13–14.

30. Both pamphlets are filed in the RSV Committee Papers. On Kaub, see Roy, *Apostles of Discord,* 244–50; on the Circuit Riders, see 325–29; and Brooks R. Walker, *The Christian Fright Peddlers: The Radical Right and the Churches* (Garden City, N.Y.: Doubleday, 1964), 17–18.

31. Weigle to Cavert, 23 February 1953, RSV Committee Papers. On the Supreme Court's gradual dismantling of McCarthyism, see Fried, *Nightmare in Red,* 184–88.

32. Cavert to Weigle, 1 April 1953, RSV Committee Papers.

33. *Plain Facts about the National Council of the Churches of Christ in the U.S.A.* (New York: National Council of Churches, 1953); Luther A. Weigle, "On Religious Freedom in Russia"; RSV Committee Papers.

34. The alleged debate between Gilbert and Stevenson is printed in Dan Gilbert, *Debate over the New Bible* (Upland, Calif., n.d.), RSV Committee Papers. (Excerpts from the alleged debate soon appeared in other anti-RSV literature, e.g., Cowan, *Revised Standard Version.*) Correspondence relating to

the Gilbert affair is in the RSV Committee Papers, with overlapping material in the Papers of the National Council of Churches, RG 17, Box 8, Folder 6; see also Larue, "Another Chapter," 304–5. On Gilbert's death, see "Excerpt from a report to the Committee on Use and Understanding of the RSV" (26 November 1962), RSV Committee Papers.

35. Correspondence relating to the Air Force manual incident is in the RSV Committee Papers, with overlapping material in the Papers of the National Council of Churches, RG 17, Box 6, Folder 23. The disputed document, *Air Reserve Center Training Manual 45–0050*, increment 5, vol. 7 (Mitchell Air Force Base, N.Y.: Continental Air Command, 1960), is reprinted in *The Churches and the Air Force Manual Issue: A Compilation by the National Council of Churches* (New York: National Council of Churches, 1960). On Billy James Hargis, see Erling Jorstad, *The Politics of Doomsday: Fundamentalists of the Far Right* (Nashville: Abingdon Press, 1970), 70–73, 83–84; and Forster and Epstein, *Danger on the Right,* 68–86.

36. *Congressional Record,* 86th Cong., 2nd sess., 1960, 106, pt. 6:8188–8284; Quigley is quoted on 8284.

37. J. Edgar Hoover, "Communist Propaganda and the Christian Pulpit" (pt. 2 of 3), *Christianity Today* 5 (24 October 1960): 5–7.

38. See Bundy's oft-reprinted *Collectivism in the Churches: A Documented Account of the Political Activities of the Federal, National, and World Councils of Churches* (Wheaton, Ill.: Church League of America, 1958), which repeated old charges against Weigle and the RSV (53–55) while inventing some new ones—for example, that Weigle had helped write a Unitarian Sunday school curriculum (a complete falsehood; see Weigle to Robert Crenshaw, 9 January 1962, RSV Committee Papers).

39. James Davison Hunter, *Evangelicalism: The Coming Generation* (Chicago: University of Chicago Press, 1987), 116–30; compare the similar scheme adopted by Clyde Wilcox, *God's Warriors: The Christian Right in Twentieth-Century America* (Baltimore: Johns Hopkins University Press, 1992), 1–20.

40. Carl McIntire, *Call to Separation* (Collingswood, N.J.: Christian Beacon Press, n.d.), RSV Committee Papers. On McIntire and 2 Corinthians 6:17, see Marsden, *Reforming Fundamentalism,* 64–65. See also the long footnote on 2 Cor. 6:17 in *The Scofield Reference Bible,* edited by C. I. Scofield et al. (New York: Oxford University Press, 1917).

41. See his marginal note to Romans 12:6 in *Tyndale's New Testament* (1534), edited by David Daniell (New Haven: Yale University Press, 1989), 237; compare Donald Dean Smeeton, *Lollard Themes in the Reformation Theology of William Tyndale* (Kirksville, Mo.: Sixteenth Century Journal Publishers, 1986), 103.

42. "The Translators to the Reader," in *Documents of the English Reformation,* edited by Gerald Bray (Minneapolis: Fortress Press, 1994), 433.

43. Philip Schaff, *A Companion to the Greek Testament and the English Version* (New York: Harper and Brothers, 1883), 307.

44. Larue makes this point in "Another Chapter," 307.

45. McIntire, *The New Bible*, 9–10.

46. [Weigle], *An Open Letter*, 11–12.

47. McIntire, *The New Bible*, 8.

48. Weigle explained the problem at length in an interview with Adon Taft, religion editor of the *Miami Herald*, 13 March 1953 (transcript in RSV Committee Papers), 3.

49. McIntire, *The New Bible*, 8–9; Weigle, *Miami Herald* interview, 5.

50. State of Michigan, *Journal of the Senate*, 67th Legislature, Regular Session of 1953 (21 January 1953), RSV Committee Papers. For biographical information on Decker and Feenstra, see State of Michigan, *Official Directory and Legislative Manual* (Lansing, 1953–54), 242–43. Interestingly, Feenstra was a member of the Christian Reformed Church, the conservative Dutch Calvinist denomination in which the RSV's primary rival, the New International Version, originated (see chapter 5).

51. Oliver B. Greene, *The RSV (of the Holy Bible) along side the King James* (Greenville, S.C., n.d.), RSV Committee Papers; Taylor, *The New Bible*, 126.

52. Cyril Hutchinson, *Why Christians Should Not Accept the New Bible* (Calgary, Alberta: Berean Bible College, n.d.), 13–14, RSV Committee Papers. The treatment of Luke 24:6 is also criticized, for example, in a pamphlet issued by Verne Kaub's organization: Robert L. Sumner, *The "New" Bible: An Appraisal of the Revised Standard Version* (Madison, Wis.: American Council of Christian Laymen, n.d.), 15, RSV Committee Papers.

53. Martin Luther Hux, *Modernism's Unholy Bible: Why Christians Cannot Accept It* (Rocky Mount, N.C., n.d.), 11, RSV Committee Papers; Homer G. Ritchie, "Tampering with the Scriptures," in William Fraser, Homer G. Ritchie, Peter Connolly, and Luther C. Peak, *Why We Reject the "National Council" Bible*, 2nd. ed. (Wichita, Kan.: Wichita Publishing, n.d.), 42, RSV Committee Papers.

54. Jewish scholars had, of course, influenced Christian translation and exegesis for centuries; see Orlinsky's own article, "Jewish Influences on Christian Translations of the Bible," in Orlinsky, *Essays in Biblical Culture and Bible Translation* (New York: KTAV Publishing, 1974), 423–40.

55. Harry M. Orlinsky, "The Hebrew Text and the Ancient Versions of the Old Testament," in *An Introduction to the Revised Standard Version of the Old Testament* (New York: Thomas Nelson and Sons, National Council of the Churches of Christ in the United States of America, 1952), 30.

56. Allis, *Revised Version or Revised Bible?* 47–48; William C. Robinson, *What Think Ye of Christ? A Study in the Christology of the RSV* (Weaverville, N.C.: Southern Presbyterian Journal, n.d.), 12–13, 15, RSV Committee Papers.

57. Ritchie, "Tampering with the Scriptures," 38.

58. [Gerald Winrod], "The New Blasphemous Bible," undated article clipping, RSV Committee Papers. On Winrod, see Roy, *Apostles of Discord,* 26–58, 208; and more recently, Leo P. Ribuffo, *The Old Christian Right: The Protestant Far Right from the Great Depression to the Cold War* (Philadelphia: Temple University Press, 1983), 80–127.

59. Wallace, *A Review of the New Versions,* vii, 269.

60. Orlinsky to Weigle, 5 May 1945, 8 May 1945; Weigle to G. Weir Hartman, 21 April 1953; RSV Committee Papers; [Weigle], *An Open Letter,* 19.

61. Weigle to Myron C. Settle, 29 December 1952, RSV Committee Papers.

62. H. H. Savage, "Comments on the Revised Standard Version," *Highland Park Evangelist,* 28 January 1953, 4, RSV Committee Papers.

63. Weigle, *Miami Herald* interview, 9.

64. John R. Rice, "God's Own Translation of Isaiah 7:14 Says 'Virgin',," *Sword of the Lord,* 25 September 1953, 11, RSV Committee Papers; on Rice, see Marsden, *Reforming Fundamentalism,* 48, 190–91.

65. Jack P. Lewis, "The New American Standard Bible," in *The English Bible from KJV to NIV: A History and Evaluation,* 2nd ed. (Grand Rapids, Mich.: Baker Book House, 1991), 165–97; compare the foreword to the New American Standard Bible (1973 ed.).

66. Millar Burrows, *An Outline of Biblical Theology* (Philadelphia: Westminster Press, 1946), 30. This passage appeared in numerous pamphlets, for example, Sumner, *The "New" Bible,* 22.

67. Preface to the Revised Standard Version (1952 ed.), x.

68. McIntire, *The New Bible,* 18.

69. E. L. Banta, radio address printed in the *Gospel of Grace Messenger,* 24 November 1952, RSV Committee Papers.

70. Clipping in RSV Committee Papers (see introduction).

71. Weigle to Albert Leininger, 30 December 1952, RSV Committee Papers.

72. Weigle to Marie Arthur, 9 May 1953, RSV Committee Papers. On the *Formula Consensus Helvetica,* see Philip Schaff, *The Creeds of Christendom, with a History and Critical Notes* (New York: Harper and Brothers, 1877), 1:487.

73. Richard A. Muller, "The Debate over the Vowel Points and the Crisis in Orthodox Hermeneutics," *Journal of Medieval and Renaissance Studies* 10 (Spring 1980): 53–72.

74. Weigle to Dale Moody, 13 December 1952, RSV Committee Papers.

75. [Weigle], *An Open Letter,* especially 3, 16–17.

76. Clovis G. Chappell, *The Revised Standard Version: A Genuine Joy* (New York: Division of Christian Education of the National Council of Churches, 1954), especially 8, RSV Committee Papers. The pamphlet appeared

in an initial print run of three hundred thousand copies. On Chappell, see the brief biographical sketch by Donald S. Armentrout in *Dictionary of Christianity in America,* edited by Daniel G. Reid et al. (Downers Grove, Ill.: InterVarsity Press, 1990), 241.

77. A. L. Goodrich, *The Revised Standard Version as Seen by a Southern Baptist* (New York: Division of Christian Education of the National Council of Churches, n.d.), RSV Committee Papers. Goodrich's article originally appeared in the *Baptist Record,* 1 January 1953.

78. Jack P. Lewis, "The Revised Standard Version after Twenty-five Years," in *The English Bible,* 118–19.

79. Weigle to William A. Irwin, 7 April 1955; compare Weigle to Paul M. Fekula, 20 March 1962; RSV Committee Papers. On the text-critical issues surrounding Matthew 1:16, see Bruce M. Metzger, *A Textual Commentary on the Greek New Testament* (London: United Bible Societies, 1971), 2–7.

80. [Weigle], *An Open Letter,* 9; Lewis, "The Revised Standard Version After Twenty-Five Years," in *The English Bible,* 119; and Luther A. Weigle, "The Standard Bible Committee," in *Translating and Understanding the Old Testament: Essays in Honor of Herbert Gordon May,* edited by Harry Thomas Frank and William L. Reed (Nashville: Abingdon Press, 1970), 35.

81. Henry H. Ness, *An Analysis of Criticisms of the New Revised Standard Version of the Bible* (Seattle, 1953), 6, 8–9, RSV Committee Papers.

82. Ness to Fuller, 4 August 1956, with carbon copy to Weigle, RSV Committee Papers.

83. A. Clay Sicher, "Is This Book 'Blasphemous'?" *Christian Herald* (March 1953), offprint in RSV Committee Papers.

84. Poling to Weigle, 30 December 1952, RSV Committee Papers.

85. Evans to Division of Christian Education, National Council of Churches, 29 January 1953, RSV Committee Papers.

86. Knoff to Weigle, 6 February 1953; Weigle to Evans, 9 February 1953; RSV Committee Papers.

87. Evans to Weigle, 20 February 1953, RSV Committee Papers.

88. Marsden, *Reforming Fundamentalism,* 89.

89. See, for example, David Otis Fuller, ed., *Which Bible?* 3rd ed. (Grand Rapids, Mich.: Grand Rapids International Publications, 1972), and its sequel, *True or False? The Westcott-Hort Textual Theory Examined* (Grand Rapids, Mich.: Grand Rapids International Publications, 1973).

90. David Otis Fuller, "The Bible—God's Character in Print; Jesus Christ—God's Character in Person," address delivered at the Spring Convention of the American Council of Christian Churches, Fort Worth, Texas, 25 April 1956, RSV Committee Papers.

91. Marsden, *Reforming Fundamentalism,* 48–49.

Chapter 5

1. John A. Abbo and Jerome D. Hannan, *The Sacred Canons: A Concise Presentation of the Current Disciplinary Norms of the Church,* vol. 2, Canons 870–2414, 2nd rev. ed. (St. Louis: Herder, 1960), 624.

2. James DeForest Murch, "Evangelicals and 'The New Version,'" *United Evangelical Action,* 15 January 1953, 5–6.

3. Stephen W. Paine, "Presidential Address," in *Report to Evangelicals: A Report of the Seventh Annual Convention of the National Association of Evangelicals, Chicago, Illinois, 19–22 April 1949* (Chicago: National Association of Evangelicals, 1949), 31.

4. *United We Stand: A Report on the Constitutional Convention of the National Association of Evangelicals,* Chicago, Illinois, 3–6 May 1943 (Boston: National Association of Evangelicals, 1943), 1; and H. H. Savage, introduction to James DeForest Murch, *Cooperation without Compromise: A History of the National Association of Evangelicals* (Grand Rapids, Mich.: Eerdmans, 1956), v.

5. H. Sheldon Smith, "Conflicting Interchurch Movements in American Protestantism," *Christendom* 12 (1947): 174.

6. Philip C. Landers to NCC executive staff, 19 April 1954, RSV Committee Papers.

7. J. Oliver Buswell, Jr., "The Revised Standard Version of the New Testament," *Sunday School Times* 94 (1 November 1952): 919–21.

8. C. I. Scofield, ed., *The Scofield Reference Bible* (New York: Oxford University Press, 1917), 1318.

9. See, for example, Justin Martyr's *Dialogue with Trypho* (c. 135 C.E.) in *Writings of Justin Martyr,* edited and translated by Thomas B. Falls (New York: Christian Heritage, 1948), chs. 66–68, pp. 253–59.

10. John Calvin, *Commentary on the Book of the Prophet Isaiah,* vol. 1, translated by William Pringle, vol. 7 of *Calvin's Commentaries* (1850; reprint, Grand Rapids, Mich.: Baker Book House, 1993), 244, 247–48. Calvin thus interpreted Isaiah 7:14 as a literal (rather than typological) reference to the virgin birth of Christ; his interpretation in this case resembled that of many modern evangelicals.

11. Martin Luther, *Lectures on Isaiah, Chapters 1–39,* edited by Jaroslav Pelikan and Hilton C. Oswald, vol. 16 of *Luther's Works* (St. Louis: Concordia, 1969), 84. On Luther and Isaiah 7:14, see John F. A. Sawyer, *The Fifth Gospel: Isaiah in the History of Christianity* (Cambridge: Cambridge University Press, 1996), 127.

12. George Rapall Noyes, "Hengstenberg's Christology," *Christian Examiner* 16 (July 1834): 344–45.

13. Harry M. Orlinsky and Robert G. Bratcher, *A History of Bible*

Translation and the North American Contribution (Atlanta: Scholars Press, 1991), 73. Compare Dale Moody, "Isaiah 7:14 in the Revised Standard Version," *Review and Expositor* 50 (January 1953): 61.

14. Smith, who translated the Old Testament with the help of Theophile J. Meek, Alexander R. Gordon, and Leroy Waterman, rendered Isaiah 7:14: "Therefore the Lord himself will give you a sign: Behold! a young woman is with child, and is about to bear a son; and she will call him 'God is with us.'"

15. Donald Grey Barnhouse, "I Have Read the RSV," *Eternity* 4 (June 1953): 10–12. Barnhouse's magazine was originally known as *Revelation;* see the biographical sketch by Joel A. Carpenter in *Dictionary of Christianity in America,* edited by Daniel G. Reid et al. (Downers Grove, Ill.: InterVarsity Press, 1990): 117–18.

16. William A. Irwin, "Method and Procedure of the Revision," in *An Introduction to the Revised Standard Version of the Old Testament* (New York: Thomas Nelson and Sons, 1952), 14.

17. Merrill F. Unger, "The Revised Standard Old Testament," *Bibliotheca Sacra* 110 (January 1953): 54–56.

18. Oswald T. Allis, "RSV Appraisal: Old Testament," *Christianity Today* 1 (8 July 1957): 23–24.

19. William A. Irwin, "That Troublesome *'Almah* and Other Matters," *Review and Expositor* 50 (July 1953): 350. Irwin's only regret, revealed privately to Luther Weigle two years later, was the RSV's footnote ("or virgin") on Isaiah 7:14. He felt that the note should have clarified that "virgin" appeared in the Greek, Syriac, and Latin versions—not in the original Hebrew (Irwin to Weigle, 2 April 1955).

20. Irwin, "That Troublesome *'Almah,*" 350, 352.

21. Weigle, interview with Adon Taft, religion editor of the *Miami Herald,* 13 March 1953 (transcript in RSV Committee Papers), 2–3, quoting Millar Burrows, "The Style and Vocabulary of the RSV of the Old Testament," in *Introduction to the Revised Standard Version of the Old Testament,* 61.

22. Irwin, "That Troublesome *'Almah,*" 354–55. Carl McIntire and other conservatives had vigorously objected to the RSV's rendering of this passage.

23. Weigle to Paul M. Fekula, 20 March 1962, RSV Committee Papers. The imminence of Immanuel's birth is based on Isaiah 7:16: "For before the child knows how to refuse the evil and choose the good, the land before whose two kings you are in dread will be deserted." Interestingly, Weigle's objection—that the birth of Christ could not have been a sign to Ahaz—had been made by earlier liberals and dismissed as "puerile" by C. I. Scofield in his note on Isaiah 7:13, *The Scofield Reference Bible,* 719.

24. George M. Marsden, *Reforming Fundamentalism: Fuller Seminary and the New Evangelicalism* (Grand Rapids, Mich.: Eerdmans, 1987), 6.

25. George Eldon Ladd, "RSV Appraisal: New Testament," *Christianity Today* 1 (8 July 1957), 7–11.

26. William Sanford LaSor, *Isaiah 7:14—"Young Woman" or "Virgin"?* (undated booklet), RSV Committee Papers.

27. Edward John Carnell, "How My Mind Has Changed," reprinted in *How My Mind Has Changed*, edited by Harold E. Fey (Cleveland: Meridian Books, 1961), 92–93, 99; the article appeared originally as "Orthodoxy: Cultic vs. Classical," *Christian Century* 77 (30 March 1960): 377–79. Carnell elaborated on his frustrations with fundamentalism in *The Case for Orthodox Theology* (Philadelphia: Westminster Press, 1959).

28. Harold Lindsell, ed., *Harper Study Bible: The Holy Bible, Revised Standard Version* (New York: Harper and Row, 1964), 1010; reviewed by Edward John Carnell in *Christianity Today* 9 (12 February 1965): 38.

29. Marsden, *Reforming Fundamentalism*, 138.

30. Joel A. Carpenter has also noted the ambiguous relationship between the NAE and the "new" evangelicals at Fuller; see his *Revive Us Again: The Reawakening of American Fundamentalism* (New York: Oxford University Press, 1997), 207.

31. Membership figures are from James D. Bratt, *Dutch Calvinism in Modern America: A History of a Conservative Subculture* (Grand Rapids, Mich.: Eerdmans, 1984), 223; Bratt's is the best overview of the CRC and Dutch-American Calvinism generally.

32. On the CRC's influence in biblical scholarship and publishing, see Mark A. Noll, *Between Faith and Criticism: Evangelicals, Scholarship, and the Bible in America* (San Francisco: Harper and Row, 1986), 100–105.

33. On the CRC and the NAE, see Bratt, *Dutch Calvinism*, 199–200; and Carpenter, *Revive Us Again*, 156–57, 299 n. 54.

34. William Hendriksen, "The Drive Is On! To Put Across the Revised Standard Version of the Bible," *Banner* 88 (2 January 1953): 6–7, 22.

35. See the reports in the *Banner* 89 (28 May 1954): 676–77; and 89 (9 July 1954): 880.

36. On the background of the committee's work, see the CRC Synod *Agenda* (Grand Rapids, Mich., 1966) ("Report 35: Bible Translation"), 241–50.

37. Bastiaan Van Elderen, "More Thoughts on Bible Translations," *The Banner* 101 (3 June 1966): 14–16; and CRC Synod *Agenda* (Grand Rapids, Mich., 1966) ("Report 35-A: Minority Report on Bible Translation"), 251–52.

38. On the events of 1966–69, see Bastiaan Van Elderen to Howard N. Woodland (copy), 6 July 1966; David E. Holwerda to Luther A. Weigle, 27 May 1968; Weigle to Holwerda, 3 July 1968; Holwerda to Weigle, 27 August 1969; RSV Committee Papers.

39. P. J. Zondervan to Gerald Knoff, 22 July 1969, RSV Committee Papers.

40. Oscar E. Feucht, "Synod's Advisory Committee on English Bible

Versions Reports on Its Study of the Revised Standard Version of the Bible," *Lutheran Witness* (15 July 1958): 8–9, 20–21; and Luther A. Weigle to Oscar E. Feucht, 28 September 1959, RSV Committee Papers.

41. For an overview of the Missouri Synod schism, see E. Clifford Nelson et al., *The Lutherans in North America,* rev. ed. (Philadelphia: Fortress Press, 1980), 531–35, 559–60; compare the more apologetic account by a leading moderate, John H. Tietjen, *Memoirs in Exile: Confessional Hope and Institutional Conflict* (Minneapolis: Fortress Press, 1990).

42. The Missouri Synod by no means countenanced fundamentalist emphasis on conversion, revival, and dispensationalism (compare Carpenter, *Revive Us Again,* 8), but its resolute defense of biblical inerrancy (see the comments of Robert Preus, hereafter), the virgin birth, and other doctrines went a long way toward ingratiating the Missourians to "oldline" fundamentalists.

43. Noll, *Between Faith and Criticism,* 156–59; Noll points out that "critical anti-critics" bore only a superficial resemblance to "popular anti-critics," or those who rejected all scholarship as inherently corrupting.

44. Ronald Youngblood, quoted in Richard Kevin Barnard, *God's Word in Our Language: The Story of the New International Version* (Colorado Springs: International Bible Society, 1989), 101.

45. Mantey to Nelson, 2 April 1953; Weigle to Mantey, 13 April 1953; RSV Committee Papers. Mantey had praised the RSV in "A View of the RSV," *Watchman-Examiner,* 30 October 1952, 1007, 1009–10.

46. Wagner to Weigle, 24 May 1953, RSV Committee Papers.

47. The NIV's history is related by two "insider" monographs: Barnard, *God's Word in Our Language;* and Burton L. Goddard, *The NIV Story: The Inside Story of the New International Version* (New York: Vantage Press, 1989). See also Carolyn Johnson Youngblood, "The New International Version Translation Project: Its Conception and Implementation," *Journal of the Evangelical Theological Society* 21 (September 1978): 239–49.

48. Barnard, *God's Word in Our Language,* 70–73. On the case for an evangelical translation, see John H. Stek, "KJV, ASV, RSV, NEB, NASB—or What?" *Banner* 101 (18 March 1966): 4–5.

49. Preface to Ronald Youngblood, ed., *Evangelicals and Inerrancy* (Nashville: Thomas Nelson, 1984), xi. Youngblood's volume is collection of papers read before the ETS and articles published in the *Journal of the Evangelical Theological Society.*

50. Robert Preus, "Notes on the Inerrancy of Scripture" (1965), reprinted in Youngblood, *Evangelicals and Inerrancy,* 101–2. On the illegitimacy of questioning Scripture, see Merrill C. Tenney, "The Legitimate Limits of Biblical Criticism" (1960), in the same volume, 32. A number of NIV translators also contributed to Norman L. Geisler, ed., *Inerrancy* (Grand Rapids, Mich.: Zondervan Publishing House, 1979).

51. Stephen W. Paine, "Background of this Bible Translation Project," re-

port delivered at the Conference on Bible Translation, Moody Church, Chicago, 27 August 1966, copy in RSV Committee Papers; Barnard, *God's Word in Our Language,* 74–75. The inerrancy requirement was formally codified in the Constitution of the Committee on Bible Translation (adopted 5 January 1968), copy supplied by Kenneth L. Barker in correspondence with the author, 7 October 1995.

52. Quoted in Barnard, *God's Word in Our Language,* 100.

53. Translators' Manual of the Committee on Bible Translation (adopted 29 November 1968), 1, 5, copy supplied by Kenneth L. Barker in correspondence with the author, 7 October 1995. I am grateful to Dr. Barker for sharing this information.

54. See, for example, the "Branch" in Isaiah 11:1 (KJV), which was lowercased in the RV, ASV, and RSV; but compare the lowercase "branch" in Isaiah 4:2 (KJV).

55. Goddard to Weigle, 28 May 1966, RSV Committee Papers.

56. Barnard, *God's Word in Our Language,* 75.

57. Ibid., 15–18.

58. Burton L. Goddard, "The Crucial Issue in Bible Translation," *Christianity Today* 14 (3 July 1970): 13. Compare Goddard's report on contemporary Bible versions in "Summary of Proceedings," Conference on Bible Translation, Moody Church, Chicago, 26–27 August 1966, 2; copy in RSV Committee Papers.

59. Among Catholics, the books are known as the Deuterocanonicals. On the complicated issue of their number and arrangement in the larger canon, see the summary in *The Oxford Dictionary of the Christian Church,* edited by F. L. Cross and E. A. Livingstone, 3rd ed. (Oxford: Oxford University Press, 1997), 83–85.

60. Westminster Confession of Faith, ch. 1, no. 3, in *The Book of Confessions* (Louisville, Ky.: Office of the General Assembly, Presbyterian Church [U.S.A.], 1991), n.p.

61. The Apocrypha was translated by a nine-member section of the RSV committee headed by Luther Weigle and including four new members: Floyd V. Filson of McCormick Theological Seminary, Bruce M. Metzger of Princeton Theological Seminary, Robert H. Pfeiffer of Harvard University, and Allen P. Wikgren of the University of Chicago. See Luther A. Weigle, "The Standard Bible Committee," in *Translating and Understanding the Old Testament: Essays in Honor of Herbert Gordon May,* edited by Harry Thomas Frank and William L. Reed (Nashville: Abingdon Press, 1970), 32–33.

62. I shall refer to the Catholic Biblical Association *of Great Britain* to distinguish it from the Catholic Biblical Association in the United States.

63. See Canons 1399 and 1400 in Abbo and Hannan, *The Sacred Canons,* 634, 638–39.

64. Morrison to Weigle, 13 August 1953, RSV Committee Papers.

65. On the events leading up to the RSV Catholic Edition, see Reginald C. Fuller, "The Revised Standard Version Catholic Edition and Its Ecumenical Significance," *One in Christ* 1 (1965): 360–66.

66. Sebastian Bullough, "Confidential Report on the Meeting on July 14 [1954] at the Connaught Hotel, London," RSV Committee Papers.

67. For example, Herbert Gordon May to Weigle, 16 June 1955; J. Philip Hyatt to Weigle, 17 June 1955; George Dahl to Weigle, 22 June 1955; compare the more critical comments in Frederick C. Grant to Weigle, 11 June 1955; William A. Irwin to Weigle, 14 June 1955; RSV Committee Papers.

68. Weigle to Edgar J. Goodspeed, 27 July 1955, RSV Committee Papers.

69. Goodspeed to Weigle, 30 July 1955, RSV Committee Papers.

70. Robert Wuthnow, *The Restructuring of American Religion: Society and Faith Since World War II* (Princeton: Princeton University Press, 1988), 72–76.

71. Luther A. Weigle, "The Revised Standard Version of the Bible," *Catholic Biblical Quarterly* 14 (1952): 310–18; compare the favorable comment on the RSV in John L. McKenzie, review of the Revised Standard Version, *Catholic Biblical Quarterly* 17 (1955): 88–90; and Edward P. Arbez, "Modern Translations of the Old Testament," *Catholic Biblical Quarterly* 17 (1955): 456–85.

72. Quoted in Gerald P. Fogarty, *American Catholic Biblical Scholarship: A History from the Early Republic to Vatican II* (San Francisco: Harper and Row, 1989), 346–47.

73. Dogmatic Constitution on Divine Revelation ("Dei Verbum"), ch. 6, no. 22, in *The Documents of Vatican II*, edited by Walter M. Abbott (Piscataway, N.J.: New Century Publishers, 1966), 126, with Grant's response, 132.

74. Frederick C. Grant, *Translating the Bible* (Greenwich, Conn.: Seabury Press, 1961), 49, 88, 93.

75. Fuller to Weigle, 15 November 1963; Weigle to the Standard Bible Committee, 5 June 1964; RSV Committee Papers; "A Protestant Bible Authorized for Use by Britain's Catholics," *New York Times*, 7 December 1963, 1, 8; compare Lewis Chester, "First Bible for All Is Near," *Times* (London), 24 November 1963.

76. Weigle to Paul VI, 28 January 1966, RSV Committee Papers; Robert Morehouse, "Rev. Luther A. Weigle Receives Papal Honor," *Yale Daily News*, 27 January 1966.

77. Brown's critique appeared in the *Baltimore Catholic Review*, 15 October 1965, clipping in RSV Committee Papers; compare his comment on the RSVCE in "The English Bible," in *The Jerome Biblical Commentary*, edited by Brown, Joseph A. Fitzmyer, and Roland E. Murphy (Englewood Cliffs, N.J.: Prentice-Hall, 1968), 587. The RSVCE's note on Luke 1:5–2:52 was later slightly modified.

78. Fuller to Knoff, 13 November 1965, RSV Committee Papers; on Isaiah

7:14 in the New American Bible, see Fogarty, *American Catholic Biblical Scholarship,* 345–46.

79. Herbert G. May and Bruce M. Metzger, eds., *The Oxford Annotated Bible with the Apocrypha: Revised Standard Version* (New York: Oxford University Press, 1965); Cushing's imprimatur (along with the handful of modified footnotes) appeared in a 1966 printing.

80. See, for example, [Luther A. Weigle], *An Open Letter Concerning the Revised Standard Version of the Bible* (New York: National Council of the Churches of Christ in the United States of America, n.d.), 8–9.

Epilogue

1. As I suggested in chapter 5, Grant may have been less sanguine by the 1960s about the impartiality of textual criticism.

2. Kenneth W. Clark, "The Theological Relevance of Textual Variation in Current Criticism of the Greek New Testament," *Journal of Biblical Literature* 85 (1966): 1–16.

3. Stanley E. Hardwick, "Do Evangelicals Need a New Bible Translation? No," *Christianity Today* 12 (27 September 1968): 11, 14–15.

4. R. Laird Harris, "Do Evangelicals Need a New Bible Translation? Yes," *Christianity Today* 12 (27 September 1968): 10, 12–14.

5. Henry Otis Dwight, *The Centennial History of the American Bible Society* (New York: Macmillan, 1916), 9, 33, 457; Richard Kevin Barnard, *God's Word in Our Language: The Story of the New International Version* (Colorado Springs: International Bible Society, 1989), 76–90 (Barnard was formerly the communications director of the NYBS, later renamed the International Bible Society); and Burton L. Goddard, *The NIV Story: The Inside Story of the New International Version* (New York: Vantage Press, 1989), 46.

6. Barnard, *God's Word in Our Language,* 167–75.

7. Edwin H. Palmer, *The Five Points of Calvinism* (Grand Rapids, Mich.: Baker Book House, 1972; enl. ed., 1980), 5–6.

8. Quoted in undated news release, New York Bible Society, copy in RSV Committee Papers. On Palmer, compare Barnard, *God's Word in Our Language,* 91–97.

9. Carolyn Johnson Youngblood, "The New International Version Translation Project: Its Conception and Implementation," *Journal of the Evangelical Theological Society* 21 (1978): 246, 249.

10. The translators and consultants are listed in Barnard, *God's Word in Our Language,* 191–98; and Goddard, *The NIV Story,* 119–24.

11. On the 1969 market-testing of John, see Frank A. Gaebelein, "Evangelicals Draft New Version," *Eternity* 21 (April 1970): 46–49. An NIV

"Commonwealth Edition" (with British spellings and usages) was published by the London firm of Hodder and Stoughton in 1979. A slightly corrected and revised edition of the entire NIV appeared in 1984; all quotations hereafter are from this edition.

12. Kenneth L. Barker, "Virgin," in *Wycliffe Bible Encyclopedia,* edited by Charles F. Pfeiffer et al., vol. 2 (Chicago: Moody Press, 1975), 1779; compare Kenneth L. Barker, *The Accuracy of the NIV* (Grand Rapids, Mich.: Baker Book House, 1996), 42.

13. Translators' preface to the NIV (1978, 1984).

14. The NIV translator Jack P. Lewis outlines some of the overtly theological aspects of the version in *The English Bible from KJV to NIV: A History and Evaluation,* 2nd ed. (Grand Rapids, Mich.: Baker Book House, 1991), 324–27.

15. Bruce Waltke, "Translation Problems in Psalms 2 and 4," in *The Making of a Contemporary Translation: New International Version,* edited by Kenneth L. Barker (London: Hodder and Stoughton, 1987), 125.

16. William Sanford LaSor, "What Kind of Version Is the New International?" *Christianity Today* 23 (20 October 1978): 18–20. As he had in the 1950s, LaSor continued to argue that passages such as Isaiah 7:14, while referring *typologically* to Christ, had entirely different meanings in their original Jewish context; see William Sanford LaSor, "The *Sensus Plenior* and Biblical Interpretation," in *Scripture, Tradition, and Interpretation: Essays Presented to Everett F. Harrison by His Students and Colleagues in Honor of His Seventy-fifth Birthday,* edited by W. Ward Gasque and William Sanford LaSor (Grand Rapids, Mich.: Eerdmans, 1978), 260–77.

17. Peter C. Craigie, "The New International Version: A Review Article," *Journal of the Evangelical Theological Society* 21 (September 1978): 251–54.

18. Robert G. Bratcher, "The New International Version," in *The Word of God: A Guide to English Versions of the Bible,* edited by Lloyd R. Bailey (Atlanta: John Knox Press, 1982), 152–67; Bratcher's article originally appeared in *Duke Divinity School Review* 44 (Spring 1979): 164–79.

19. See, for example, the comment by NIV executive secretary Edwin Palmer in an interview with Stephen Board and Clifford Swanson, *Eternity* 29 (October 1978): 42.

20. Sales figures from Barnard, *God's Word in Our Language,* 180; and Barker, *The Accuracy of the NIV,* 11.

21. Barnard, *God's Word in Our Language,* 188–89; and "Transforming the World with the Word," International Bible Society brochure, n.d. The evangelical organizations headquartered in Colorado Springs are listed in a memorandum from Jeanene Moore to International Bible Society staff, 2 August 1995 (copy supplied by Moore in correspondence with the author).

22. *The Holy Bible, Revised Standard Version: An Ecumenical Edition*

(New York and Glasgow: Collins, 1973); the title "RSV Common Bible" appeared only on the book jacket.

23. Herbert G. May and Bruce M. Metzger, eds., *The New Oxford Annotated Bible with the Apocrypha: Revised Standard Version* (New York: Oxford University Press, 1977); compare Bruce M. Metzger, "The RSV—Ecumenical Edition," *Theology Today* 34 (1977): 315-17.

24. See Bruce M. Metzger, Robert C. Dentan, and Walter Harrelson, *The Making of the New Revised Standard Version of the Bible* (Grand Rapids, Mich.: Eerdmans, 1991), especially 73-84; compare Bruce Manning Metzger, "Translating the Bible: The New Revised Standard Version," in *Reminiscences of an Octogenarian* (Peabody, Mass.: Hendrickson, 1997), 89-102.

25. Sales figure from Richard N. Ostling, "Farewell to Thee's and He's," *Time,* 7 May 1990, 117.

26. General introduction to *The New Testament and Psalms: An Inclusive Version,* edited by Victor Roland Gold et al. (New York: Oxford University Press, 1995), xii.

27. For a defense of the rendering "religious authorities," see the otherwise negative review of the Inclusive Version by Gail R. O'Day, "Probing an Inclusive Scripture," *Christian Century* 113 (3-10 July 1996): 692-94.

28. Quoted in Aida Besançon Spencer, "Power Play," *Christian Century* 114 (2-9 July 1997): 618. On the debate over inclusive Scripture among evangelicals, see the companion articles by Wayne Grudem and Grant Osborne, "Do Inclusive-Language Bibles Distort Scripture?" *Christianity Today* 41 (27 October 1997): 26-39.

29. *The NIV Women's Devotional Bible* (Grand Rapids, Mich.: Zondervan, 1990); *The NIV Men's Devotional Bible* (Zondervan, 1993); *The Original African Heritage Study Bible: King James Version* (Nashville: James C. Winston, 1993); *The African-American Devotional Bible* (Zondervan, 1997; available in either NIV or KJV); *The Student Bible* (Zondervan, 1986; NIV); *The Young Explorer's Bible: New International Version* (Zondervan, 1995); *The Wesley Bible: New King James Version* (Nashville: Thomas Nelson, 1990); *Concordia Reference Bible: New International Version* (St. Louis: Concordia, 1989); *Recovery Devotional Bible: New International Version* (Zondervan, 1993); and *New Believer's Bible: New Living Translation* (Wheaton, Ill.: Tyndale House, 1996).

30. This is a point made rather forcefully (and often polemically) in James Barr, *Fundamentalism* (Philadelphia: Westminster Press, 1978), especially chapter 8, "Miracles and the Supernatural," 234-59.

31. For Frei's use of the term "aesthetic," see "Remarks in Connection with a Theological Proposal," in Hans W. Frei, *Theology and Narrative: Selected Essays,* edited by George Hunsinger and William C. Placher (New York: Oxford University Press, 1993), 26-44, especially 32-33.

32. On the concurrence of literal and typological (or figural) reading, see Hans W. Frei, *The Eclipse of Biblical Narrative: A Study in Eighteenth and Nineteenth Century Hermeneutics* (New Haven: Yale University Press, 1974), 27–30.

33. On the problem of "reference," see Frei's "Response to 'Narrative Theology: An Evangelical Appraisal,'" in *Theology and Narrative*, 207–12.

34. It is interesting to speculate on whether Frei would have favored highlighting the biblical narrative's overarching unity by translating the Old Testament christologically. I suspect he would have regarded christological translation as simply unnecessary: the Old Testament's intimate relationship to the New emerges clearly enough even when Christology is not made a criterion of translation. A far more serious objection to christological translation, and one beyond the purview of this study, is Hebrew Scripture's self-integrity as a Jewish document.

35. The truth-question has been particularly acute in relation to the closely allied work of George A. Lindbeck, *The Nature of Doctrine: Religion and Theology in a Postliberal Age* (Philadelphia: Westminster Press, 1984). For a good survey of the issues, see the essays in Timothy R. Phillips and Dennis L. Okholm, eds., *The Nature of Confession: Evangelicals and Postliberals in Conversation* (Downers Grove, Ill.: InterVarsity Press, 1996). See also the critique of Lindbeck in Alister E. McGrath, *The Genesis of Doctrine: A Study in the Foundations of Doctrinal Criticism* (Oxford: Basil Blackwell, 1990), 14–34.

Bibliography

Note on Archival Sources

The primary archival sources for this study are the Papers of the Revised Standard Version Committee (cited as RSV Committee Papers), Princeton Theological Seminary Library, Princeton, New Jersey. I gratefully acknowledge permission from Bruce M. Metzger, chairman of the NRSV committee, to use this uncatalogued collection before it was deposited in 1997 in Princeton Seminary's Department of Archives and Special Collections. Since 1979, a major portion of the collection has been available on twenty-two reels of microfilm at the Oberlin College Archives, Oberlin, Ohio, with duplicate sets at Princeton Seminary and the Library of Congress. A smaller, overlapping collection, the Papers of the Standard Bible Committee, Yale Divinity School Library, contains the RSV committee's drafts of biblical books. Additional overlapping materials on the RSV controversy appear in two collections: the Papers of the National Council of the Churches of Christ in the United States of America, Presbyterian Historical Society, Philadelphia; and the Papers of Luther Allan Weigle, Sterling Memorial Library, Yale University. In citing archival sources, I have deemed it unnecessary to specify where carbon copies of letters, rather than originals, are quoted.

Published Works Cited
(Excluding pamphlets from the RSV Committee Papers and other archival materials)

Abbo, John A., and Jerome D. Hannan, eds. *The Sacred Canons: A Concise Presentation of the Current Disciplinary Norms of the Church.* Vol. 2: Canons 870–2414. 2nd rev. ed. St. Louis: Herder, 1960.
Abbott, Walter M., and Joseph Gallagher, eds. *The Documents of Vatican II.* Piscataway, N.J.: Association Press, 1966.

Ackroyd, P. R., C. F. Evans, G. W. H. Lampe, and S. L. Greenslade, eds. *The Cambridge History of the Bible*. 3 vols. Cambridge: Cambridge University Press, 1963–70.

Air Reserve Center Training Manual 45–0050. Increment 5. Vol. 7. Mitchell Air Force Base, N.Y.: Continental Air Command, 1960.

Albright, William Foxwell. "The War in Europe and the Future of Biblical Studies." In *The Study of the Bible Today and Tomorrow*, edited by Harold R. Willoughby. Chicago: University of Chicago Press, 1947.

———. *From the Stone Age to Christianity: Monotheism and the Historical Process*. 2nd ed. Garden City, N.Y.: Anchor Books, 1957.

Allis, Oswald T. *Revised Version or Revised Bible? A Critique of the Revised Standard Version of the Old Testament*. Philadelphia: Presbyterian and Reformed Publishing, 1953.

———. "RSV Appraisal: Old Testament." *Christianity Today* 1 (8 July 1957): 6–7, 21–24.

Anderson, Benedict. *Imagined Communities: Reflections on the Origin and Spread of Nationalism*. Rev. ed. London: Verso, 1991.

Anderson, Christopher. *The Annals of the English Bible*. 2 vols. London: William Pickering, 1845.

Anglo-American Bible Revision: Its Necessity and Purpose. By the Members of the American Revision Committee. Rev. ed. Philadelphia: American Sunday-School Union, 1879.

An Introduction to the Revised Standard Version of the New Testament. New York: International Council of Religious Education, 1946.

An Introduction to the Revised Standard Version of the Old Testament. New York: Thomas Nelson and Sons, 1952.

Arbez, Edward P. "Modern Translations of the Old Testament." *Catholic Biblical Quarterly* 17 (1944): 456–85.

Auerbach, Erich. *Mimesis: The Representation of Reality in Western Literature*. Translated by Willard R. Trask. Princeton: Princeton University Press, 1953.

Aston, Margaret. *England's Iconoclasts*. Vol. 1. *Laws against Images*. Oxford: Clarendon Press, 1988.

Bacon, Margaret Hope. *Let This Life Speak: The Legacy of Henry Joel Cadbury*. Philadelphia: University of Pennsylvania Press, 1987.

Baikie, James. *The English Bible and Its Story: Its Growth, Its Translators and Their Adventures*. Philadelphia: Lippincott, 1928.

Bailey, Lloyd R., ed. *The Word of God: A Guide to English Versions of the Bible*. Atlanta: John Knox Press, 1982.

Bainton, Roland H. *The Reformation of the Sixteenth Century*. Enlarged ed. Boston: Beacon Press, 1985.

Balmer, Randall H. "The Princetonians and Scripture: A Reconsideration." *Westminster Theological Journal* 44 (1982): 352–65.

Barker, Kenneth L. "Virgin." In *Wycliffe Bible Encyclopedia*, edited by Charles F. Pfeiffer et al. Vol. 2. Chicago: Moody Press, 1975.

———, ed. *The Making of a Contemporary Translation: New International Version*. London: Hodder and Stoughton, 1987.

———. *The Accuracy of the NIV*. Grand Rapids, Mich.: Baker Book House, 1996.

Barker, Kenneth L., Donald Burdick, John Stek, Walter Wessel and Ronald

Youngblood, eds. *The NIV Study Bible.* Grand Rapids, Mich.: Zondervan, 1985.

Barlow, Philip L. *Mormons and the Bible: The Place of the Latter-day Saints in American Religion.* New York: Oxford University Press, 1991.

Barnard, Richard Kevin. *God's Word in Our Language: The Story of the New International Version.* Colorado Springs: International Bible Society, 1989.

Barnhouse, Donald Grey. "I Have Read the RSV." *Eternity* 4 (June 1953): 10–12.

Barr, James. *Fundamentalism.* Philadelphia: Westminster Press, 1978.

Bauer, Walter. *A Greek-English Lexicon of the New Testament.* Edited and translated by William F. Arndt, F. Wilbur Gingrich, and Frederick W. Danker. 2nd ed. Chicago: University of Chicago Press, 1979.

Beck, T. Romeyn. "Comparative Merits of the Authorized Version of the English New Testament and the Revised Version as Translations." *Reformed Quarterly Review* 28 (1881): 535–58.

Becker, Carl L. *The Heavenly City of the Eighteenth-Century Philosophers.* New Haven: Yale University Press, 1932.

Bederman, Gail. *Manliness and Civilization: A Cultural History of Gender and Race in the United States, 1880–1917.* Chicago: University of Chicago Press, 1995.

Bendroth, Margaret Lamberts. *Fundamentalism and Gender, 1875 to the Present.* New Haven: Yale University Press, 1993.

Bercovitch, Sacvan, ed. *Typology and Early American Literature.* Amherst: University of Massachusetts Press, 1972.

Billington, Ray Allen. *The Protestant Crusade, 1800–1860: A Study of the Origins of American Nativism.* New York: Macmillan, 1938. Reprint, Chicago: Quadrangle Books, 1964.

Bledstein, Burton J. *The Culture of Professionalism: The Middle Class and the Development of Higher Education in America.* New York: Norton, 1976.

Blumenberg, Hans. *The Legitimacy of the Modern Age.* Translated by Robert M. Wallace. Cambridge: MIT Press, 1983.

Board, Stephen, and Clifford Swanson. "Will the New International Version Win the Translation Race? Interview with Edwin Palmer." *Eternity* 29 (October 1978): 28–30, 28–30, 42–45.

Bonhoeffer, Dietrich. "Protestantism without Reformation." In *Dietrich Bonhoeffer: Witness to Jesus Christ,* edited by John de Gruchy. The Making of Modern Theology Series. Minneapolis: Fortress Press, 1991.

The Book of Confessions. Louisville, Ky.: Office of the General Assembly, Presbyterian Church (U.S.A.), 1991.

Boone, Kathleen C. *The Bible Tells Them So: The Discourse of Protestant Fundamentalism.* Albany: State University of New York Press, 1989.

Boylan, Anne M. *Sunday School: The Formation of an American Institution.* New Haven: Yale University Press, 1988.

Bozeman, Theodore Dwight. *Protestants in an Age of Science: The Baconian Ideal and Antebellum Religious Thought.* Chapel Hill: University of North Carolina Press, 1977.

———. *To Live Ancient Lives: The Primitivist Dimension in Puritanism.* Chapel Hill: University of North Carolina Press, 1988.

Bratt, James D. *Dutch Calvinism in Modern America: A History of a Conservative Subculture.* Grand Rapids, Mich.: Eerdmans, 1984.

Bray, Gerald, ed. *Documents of the English Reformation*. Minneapolis: Fortress Press, 1994.

Brereton, Virginia Lieson. *Training God's Army: The American Bible School, 1880–1940*. Bloomington: Indiana University Press, 1988.

Bridges, Ronald, and Luther A. Weigle. *The Bible Word Book: Concerning Obsolete or Archaic Words in the King James Version of the Bible*. New York: Thomas Nelson and Sons, 1960.

Brown, Ira V. "The Higher Criticism Comes to America, 1880–1900." *Journal of Presbyterian History* 38 (1960): 192–212.

Brown, John. *The History of the English Bible*. Cambridge: Cambridge University Press, 1911.

Brown, Raymond E. "The English Bible." In *The Jerome Biblical Commentary*, edited by Raymond E. Brown, Joseph A. Fitzmyer, and Roland E. Murphy. Englewood Cliffs, N.J.: Prentice-Hall, 1968.

Bruce, F. F. *History of the Bible in English*. 3rd. ed. Cambridge, England: Lutterworth Press, 1978.

Bundy, Edgar C. *Collectivism in the Churches: A Documented Account of the Political Activities of the Federal, National, and World Councils of Churches*. Wheaton, Ill.: Church League of America, 1958.

Burgon, John William. *The Last Twelve Verses of the Gospel According to S. Mark, Vindicated against Recent Critical Objectors and Established*. Oxford: Parker, 1871.

———. *The Revision Revised: Three Articles Reprinted from the "Quarterly Review."* London: John Murray, 1883.

Burrows, Millar. *An Outline of Biblical Theology*. Philadelphia: Westminster Press, 1946.

———. *Diligently Compared: The Revised Standard Version and the King James Version of the Old Testament*. New York: Thomas Nelson and Sons, 1964.

Buswell, J. Oliver, Jr. "The Revised Standard Version of the New Testament." *Sunday School Times* 94 (1 November 1952): 919–21.

Buttz, H. A. "The Revised Version of the New Testament." *Methodist Quarterly Review* 63 (October 1881): 715–38.

Calvin, John. *Commentary on the Book of the Prophet Isaiah*. Vol. 1. Translated by William Pringle. Vol. 7 of *Calvin's Commentaries*. 1850. Reprint, Grand Rapids, Mich.: Baker Book House, 1993.

Campbell, Alexander. "A Restoration of the Ancient Order of Things, No. 1." *Christian Baptist* 2 (1825). Reprint, Cincinnati: D. S. Burnet and Benjamin Franklin, 1852.

Canton, William. *The Bible and the Anglo-Saxon People*. London: Dent, 1914.

Cantor, Norman F. *Inventing the Middle Ages: The Lives, Works, and Ideas of the Great Medievalists of the Twentieth Century*. New York: Quill, 1991.

———. *Civilization of the Middle Ages*. Rev. ed. New York: HarperCollins, 1993.

Carlen, Claudia, ed. *The Papal Encyclicals*. Vol. 4: 1939–58. Wilmington, N.C.: Consortium, 1981.

Carnell, Edward John. *The Case for Orthodox Theology*. Philadelphia: Westminster Press, 1959.

———. "Orthodoxy: Cultic vs. Classical." *Christian Century* 77 (30 March 1960): 377–79.

————. Review of *Harper Study Bible: The Holy Bible, Revised Standard Version,* edited by Harold Lindsell. *Christianity Today* 9 (12 February 1965): 38.

Carpenter, Joel A. *Revive Us Again: The Reawakening of American Fundamentalism.* New York: Oxford University Press, 1997.

Cashdollar, Charles D. *The Transformation of Theology, 1830–1890: Positivism and Protestant Thought in Britain and America.* Princeton: Princeton University Press, 1989.

Cavert, Samuel McCrea. *The American Churches in the Ecumenical Movement, 1900–1968.* New York: Association Press, 1968.

Chamberlin, William J. *Catalogue of English Bible Translations: A Classified Bibliography of Versions and Editions Including Books, Parts, and Old and New Testament Apocrypha and Apocryphal Books.* Westport, Conn.: Greenwood Press, 1991.

Cherry, Conrad. *Hurrying toward Zion: Universities, Divinity Schools, and American Protestantism.* Bloomington: Indiana University Press, 1995.

Chew, Peter. "The Great Bible Controversy." *Look,* 2 November 1952, 97–98.

Christian Education Today: A Statement of Basic Philosophy. Chicago: International Council of Religious Education, 1940.

Christian Reformed Church. Synod. *Agenda.* Grand Rapids, Mich., 1966.

The Churches and the Air Force Manual Issue: A Compilation by the National Council of Churches. New York: National Council of the Churches of Christ in the United States of America, 1960.

Clabaugh, Gary K. *Thunder on the Right: The Protestant Fundamentalists.* Chicago: Nelson-Hall, 1974.

Clark, Kenneth W. "The Theological Relevance of Textual Variation in Current Criticism of the Greek New Testament." *Journal of Biblical Literature* 85 (1966): 1–16.

Cmiel, Kenneth. *Democratic Eloquence: The Fight over Popular Speech in Nineteenth-Century America.* New York: William Morrow, 1990.

Collingwood, R. G. *An Essay on Metaphysics.* Oxford: Clarendon Press, 1940.

————. *The Idea of History.* Oxford: Clarendon Press, 1946.

Conant, H. C. *The English Bible: History of the Translation of the Holy Scriptures into the English Tongue: With Specimens of the Old English Versions.* New York: Sheldon, Blakeman, 1856.

Conant, H. C. and T. J. *The Popular History of the Translation of the Holy Scriptures into the English Tongue.* New York: I. K. Funk, 1881.

Congressional Record. 86th Congress, 2nd sess., 1960. Vol. 106, pt. 6.

Cook, James I. *Edgar Johnson Goodspeed: Articulate Scholar.* Chico, Calif.: Society of Biblical Literature, 1981.

Coriden, James A., Thomas J. Green, and Donald E. Heintschel, eds. *The Code of Canon Law: A Text and Commentary.* Mahwah, N.J.: Paulist Press, 1985.

Craig, Clarence Tucker. *The One Church in Light of the New Testament.* New York: Abingdon-Cokesbury Press, 1951.

Craigie, Peter C. "The New International Version: A Review Article." *Journal of the Evangelical Theological Society* 21 (1978): 251–54.

Cross, F. L., and E. A. Livingstone, eds. *The Oxford Dictionary of the Christian Church.* 3rd ed. Oxford: Oxford University Press, 1997.

Dabney, Robert Lewis. "The Revised Version of the New Testament." *Southern Presbyterian Review* 32 (1881): 575–83.

Dallmann, William. *William Tyndale: The Translator of the English Bible*. St. Louis: Concordia, 1904.

Daniell, David, ed. *Tyndale's New Testament*. New Haven: Yale University Press, 1989.

———. *William Tyndale: A Biography*. New Haven: Yale University Press, 1994.

Davies, Clifford S. L. "Henry VIII." In *The Oxford Encyclopedia of the Reformation*, edited by Hans J. Hillerbrand. Vol. 2. Oxford: Oxford University Press, 1996.

Davies, Horton. *Worship and Theology in England*. Vol. 1. *From Cranmer to Hooker, 1534–1603*. Princeton: Princeton University Press, 1970.

———. *Worship and Theology in England*. Vol. 2. *From Andrewes to Baxter and Fox, 1603–1690*. Princeton: Princeton University Press, 1975.

DeBerg, Betty A. *Ungodly Women: Gender and the First Wave of American Fundamentalism*. Minneapolis: Fortress Press, 1990.

Dickens, A. G. *The English Reformation*. 2nd ed. University Park: Pennsylvania State University Press, 1989.

Documentary History of the American Committee on Revision. New York, 1885.

Donagan, Alan. *The Later Philosophy of R. G. Collingwood*. Oxford: Clarendon Press, 1962.

Drake, Charles. "The Battle on the Revised Standard Version." *Christianity and Crisis* 13 (22 June 1953): 90–92.

Duffy, Eamon. *The Stripping of the Altars: Traditional Religion in England, 1400–1580*. New Haven: Yale University Press, 1992.

Dwight, Henry Otis. *The Centennial History of the American Bible Society*. New York: Macmillan, 1916.

Eadie, John. *The English Bible: An External and Critical History of the Various English Translations of Scripture*. 2 vols. London: Macmillan, 1876.

Eco, Umberto. *Art and Beauty in the Middle Ages*. Translated by Hugh Bredin. New Haven: Yale University Press, 1986.

Ehrman, Bart D. *The Orthodox Corruption of Scripture: The Effect of Early Christological Controversies on the Text of the New Testament*. New York: Oxford University Press, 1993.

Eighty-eighth Annual Report of the American Bible Society. New York, 1904.

Eire, Carlos M. N. *War Against the Idols: The Reformation of Worship from Erasmus to Calvin*. Cambridge: Cambridge University Press, 1986.

Farrar, F. W. "Fidelity and Bias in Versions of the Bible." *Expositor* 3, series 2 (1882): 280–302.

Feucht, Oscar E. "Synod's Advisory Committee on English Bible Versions Reports on Its Study of the Revised Standard Version of the Bible." *Lutheran Witness*, 15 July 1958, 8–9, 20–21.

Fogarty, Gerald P. *American Catholic Biblical Scholarship: A History from the Early Republic to Vatican II*. San Francisco: Harper and Row, 1989.

Forster, Arnold, and Benjamin R. Epstein. *Danger on the Right*. New York: Random House, 1964.

Fox, William L. *Willard L. Sperry: The Quandaries of a Liberal Protestant Mind, 1914–1939*. New York: Lang, 1991.

Foxe, John. *Acts and Monuments*. Vol. 5. Edited by George Townsend and Stephen Reed Cattley. London, 1838.

Frei, Hans W. *The Eclipse of Biblical Narrative: A Study in Eighteenth and Nineteenth Century Hermeneutics.* New Haven: Yale University Press, 1974.

———. *Types of Christian Theology.* Edited by George Hunsinger and William C. Placher. New Haven: Yale University Press, 1992.

———. *Theology and Narrative: Selected Essays.* Edited by George Hunsinger and William C. Placher. New York: Oxford University Press, 1993.

Fried, Richard M. *Nightmare in Red: The McCarthy Era in Perspective.* New York: Oxford University Press, 1990.

Froude, James Anthony. *History of England from the Fall of Wolsey to the Defeat of the Spanish Armada.* Vol. 3. New ed. London: Longmans, Green, 1873.

Frye, Northrop. *The Great Code: The Bible and Literature.* San Diego: Harcourt Brace Jovanovich, 1982.

Fulke, William. *Confutation of the Rhemish Testament.* New York, 1834.

Fuller, David Otis. *True or False? The Westcott-Hort Textual Theory Examined.* Grand Rapids, Mich.: Grand Rapids International Publications, 1973.

———, ed. *Which Bible?* 3rd ed. Grand Rapids, Mich.: Grand Rapids International Publications, 1972.

Fuller, Reginald C. "The Revised Standard Version Catholic Edition and Its Ecumenical Significance." *One in Christ* 1 (1965): 360–66.

The Fundamentals: A Testimony to the Truth. 12 vols. Chicago: Testimony Publishing, 1910–15. Reprint, New York: Garland, 1988.

Funk, Robert W. "The Watershed of the American Biblical Tradition: The Chicago School, First Phase, 1892–1920." *Journal of Biblical Literature* 95 (1976): 4–22.

Gaebelein, Frank A. "Evangelicals Draft New Version." *Eternity* 21 (April 1970): 46–49.

Garrison, W. E. "A New New Testament—Coming." *Christian Century* 63 (1946): 171–72.

———. "The New New Testament—Here." *Christian Century* 63 (1946): 202–4.

Garside, Charles, Jr. *Zwingli and the Arts.* New Haven: Yale University Press, 1966.

Gasper, Louis. *The Fundamentalist Movement, 1930–1956.* The Hague: Mouton, 1963. Reprint, Grand Rapids: Baker Book House, 1981.

Gaustad, Edwin S., and Walter Harrelson, eds. *The Bible in American Culture.* 6 vols. Philadelphia: Fortress Press, 1982–85.

Geisler, Norman L., ed. *Inerrancy.* Grand Rapids, Mich.: Zondervan Publishing House, 1979.

The Geneva Bible: A Facsimile of the 1560 Edition. With an introduction by Lloyd E. Berry. Madison: University of Wisconsin Press, 1969.

Goddard, Burton L. "The Crucial Issue in Bible Translation." *Christianity Today* 14 (3 July 1970): 900–901.

———. *The NIV Story: The Inside Story of the New International Version.* New York: Vantage Press, 1989.

Gold, Victor Roland, et al., eds. *The New Testament and Psalms: An Inclusive Version.* New York: Oxford University Press, 1995.

Goodspeed, Edgar J. *The New Testament: An American Translation.* Chicago: University of Chicago Press, 1923.

———. *The Making of the English New Testament.* Chicago: University of Chicago Press, 1925.

————. *How Came the Bible?* New York: Abingdon-Cokesbury Press, 1940.

————. *As I Remember.* New York: Harper and Brothers, 1953.

Goodspeed, Edgar J., and J. M. Powis Smith, eds. *The Bible: An American Translation.* Chicago: University of Chicago Press, 1931.

Graff, Gerald. *Professing Literature: An Institutional History.* Chicago: University of Chicago Press, 1987.

Graham, Stephen R. *Cosmos in the Chaos: Philip Schaff's Interpretation of Nineteenth-Century American Religion.* Grand Rapids, Mich.: Eerdmans, 1995.

Grant, Frederick C. *Translating the Bible.* Greenwich, Conn.: Seabury Press, 1961.

Green, Ian. *The Christian's ABC: Catechisms and Catechizing in England c. 1530–1740.* Oxford: Clarendon Press, 1996.

Green, William Henry. "The Authorized Version and the Present Revision." *The Wycliffe Semi-Millennial Bible Celebration.* Proceedings of the Convention of the Bible Societies of New Jersey, Trenton, N.J., 21–22 September 1880. Newark, N.J., n.d.

Greenblatt, Stephen. *Renaissance Self-Fashioning: From More to Shakespeare.* Chicago: University of Chicago Press, 1980.

Greenfeld, Liah. *Nationalism: Five Roads to Modernity.* Cambridge: Harvard University Press, 1992.

Grudem, Wayne, and Grant Osborne. "Do Inclusive-Languages Bibles Distort Scripture?" *Christianity Today* 41 (27 October 1997): 26–39.

Gutjahr, Paul C. *An American Bible: A History of the Good Book in the United States, 1777–1880.* Stanford, Calif.: Stanford University Press, 1999.

Habermas, Jürgen. *The Philosophical Discourse of Modernity.* Translated by Frederick G. Lawrence. Cambridge: MIT Press, 1992.

Haigh, Christopher, ed. *The English Reformation Revised.* Cambridge: Cambridge University Press, 1987.

Hall, Basil. "Martin Bucer in England." In *Martin Bucer: Reforming Church and Community,* edited by David F. Wright. Cambridge: Cambridge University Press, 1994.

Haller, William. *The Elect Nation: The Meaning and Relevance of Foxe's Book of Martyrs.* New York: Harper and Row, 1963.

Hamilton-Hoare, H. W. *The Evolution of the English Bible: An Historical Sketch of the Successive Versions from 1382 to 1885.* London: John Murray, 1901.

Handy, Robert T. *A Christian America: Protestant Hopes and Historical Realities.* 2nd ed. New York: Oxford University Press, 1984.

————. *Undermined Establishment: Church-State Relations in America, 1880–1920.* Princeton, N.J.: Princeton University Press, 1991.

Hardwick, Stanley E. "Do Evangelicals Need a New Bible Translation? No." *Christianity Today* 12 (27 September 1968): 11, 14–15.

Harris, R. Laird. "Do Evangelicals Need a New Bible Translation? Yes." *Christianity Today* 12 (27 September 1968): 10, 12–14.

Harrisville, Roy A., and Walter Sundberg. *The Bible in Modern Culture: Theology and Historical-Critical Method from Spinoza to Käsemann.* Minneapolis: Fortress Press, 1995.

Hart, D. G. *Defending the Faith: J. Gresham Machen and the Crisis of Conservative Protestantism in Modern America.* Baltimore: Johns Hopkins University Press, 1994.

Hatch, Nathan O. *The Democratization of American Christianity.* New Haven: Yale University Press, 1989.

Hatch, Nathan O., and Mark A. Noll, eds. *The Bible in America: Essays in Cultural History.* New York: Oxford University Press, 1982.

Hendriksen, William. "The Drive Is On! To Put across the Revised Standard Version of the Bible." *Banner* 88 (2 January 1953): 6–7, 22.

Henry, Carl F. H., ed. *Revelation and the Bible: Contemporary Evangelical Thought.* Grand Rapids, Mich.: Baker Book House, 1958.

Hentz, John P. *History of the Lutheran Version of the Bible.* Columbus, Ohio: F. J. Heer, 1910.

Hill, Christopher. *The Century of Revolution, 1603–1714.* Norton Library History of England. New York: Norton, 1961.

———. *The English Bible and the Seventeenth-Century Revolution.* London: Penguin Books, 1993.

Hills, Margaret T., ed. *The English Bible in America: A Bibliography of Editions of the Bible and the New Testament Published in America 1777–1957.* New York: American Bible Society, 1961.

Hodge, A. A., and B. B. Warfield. "Inspiration." *Presbyterian Review* 2 (1881): 225–60.

Hodge, Archibald Alexander. *The Life of Charles Hodge D.D. LL.D.* New York: Scribner's, 1880.

Hoover, J. Edgar. "Communist Propaganda and the Christian Pulpit." *Christianity Today* 5 (24 October 1960): 5–7.

Huelster, A. "A Bird's Eye View of the Revised New Testament." *Evangelical Messenger* 34, no. 27 (5 July 1881).

Hunter, James Davison. *Evangelicalism: The Coming Generation.* Chicago: University of Chicago Press, 1987.

———. *Culture Wars: The Struggle to Define America.* New York: Basic Books, 1991.

Hutchison, William R., ed. *Between the Times: The Travail of the Protestant Establishment in America, 1900–1960.* Cambridge: Cambridge University Press, 1989.

Irwin, William A. "That Troublesome '*Almah* and Other Matters." *Review and Expositor* 50 (July 1953): 337–60.

Jacobsen, Douglas, and William Vance Trollinger, Jr., eds. *Re-Forming the Center: American Protestantism, 1900 to the Present.* Grand Rapids, Mich.: Eerdmans, 1998.

Jorstad, Erling. *The Politics of Doomsday: Fundamentalists of the Far Right.* Nashville: Abingdon Press, 1970.

Junghans, Helmar. *Wittenberg als Lutherstadt.* Göttingen: Vandenhoeck and Ruprecht, 1979.

Justin Martyr. *Dialogue with Trypho.* In *Writings of Saint Justin Martyr,* edited and translated by Thomas B. Falls. New York: Christian Heritage, 1948.

Kannengiesser, Charles, ed. *Bible de tous les temps.* 8 vols. Paris: Éditions Beauchesne, 1984–85.

Kibbey, Ann. *The Interpretation of Material Shapes in Puritanism: A Study of Rhetoric, Prejudice and Violence.* Cambridge: Cambridge University Press, 1986.

King, John N. *Tudor Royal Iconography: Literature and Art in an Age of Religious Crisis.* Princeton: Princeton University Press, 1989.

Kittel, Gerhard, ed., and Geoffrey W. Bromiley, trans. *Theological Dictionary of the New Testament*. Grand Rapids, Mich.: Eerdmans, 1965.

Kooiman, Willem Jan. *Luther and the Bible*. Translated by John Schmidt. Philadelphia: Muhlenberg Press, 1961.

Kretzmann, P. E. *The Story of the German Bible: A Contribution to the Quadricentennial of Luther's Translation*. St. Louis: Concordia, 1934.

Kuklick, Bruce. *Puritans in Babylon: The Ancient Near East and American Intellectual Life, 1880–1930*. Princeton: Princeton University Press, 1996.

Ladd, George Eldon. "RSV Appraisal: New Testament." *Christianity Today* 1 (8 July 1957): 7–11.

Larue, Gerald A. "Another Chapter in the History of Bible Translation: Attacks upon the RSV." *Journal of Bible and Religion* 31 (1963): 301–10.

LaSor, William Sanford. "The *Sensus Plenior* and Biblical Interpretation." In *Scripture, Tradition, and Interpretation: Essays Presented to Everett F. Harrison by His Students and Colleagues in Honor of His Seventy-fifth Birthday*, edited by W. Ward Gasque and William Sanford LaSor. Grand Rapids, Mich.: Eerdmans, 1978.

———. "What Kind of Version Is the New International?" *Christianity Today* 23 (20 October 1978): 18–20.

Lea, John W. *The Book of Books and Its Wonderful Story: A Popular Handbook for Colleges, Bible Classes, Sunday Schools, and Private Students*. Philadelphia: John C. Winston, 1922.

Lee, Robert. *The Social Sources of Church Unity: An Interpretation of Unitive Movements in American Protestantism*. New York: Abingdon Press, 1960.

Lewis, Jack P. *The English Bible from KJV to NIV: A History and Evaluation*. 2nd ed. Grand Rapids, Mich.: Baker Book House, 1991.

Lewis, John. *A Complete History of the Several Translations of the Holy Bible, and New Testament, into English, Both in MS. and in Print: And of the most Remarkable Editions of them since the Invention of Printing*. 2nd ed. London, 1739.

Lietzmann, Hans, Heinrich Bornkamm, Hans Volz, and Ernst Wolf, eds. *Die Bekenntnisschriften der Evangelisch-Lutherischen Kirche*. 11th ed. Göttingen: Vandenhoeck and Ruprecht, 1992.

Lightfoot, J. B., Richard Chenevix Trench, and C. J. Ellicott. *The Revision of the English Version of the New Testament*. New York: Harper and Brothers, 1873.

Lindbeck, George A. *The Nature of Doctrine: Religion and Theology in a Postliberal Age*. Philadelphia: Westminster Press, 1984.

Lindberg, Carter. *The European Reformations*. Oxford: Blackwell, 1996.

Lindsell, Harold, ed. *Harper Study Bible: The Holy Bible, Revised Standard Version*. New York: Harper and Row, 1964.

Lippy, Charles H., ed. *Twentieth-Century Shapers of American Popular Religion*. Westport, Conn.: Greenwood Press, 1989.

Lockridge, Kenneth A. *Literacy in Colonial New England: An Enquiry into the Social Context of Literacy in the Early Modern West*. New York: Norton, 1974.

Loetscher, Lefferts A. *The Broadening Church: A Study of Theological Issues in the Presbyterian Church since 1869*. Philadelphia: University of Pennsylvania Press, 1954.

Long, Burke O. *Planting and Reaping Albright: Politics, Ideology, and Interpreting the Bible.* University Park: Pennsylvania State University Press, 1997.

Longfield, Bradley J. *The Presbyterian Controversy: Fundamentalists, Modernists, and Moderates.* New York: Oxford University Press, 1991.

Lotz, David W., Donald W. Shriver, Jr., and John F. Wilson, eds. *Altered Landscapes: Christianity in America, 1935–1985.* Grand Rapids, Mich.: Eerdmans, 1989.

Luther, Martin. *Sermons.* Vol. 1. In *Luther's Works.* Vol. 51. Edited and translated by John W. Doberstein. Philadelphia: Muhlenberg Press, 1959.

———. *Lectures on Isaiah, Chapters 1–39.* In *Luther's Works.* Vol. 16. Edited by Jaroslav Pelikan and Hilton C. Oswald. St. Louis: Concordia, 1969.

———. *Martin Luther's Basic Theological Writings.* Edited by Timothy F. Lull. Minneapolis: Fortress Press, 1989.

Lynn, Robert W., and Elliott Wright. *The Big Little School: Two Hundred Years of the Sunday School.* Birmingham, Ala.: Religious Education Press, 1980.

MacCulloch, Diarmaid. *Thomas Cranmer: A Life.* New Haven: Yale University Press, 1996.

Machen, J. Gresham. *Christianity and Liberalism.* New York: Macmillan, 1929.

———. *The Virgin Birth of Christ.* New York: Harper and Brothers, 1930.

Mantey, Julius Robert. "A View of the RSV." *Watchman-Examiner,* 30 October 1952, 1007, 1009–10.

Marsden, George M. *Fundamentalism and American Culture: The Shaping of Twentieth-Century American Evangelicalism, 1870–1925.* New York: Oxford University Press, 1980.

———. *Reforming Fundamentalism: Fuller Seminary and the New Evangelicalism.* Grand Rapids, Mich.: Eerdmans, 1987.

Martin, Gregory. *A Discoverie of the Manifold Corruptions of the Holy Scriptures by the Heretikes of Our Daies.* Rheims, 1582.

Marty, Martin E. *Pilgrims in Their Own Land: Five Hundred Years of Religion in America.* New York: Penguin Books, 1984.

———. *Modern American Religion.* Vol. 1. *The Irony of It All, 1893–1919.* Chicago: University of Chicago Press, 1986.

———. *Modern American Religion.* Vol. 3. *Under God, Indivisible, 1941–1960.* Chicago: University of Chicago Press, 1996.

Mauro, Philip. "A Personal Testimony." In *The Fundamentals: A Testimony to the Truth.* Edited by A. C. Dixon, Louis Meyer, and Reuben Torrey. Vol. 4. Chicago: Testimony Publishing, 1910–15.

———. "Life in the Word." In *The Fundamentals: A Testimony to the Truth.* Edited by A. C. Dixon, Louis Meyer, and Reuben Torrey. Vol. 5. Chicago: Testimony Publishing, 1910–15.

———. *Evolution at the Bar.* Boston: Hamilton Brothers, 1917.

———. *Which Version? Authorized or Revised?* Boston: Hamilton Brothers. 1924.

May, Henry F. *The Enlightenment in America.* New York: Oxford University Press, 1976.

May, Herbert Gordon. *Our English Bible in the Making: The Word of Life in Living Language.* Philadelphia: Westminster Press, 1952.

May, Herbert G., and Bruce M. Metzger, eds. *The Oxford Annotated Bible with the Apocrypha: Revised Standard Version.* New York: Oxford University Press, 1965.

————, eds. *The New Oxford Annotated Bible with the Apocrypha: Revised Standard Version*. New York: Oxford University Press, 1977.

McDannell, Colleen. *Material Christianity: Religion and Popular Culture in America*. New Haven: Yale University Press, 1995.

McGrath, Alister. *The Intellectual Origins of the European Reformation*. Oxford: Blackwell, 1987.

————. *The Genesis of Doctrine: A Study in the Foundations of Doctrinal Criticism*. Oxford: Basil Blackwell, 1990.

McKenzie, John L. Review of *The Holy Bible, Revised Standard Version*. *Catholic Biblical Quarterly* 17 (1955): 88–90.

McNeill, John T. *The History and Character of Calvinism*. Oxford: Oxford University Press, 1954.

Metzger, Bruce M. *A Textual Commentary on the Greek New Testament*. London: United Bible Societies, 1971.

————. "The RSV—Ecumenical Edition," *Theology Today* 34 (1977): 315–17.

————. *The Text of the New Testament: Its Transmission, Corruption, and Restoration*. 3rd ed. New York: Oxford University Press, 1992.

————. *Reminiscences of an Octogenarian*. Peabody, Mass.: Hendrickson, 1997.

Metzger, Bruce M., Robert C. Dentan, and Walter Harrelson. *The Making of the New Revised Standard Version of the Bible*. Grand Rapids, Mich.: Eerdmans, 1991.

Michigan, State of. *Official Directory and Legislative Manual*. Lansing, 1953–54.

Miles, Margaret R. *Image as Insight: Visual Understanding in Western Christianity and Secular Culture*. Boston: Beacon Press, 1985.

Miller, Perry. *The New England Mind: The Seventeenth Century*. Cambridge: Harvard University Press, 1939.

Minkema, Kenneth P. "The Other Unfinished 'Great Work': Jonathan Edwards, Messianic Prophecy, and 'The Harmony of the Old and New Testament.'" In *Jonathan Edwards's Writings: Text, Context, Interpretation*, edited by Stephen J. Stein. Bloomington: Indiana University Press, 1996.

Moffatt, James. *The New Testament: A New Translation*. New York: Hodder and Stoughton, 1913.

————. *The Old Testament: A New Translation*. New York: George H. Doran, 1924–25.

Moody, Dale. "Isaiah 7:14 in the Revised Standard Version." *Review and Expositor* 50 (1953): 61–68.

More, Thomas. "Confutation of Tyndale's Answer." In *The Complete Works of St. Thomas More*, vol. 8, pt. 1, edited by Louis A. Schuster, Richard C. Marius, James P. Lusardi, and Richard J. Schoeck. New Haven: Yale University Press, 1993.

Morgan, David, ed. *Icons of American Protestantism: The Art of Warner Sallman*. New Haven: Yale University Press, 1996.

Mozley, J. F. *John Foxe and His Book*. London: Society for Promoting Christian Knowledge, 1940.

Mullen, Tobias. *The Canon of the Old Testament*. New York: Frederick Pustet, 1892.

Muller, Richard A. "The Debate over the Vowel Points and the Crisis in Orthodox Hermeneutics." *Journal of Medieval and Renaissance Studies* 10 (Spring 1980): 53–72.

Mullin, Robert Bruce. *Miracles and the Modern Religious Imagination.* New Haven: Yale University Press, 1996.

Murch, James DeForest. "Evangelicals and 'The New Version.'" *United Evangelical Action,* 15 January 1953, 5–6.

Neill, Stephen, and Tom Wright. *The Interpretation of the New Testament, 1861–1986.* 2nd ed. Oxford: Oxford University Press, 1988.

Nelson, E. Clifford, et al. *The Lutherans in North America.* Rev. ed. Philadelphia: Fortress Press, 1980.

Nichols, James Hastings. *Romanticism in American Theology: Nevin and Schaff at Mercersburg.* Chicago: University of Chicago Press, 1961.

Niebuhr, H. Richard, "The Anachronism of Jonathan Edwards." In *H. Richard Niebuhr: Theology, History, and Culture: Major Unpublished Writings,* edited by William Stacy Johnson. New Haven: Yale University Press, 1996.

Noll, Mark A. "Common Sense Traditions and American Evangelical Thought." *American Quarterly* 37 (1985): 216–38.

———. *Between Faith and Criticism: Evangelicals, Scholarship, and the Bible in America.* San Francisco: Harper and Row, 1986.

———. *Princeton and the Republic, 1768–1822: The Search for a Christian Enlightenment in the Era of Samuel Stanhope Smith.* Princeton: Princeton University Press, 1989.

———. "Ethnic, American, or Lutheran? Dilemmas for a Historic Confession in the New World." *Lutheran Theological Seminary Bulletin* [Gettysburg, Pa.] 71, no. 1 (1991): 17–38.

———, ed. *The Princeton Theology, 1812–1921: Scripture, Science, and Theological Method from Archibald Alexander to Benjamin Warfield.* Grand Rapids, Mich.: Baker Book House, 1983.

———, ed. *The Princeton Defense of Plenary Verbal Inspiration.* Fundamentalism in American Religion Series. New York: Garland, 1988.

Noyes, George Rapall. "Hengstenberg's Christology." *Christian Examiner* 16 (July 1834): 321–64.

Oberman, Heiko A. *Luther: Man between God and the Devil.* Translated by Eileen Walliser-Schwarzbart. New York: Image Books, 1992.

O'Day, Gail R. "Probing an Inclusive Scripture." *Christian Century* 113 (3–10 July 1996): 692–94.

Orlinsky, Harry M. *Essays in Biblical Culture and Bible Translation.* New York: KTAV Publishing, 1974.

Orlinsky, Harry M., and Robert G. Bratcher. *A History of Bible Translation and the North American Contribution.* Atlanta: Scholars Press, 1991.

Ostling, Richard N. "Farewell to Thee's and He's." *Time,* 7 May 1990, 17.

Painter, Nell Irvin. *Standing at Armageddon: The United States, 1877–1919.* New York: Norton, 1987.

Palmer, Edwin H. *The Five Points of Calvinism.* Grand Rapids, Mich.: Baker Book House, 1980.

Patrick, James. *The Magdalen Metaphysicals: Idealism and Orthodoxy at Oxford, 1901–1945.* Macon, Ga.: Mercer University Press, 1985.

Pattison, T. Harwood. *The History of the English Bible.* London: Baptist Tract and Book Society, 1894.

Penzel, Klaus. "Church History and the Ecumenical Quest: A Study of the German

Background and Thought of Philip Schaff." Th.D. diss., Union Theological Seminary [New York], 1962.

————, ed. *Philip Schaff: Historian and Ambassador of the Universal Church: Selected Writings*. Macon, Ga.: Mercer University Press, 1991.

Phillips, John. *The Reformation of Images: Destruction of Art in England, 1535–1660*. Berkeley: University of California Press, 1973.

Phillips, Timothy R., and Dennis L. Okholm, eds. *The Nature of Confession: Evangelicals and Postliberals in Conversation*. Downers Grove, Ill.: Inter-Varsity Press, 1996.

Pollard, Alfred W. *Records of the English Bible: The Documents Relating to the Translation and Publication of the Bible in English, 1525–1611*. London: Oxford University Press, 1911.

Pope, Hugh. *The Catholic Church and the Bible*. New York: Macmillan, 1928.

————. *English Versions of the Bible*. Edited by Sebastian Bullough. St. Louis: Herder, 1952.

Price, Ira Maurice, William A. Irwin, and Allen P. Wikgren. *The Ancestry of Our English Bible: An Account of Manuscripts, Texts, and Versions of the Bible*. 3rd ed. New York: Harper and Brothers, 1956.

Reardon, Bernard M. G. *Religious Thought in the Reformation*. 2nd ed. London: Longman, 1995.

Reich, Jutta. *Amerikanischer Fundamentalismus: Geschichte und Erscheinung der Bewegung um Carl McIntire*. 2nd ed. Hildesheim: Dr. H. A. Gerstenberg, 1972.

Reid, Daniel G., Robert D. Linder, Bruce L. Shelley, and Harry S. Stout, eds., *Dictionary of Christianity in America*. Downers Grove, Ill.: InterVarsity Press, 1990.

Report to Evangelicals: A Report of the Seventh Annual Convention of the National Association of Evangelicals, Chicago, Illinois, 19–22 April 1949. Chicago: National Association of Evangelicals, 1949.

Reu, Johann Michael. *Luther's German Bible: An Historical Presentation Together with a Collection of Sources*. Columbus, Ohio: Lutheran Book Concern, 1934.

Reventlow, Henning Graf. *The Authority of the Bible and the Rise of the Modern World*. Translated by John Bowden. Philadelphia: Fortress Press, 1985.

"The Revision of the New Testament," *Dublin Review*. 3rd ser. 6 (July 1881): 127–44.

Rex, Richard. *Henry VIII and the English Reformation*. London: Macmillan, 1993.

Ribuffo, Leo P. *The Old Christian Right: The Protestant Far Right from the Great Depression to the Cold War*. Philadelphia: Temple University Press, 1983.

Riddle, Matthew Brown. *The Story of the Revised New Testament, American Standard Edition*. Philadelphia: Sunday School Times, 1908.

Roberts, Alexander. *Companion to the Revised Version of the New Testament, Explaining the Reasons for the Changes Made on the Authorized Version*. New York: I. K. Funk, 1881.

Roberts, Jon H. *Darwinism and the Divine in America: Protestant Intellectuals and Organic Evolution, 1859–1900*. Madison: University of Wisconsin Press, 1988.

Robinson, C. S. "The Bible Society and the New Revision." *Scribner's Monthly* (January 1881): 447–56.

Rockwood, Raymond O., ed. *Carl Becker's Heavenly City Revisited*. Ithaca, N.Y.: Cornell University Press, 1958. Reprint, Hamden, Conn.: Archon Books, 1968.

Roosevelt, Theodore. *The Winning of the West.* 4 vols. New York: Putnam's, 1889–96.

Rorem, Paul. *Pseudo-Dionysius: A Commentary on the Texts and an Introduction to Their Influence.* New York: Oxford University Press, 1993.

Rouse, Ruth, and Stephen Charles Neill, eds. *A History of the Ecumenical Movement, 1517–1948.* 3rd ed. Geneva: World Council of Churches, 1986.

Roy, Ralph Lord. *Apostles of Discord: A Study of Organized Bigotry and Disruption on the Fringes of Protestantism.* Boston: Beacon Press, 1953.

Sandeen, Ernest R. *The Roots of Fundamentalism: British and American Millenarianism, 1800–1930.* Chicago: University of Chicago Press, 1970.

Saunders, Ernest W. *Searching the Scriptures: A History of the Society of Biblical Literature.* Chico, Calif.: Scholars Press, 1982.

Savage, H. H. Introduction to *Cooperation without Compromise: A History of the National Association of Evangelicals* by James DeForest Murch. Grand Rapids, Mich.: Eerdmans, 1956.

Sawyer, John F. A. *The Fifth Gospel: Isaiah in the History of Christianity.* Cambridge: Cambridge University Press, 1996.

Schaff, David S. *The Life of Philip Schaff, in Part Autobiographical.* New York: Scribner's, 1897.

Schaff, Philip. *The Creeds of Christendom, with a History and Critical Notes.* New York: Harper and Brothers, 1877.

———. *A Companion to the Greek Testament and English Version.* New York: Harper and Brothers, 1883.

———. *History of the Christian Church.* Vol. 1: Apostolic Christianity A.D. 1–100. 3rd ed. New York: Scribner's, 1891.

Scholder, Klaus. *The Birth of Modern Critical Theology: Origins and Problems of Biblical Criticism in the Seventeenth Century.* Translated by John Bowden. London: SCM Press, 1990.

Schrecker, Ellen. *The Age of McCarthyism: A Brief History with Documents.* Boston: Bedford Books, 1994.

Schweitzer, Albert. *The Quest of the Historical Jesus: A Critical Study of Its Progress from Reimarus to Wrede.* Translated by W. Montgomery. New York: Macmillan, 1968.

Scofield, C. I., et al., eds. *The Scofield Reference Bible.* 1909. New York: Oxford University Press, 1917.

Shriver, George H. *Philip Schaff: Christian Scholar and Ecumenical Prophet.* Macon, Ga.: Mercer University Press, 1987.

Simms, P. Marion. *The Bible from the Beginning.* New York: Macmillan, 1929.

———. *The Bible in America: Versions that Have Played Their Part in the Making of the Republic.* New York: Wilson-Erickson, 1936.

Smalley, Beryl. *The Study of the Bible in the Middle Ages.* 3rd ed. Oxford: Basil Blackwell, 1983.

Smeeton, Donald Dean. *Lollard Themes in the Reformation Theology of William Tyndale.* Sixteenth Century Essays and Studies, vol. 6. Kirksville, Mo.: Sixteenth Century Journal Publishers, 1986.

Smith, H. Sheldon. "Conflicting Interchurch Movements in American Protestantism." *Christendom* 12 (1947): 165–76.

Smith, J. M. Powis, ed. *The Old Testament: An American Translation.* Chicago: University of Chicago Press, 1927.

Smyth, J. Paterson. *How We Got Our Bible*. Rev. ed. Philadelphia: Westminster Press, 1889.

Spencer, Aida Besançon. "Power Play." *Christian Century* 114 (2–9 July 1997): 618–19.

Sperry, Willard L. *Religion in America*. New York: Macmillan, 1946.

Spitz, Lewis W. *The Protestant Reformation, 1517–1559*. New York: Harper and Row, 1985.

Stein, Stephen J. "America's Bibles: Canon, Commentary, and Community." *Church History* 64 (1995): 169–84.

———. Introduction to *The Works of Jonathan Edwards*. Vol. 15. *Notes on Scripture*. New Haven: Yale University Press, 1998.

Steinmetz, David C. *Luther in Context*. Bloomington: Indiana University Press, 1986. Reprint, Grand Rapids, Mich.: Baker Books, 1995.

Stek, John H. "KJV, ASV, RSV, NEB, NASB—or What?" *Banner* 101 (18 March 1966): 4–5.

Stock, Brian. *Listening for the Text: On the Uses of the Past*. Baltimore: Johns Hopkins University Press, 1990.

Stoughton, John. *Our English Bible: Its Translations and Translators*. London: Religious Tract Society, 1878.

Stout, Harry S. *The New England Soul: Preaching and Religious Culture in Colonial New England*. New York: Oxford University Press, 1986.

Strong, Josiah. *Our Country: Its Possible Future and Its Present Crisis*. New York: Baker and Taylor, American Home Missionary Society, 1885.

Szasz, Ferenc Morton. *The Divided Mind of Protestant America, 1880–1930*. University, Ala.: University of Alabama Press, 1982.

Tappert, Theodore, ed. *The Book of Concord: The Confessions of the Evangelical Lutheran Church*. Philadelphia: Fortress Press, 1959.

Taylor, William Carey. *The New Bible: Pro and Con*. New York: Vantage Press, 1955.

Tietjen, John H. *Memoirs in Exile: Confessional Hope and Institutional Conflict*. Minneapolis: Fortress Press, 1990.

Trinterud, Leonard J. "The Origins of Puritanism." *Church History* 31 (1962): 24–45.

———. "A Reappraisal of William Tyndale's Debt to Martin Luther." *Church History* 20 (1950): 37–57.

Turner, James. *Without God, Without Creed: The Origins of Unbelief in America*. Baltimore: Johns Hopkins University Press, 1985.

Tyndale, William. *An Answer to Sir Thomas More's Dialogue*. Edited by Henry Walter. Cambridge: Cambridge University Press, 1850.

Unger, Merrill F. "The Revised Standard Version Old Testament." *Bibliotheca Sacra* 110 (January 1953): 54–61.

United We Stand: A Report on the Constitutional Convention of the National Association of Evangelicals. Chicago, Illinois, 3–6 May 1943. Boston: National Association of Evangelicals, 1943.

Valentine, M. "The Revised English New Testament," *Lutheran Quarterly* 12 (January 1882): 43–60.

Van Elderen, Bastiaan. "More Thoughts on Bible Translations." *Banner* 101 (3 June 1966): 14–16.

Van Til, Cornelius. *The New Modernism: An Appraisal of the Theology of Barth and Brunner.* Philadelphia: Presbyterian and Reformed Publishing, 1946.

Vaughan, C. J. *Authorized or Revised? Sermons on Some of the Texts in Which the Revised Version Differs from the Authorized.* London: Macmillan, 1882.

Vincent, Marvin R. "Notes on the Revised New Testament." *Presbyterian Review* 2, no. 8 (October 1881): 633–86.

Von Simson, Otto. *The Gothic Cathedral: Origins of Gothic Architecture and the Medieval Concept of Order.* 3rd ed. Bollingen Series, no. 48. Princeton: Princeton University Press, 1988.

Walker, Brooks R. *The Christian Fright Peddlers: The Radical Right and the Churches.* Garden City, N.Y.: Doubleday, 1964.

Wallace, Foy E., Jr. *A Review of the New Versions: Consisting of an Exposure of the Multiple New Translations.* Fort Worth, Tex.: Foy E. Wallace, Jr., Publications, 1973.

Ward, Thomas. *The Errata to the Protestant Bible.* London, 1688.

Warfield, Benjamin B. Review of *The Holy Bible, American Standard Version. Presbyterian and Reformed Review* 13 (1902): 645–48.

Weigle, Luther A. *The Pupil and the Teacher.* New York: Hodder and Stoughton, 1911.

———. *The Training of Children in the Christian Family.* Boston: Pilgrim Press, 1922.

———. *Talks to Sunday-School Teachers.* New York: Richard R. Smith, 1930.

———. *Jesus and the Educational Method.* New York: Abingdon Press, 1939.

———. "The Making of the Revised Standard Version of the New Testament." *Religion in Life* 15 (1946): 163–73.

———. Introduction to Horace Bushnell, *Christian Nurture.* New Haven: Yale University Press, 1947.

———. *The English New Testament from Tyndale to the Revised Standard Version.* New York: Abingdon-Cokesbury Press, 1949.

———. "The Revised Standard Version of the Bible." *Catholic Biblical Quarterly* 14 (1952): 310–18.

———. "The Standard Bible Committee." In *Translating and Understanding the Old Testament: Essays in Honor of Herbert Gordon May.* Edited by Harry Thomas Frank and William L. Reed. Nashville: Abingdon Press, 1970.

[Weigle, Luther A.] *An Open Letter Concerning the Revised Standard Version of the Bible.* New York: National Council of the Churches of Christ, n.d.

Weigle, Richard D., ed. *The Glory Days: From the Life of Luther Allan Weigle.* New York: Friendship Press, 1976.

Westcott, Brooke Foss. *A General View of the History of the English Bible.* 3rd ed. Edited by William Aldis Wright. New York: Macmillan, 1927.

Westcott, Brooke Foss, and Fenton John Anthony Hort, eds. *The New Testament in the Original Greek.* New York: Harper and Brothers, 1881.

Where the Old and New Versions Differ: The Actual Changes in the Authorized and Revised New Testament. New York: Anson D. F. Randolph, 1881.

Wilcox, Clyde. *God's Warriors: The Christian Right in Twentieth-Century America.* Baltimore: Johns Hopkins University Press, 1992.

Wilkinson, Benjamin G. *Our Authorized Bible Vindicated.* Washington, D.C., 1930.

Willoughby, Harold R. *Soldiers' Bibles through Three Centuries*. Chicago: University of Chicago Press, 1944.

Wilson, John F. *Public Religion in American Culture*. Philadelphia: Temple University Press, 1979.

Winn, Herbert E., ed. *Wyclif: Select English Writings*. London: Oxford University Press, 1929.

Wosh, Peter J. *Spreading the Word: The Bible Business in Nineteenth-Century America*. Ithaca, N.Y.: Cornell University Press, 1994.

Wright, David F. "Martin Bucer and England—and Scotland." In *Martin Bucer and Sixteenth-Century Europe,* edited by Christian Krieger and Marc Lienhard. Vol. 2. Leiden: Brill, 1993.

Wuthnow, Robert. *The Restructuring of American Religion: Society and Faith Since World War II*. Princeton: Princeton University Press, 1988.

Youngblood, Carolyn Johnson. "The New International Version Translation Project: Its Conception and Implementation." *Journal of the Evangelical Theological Society* 21 (1978): 239–49.

Youngblood, Ronald, ed. *Evangelicals and Inerrancy*. Nashville: Thomas Nelson, 1984.

Index